Voices of the Civil War

Voices of the Civil War · Fredericksburg

By the Editors of Time-Life Books, Alexandria, Virginia

THE FIELD AT FREDERICKSBURG

In December 1862 Fredericksburg and its surroundings were the setting for the bloody repulse of the Army of the Potomac at the hands of Lee's Confederates. This artist's rendering shows the principal features of the battlefield, including the Federal pontoon bridges and the Rebel earthworks on the high ground west of the city.

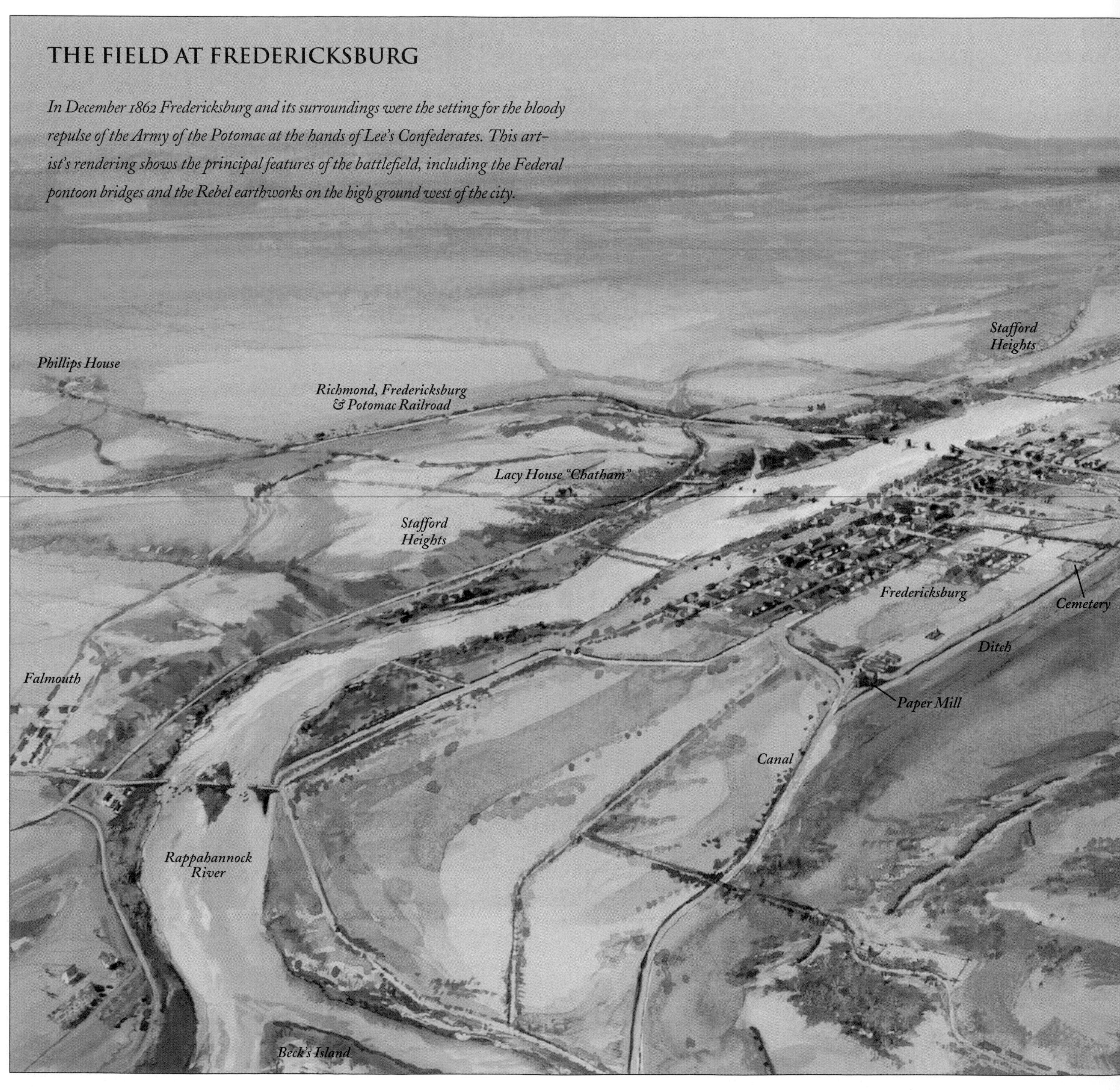

Hamilton's Crossing
E
S
N
W
Richmond Stage Road
Bernard House
"Mansfield"
Richmond, Fredericksburg
& Potomac Railroad
Hazel Run
Lee Hill
Stone Wall
Marye's Heights
Telegraph Road
Tannery
Marye House
"Brompton"
Unfinished Railroad
Plank Road

A Gathering on the Rappahannock

On the night of November 7, 1862, as an unseasonable snowfall blanketed the camps of the Union's Army of the Potomac around Warrenton, Virginia, two visitors entered the tent of Major General George B. McClellan to deliver bad news. McClellan was finished as the army's commander. His good friend Major General Ambrose E. Burnside—one of the bearers of the ill tidings that stormy night—had been appointed as his replacement.

Less than two months earlier at Antietam McClellan had successfully turned back Robert E. Lee's invasion of Maryland and had seriously weakened the Rebel Army of Northern Virginia. If McClellan had then acted to bring the retreating Confederates to bay and smash them again, the war might have been shortened drastically. But despite President Abraham Lincoln's urging, the cautious "Little Mac" refused to move, allowing Lee to retreat into the Shenandoah Valley, where he could rest and reorganize his battered forces.

The exasperated Lincoln then presented McClellan with a new plan of action. The Army of the Potomac was to follow Lee southward, staying east of the Blue Ridge, between the Rebel army and Washington. The goal was now to capture Richmond, and Lincoln figured that McClellan should be able to beat Lee in the race for the Confederate capital by staying on this more direct "inside track."

To Lincoln's dismay, however, McClellan allowed six weeks to pass before finally setting his reinforced army in motion and moving ponderously back into Virginia. The delay gave Lee plenty of time to prepare for the Federal pursuit. Using a familiar tactic, the daring Rebel commander decided to confuse the Federals by dividing his army. He left about half his forces—one corps commanded by General Thomas J. "Stonewall" Jackson—in the Shenandoah Valley and dispatched the other corps, under James Longstreet, eastward across the Blue Ridge.

By the time the vanguard of McClellan's army reached Warrenton, where he intended to pause yet again and regroup before moving on, Longstreet had established a position about 20 miles to the southwest, near Culpep-

Fredericksburg's once bustling riverfront lies idle, shut down in the first year of war when the town found itself in the front lines. Visible are two stone piers of the railroad bridge wrecked by retreating Confederates in April 1862.

er Court House, directly in the path of the Union army. McClellan's "inside track" to Richmond was now blocked, and if he wanted to reach the Southern capital, he would have to fight his way through. To Lincoln, this was the last straw. Little Mac had to go.

The change of command not only ended McClellan's military career at a stroke but also thrust Burnside into what was for him a most unwelcome position of leadership. In a milieu rife with ambitious men, Burnside seemed an almost modest soul. He candidly acknowledged his limitations and had seemed quite content to serve under his mentor and comrade McClellan. Indeed, no Union general in 1862 was more eager than Burnside to avoid being elevated in command. In fact, earlier that year President Lincoln had twice offered him the Army of the Potomac and Burnside had turned him down each time, professing doubts that he could handle such heavy responsibility.

Now, offered the post for yet a third time, Burnside finally accepted—not because of any surge of self-confidence, but because he knew that if he refused again, the job would go to a bitter rival, the arrogant and conniving Joseph Hooker.

Although McClellan had suspected that he might be fired and took the news calmly, he was stunned to learn that he was being replaced by his old friend Burnside, whom he now regarded as "not fit to command more than a regiment." While that barb may have been hurled in anger, there was truly nothing in Burnside's background to indicate that he would be capable of leading an army of more than 100,000 men.

The son of an Indiana state senator, Burnside won an appointment to West Point and graduated in the middle of the class of 1847, one year behind McClellan. He was ordered to join the U.S. Army forces fighting in Mexico but arrived too late to see action in a conflict that brought many of his fellow officers acclaim and promotion.

He spent the next six years in various frontier assignments that afforded him the spare time to indulge in his habit of tinkering. During that period he invented a breech-loading rifle, and in 1853 he resigned from the army to manufacture his new weapon.

Settling in Bristol, Rhode Island, with a new bride, Burnside founded the Bristol Firearms Company—which lasted only two years before collapsing financially. Nearly bankrupt, Burnside asked for help from McClellan, who had also left the army and was now vice president of the Illinois Central Railroad. McClellan got his ill-starred friend a job with the railroad and even took him and his wife into his home for a time.

When the Civil War broke out, Burnside assumed command of the 1st Rhode Island Infantry and later led a brigade at Bull Run, performing sufficiently well to earn a promotion to brigadier general. Early in 1862 he added to his reputation by commanding an amphibious operation that wrested control of the coastal waterways of North Carolina from the Confederates. This venture secured a Union base of operations in the South and won for Burnside a promotion to major general and command of the IX Corps. At the Battle of Antietam, however, Burnside showed poor judgment and lackluster leadership, causing his standing to slip several notches in the eyes of some of his fellow officers.

Whatever his flaws, Burnside was adept at concealing them behind a facade of charm. He was affable, he smiled often, and he had a politician's penchant for remembering names. In appearance he cut something of a dashing figure with his low-slung pistol belt, broad-brimmed hat on his massive bald head, and abundant cheek whiskers—a style known throughout the army as *sideburns* in a play on the general's name.

Some officers applauded Burnside's ascent to high command. General Herman Haupt, field commander of U.S. Military Railroads, told his wife, "I like Burnside very well. I think he will go ahead. He talks right at any rate and I feel more encouraged than I have for a long time."

But others, particularly those who had known him long enough to perceive in him a stubborn streak and a lack of imagination, considered him unsuited to the post. "You would think he had a great deal more intelligence than he really possessed," remarked Charles A. Dana, assistant U.S. secretary of war. "You had to know him some time before you really took his measure." Colonel Francis W. Palfrey of the 20th Massachusetts Infantry believed that "few men, probably, have risen so high upon so slight a foundation."

President Lincoln may have harbored his own doubts about Burnside's ability, but he had scarcely anywhere else to turn. The army's other corps commanders had shortcomings that disqualified them for high command: William B. Franklin was, like McClellan, overcautious and slow to take action; Edwin V. Sumner at 65 was too old; Joseph Hooker was known to be a schemer and troublemaker. At least Burnside had shown some mettle on the North Carolina expedition. Although he may not have been the ideal candidate to lead the army, he seemed to possess fewer liabilities than the others.

Immediately after his appointment, Burnside received his first order from the general in chief, Henry W. Halleck: "Report the position of your troops, and what you propose doing with them." It was a simple enough directive, but Burnside was woefully unprepared to respond. About such matters, as he later put it, "I probably knew less than any other corps commander."

What was worse, Burnside did not have the option of taking his new command into action slowly and cautiously. President Lincoln had run out of patience with his generals. He wanted to strike a blow that would end the Confederate rebellion, and he wanted to do it immediately. As Burnside well knew, timidity and inaction had been McClellan's downfall.

The responsibility of command weighed so heavily on Burnside that it made him physically ill. Yet, to the surprise of many, he managed to get started on his new duties quickly and vigorously. On November 9 he sent to Washington a new strategy for taking the Confederate capital. Burnside would concentrate his forces along the route southwest to Gordonsville to convince Lee that he intended to move in that direction. Then he would swiftly sidestep to the east, sending his army toward Fredericksburg on the Rappahannock River.

The eastward shift would put the army closer to Washington and its supply base and on the main road between Washington and Richmond, a much more direct route to the Confederate capital. Once at Fredericksburg, Burnside's forces would cross the Rappahannock before Lee could get into a blocking position. Then they would secure the town and plunge southward to seize Richmond.

In Washington, Burnside's new scheme got a tepid reception. Halleck came down to Warrenton for a conference and argued for retaining the Gordonsville route of march, though, as usual, he declined to commit himself officially, leaving it up to Lincoln to decide. The president, after some wavering, finally agreed to let Burnside have his way. Lincoln sensed, however, that everything hinged on speed—he commented that the plan "will succeed, if you move rapidly; otherwise not."

Burnside well knew that speed was of the essence. He had to get to Fredericksburg and cross the river before Lee could move to block him. The attack on the town, he directed, should come "as soon as the army arrives in front of [the] place."

In an effort to streamline his operations, Burnside reorganized his cumbersome army, creating three large groupings of two corps each that he called grand divisions, commanded, respectively, by Generals Sumner, Hooker, and Franklin. Burnside also tackled the problem of feeding and equipping his huge army, directing that a new supply base be established on the Potomac at Belle Plain, 10 miles northeast of Fredericksburg. He would need a flotilla of barges filled with goods, as well as wagon trains to carry supplies overland from Washington.

More than anything else, however, Burnside would need a train of pontoons. He knew that the Rappahannock bridges at Fredericksburg had been destroyed by the Confederates. In order to get his troops across the river, his engineers would have to use pontoons to lay down new spans. He was assured by Halleck that the vital bridging equipment would be waiting for him when he arrived in Fredericksburg.

Burnside's campaign got off to an impressive start. At dawn on November 15 Sumner's grand division vacated its Warrenton camps and moved out rapidly toward Fredericksburg, with the other two grand divisions following the next day. After only two days of marching, Sumner's troops entered the town of Falmouth on the north bank of the Rappahannock, just about a mile upriver from Fredericksburg. Hooker's and Franklin's divisions were about eight miles behind.

Such a lightning-fast march was something new for the Army of the Potomac—quite different from McClellan's ponderous movements. A correspondent for the New York *Tribune* noted on November 18, "Officers wont to believe that a great command cannot move more than six miles a day, and accustomed to our old method of waiting [a] week for the issue of new clothing or a month for the execution of an order to advance, rub their eyes in mute astonishment. We have marched from Warrenton forty miles, in two days and a half."

Now the army stood poised before its objective, facing only light opposition. Fredericksburg and the hills beyond were defended by four companies of Rebel infantry, a battery of light artillery, and a cavalry regiment. Burnside had merely to get his troops across the Rappahannock to take the town and have an open road to Richmond. The commanding general seemed on the verge of a great triumph.

But there were problems. Soon after Burnside arrived at Falmouth, it began raining and poured for several days. The river rose, threatening the fords, and the mud would slow any troop movement to a crawl. These troubles paled, however, before the worst problem of all. The pontoons—the key to crossing the Rappahannock—had failed to arrive.

Apparently Halleck had misunderstood the need for urgency, and the pontoon trains did not roll out of Washington until November 19. Meanwhile the rains had turned the northern Virginia roads to muck, and the wagons carrying the bridging materials made painfully slow headway and stopped entirely when they encountered washed-out bridges at Occoquan Creek. Some of the pontoons would be transferred to a steamboat and delivered to Belle Plain on November 24, but the bulk of the bridging material would not reach the army until the afternoon of November 27.

Pontoons or no, Burnside's generals favored an immediate strike. Sumner asked permission to cross his troops at a ford near Falmouth. But the river was already high, and rain continued to fall. Burnside fretted that any troops that managed to ford the river would be trapped on the far bank by rising water. He ordered Sumner to stay put.

Hooker also yearned to move—to carry out a scheme of his own. If allowed, he would cross upstream at United States Ford and strike out for the town of Bowling Green, south of Fredericksburg and only 35 miles from Richmond. Not satisfied to seek permission from Burnside alone, Hooker dispatched a message to Secretary of War Edwin M. Stanton, explaining his plan—and criticizing Burnside for delaying the attack. Stanton never replied, and Burnside rejected Hooker's request, contriving to overlook the flagrant insubordination.

While Burnside remained stalled, Robert E. Lee had been awakening to the Yankee threat. He had known that the Federals were moving, but where? And for what? The Rebel commander had a reputation for being able to foresee his opponent's plans, but his opponent up to now had been McClellan, who was very predictable—so much so, in fact, that Lee expressed disappointment at his departure. "We always understood each other so well," he told Longstreet. "I fear they may continue to make these changes till they find someone who I don't understand."

Lee learned of Sumner's departure from Warrenton on November 15 but was uncertain of what it meant. Subsequent scouting reports, fragmentary or false, added to his confusion. Then, at dusk on November 17 he discovered that Sumner's brigades were approaching Fredericksburg. But still Lee could not determine whether the movement was a feint or a genuine advance on Richmond.

The next day Lee instructed Longstreet to dispatch two of his divisions from Culpeper eastward in the direction of Fredericksburg. And he sent a message to Stonewall Jackson suggesting that he shift a part of his command east of the Blue Ridge to be closer at hand. That same day a Rebel cavalry trooper scouting north of the Rappahannock reported that the entire Federal army was approaching Fredericksburg. Lee did not hesitate; on November 19 he ordered Longstreet's remaining three divisions to the town.

As Longstreet's troops began to arrive and take positions in the hills beyond Fredericksburg on November 20, they found the populace in a state of agitation—the Yankees were just across the river, and in great profusion. Their fear only increased on the next day, when General Sumner issued an ultimatum to the town's mayor and council. "Under cover of the houses of your city," his note read, "shots have been fired upon the troops of my command. Your mills and manufactories are furnishing provision and the material for clothing for armed bodies in rebellion against the Government of the United States. Your railroads and other means of transportation are removing supplies to depots of such troops." Sumner demanded the surrender of the city—if there was no surrender, he would give the authorities 16 days to evacuate the civilians and then he would begin a bombardment.

Speaking for the Confederates, Longstreet assured the citizenry that he had no intention of occupying the town for military purposes, but that he intended to fight the Yankees if they tried to enter it. The mayor resolved the situation—for the time being—by promising to stop the sniping and the supplying of Confederate troops. Sumner withdrew his ultimatum.

When Lee arrived he was appalled to find that his few divisions faced the entire Federal Army of the Potomac across the river. He was also puzzled, if thankful, over the lack of action on the part of the enemy. Why had Burnside failed to attack during the first 48 hours when he faced only paltry opposition? On November 23 Lee sent word to Stonewall Jackson to hurry his divisions east to Fredericksburg. Then he began to deploy Longstreet's forces to meet the Union onslaught, which could come at any time.

Earlier Lee had wanted to fall back to the North Anna River, which promised better terrain for making a strong defensive stand, but he had bowed to President Jefferson Davis' insistence on a line at the Rappahannock. He had no intention, however, of trying to defend Fredericksburg proper. Federal artillery arrayed on Stafford Heights on the far bank of the river dominated the town.

On the other hand, just west of the city's streets and buildings lay a high, wooded ridge that ran from the Rappahannock southward in a slight curve for about seven miles. The ridge was mostly out of range of the Federal guns. It seemed to offer excellent defensive possibilities, and there, Lee decided, the Confederates would make a stand. He ordered the construction of rifle pits and earthworks on the ridge, arranged his troops, and waited.

On November 29 Confederate prospects brightened considerably with the arrival of Stonewall Jackson in the vanguard of his four divisions after a fast march from the Blue Ridge. Lee immediately deployed Jackson's troops downriver to guard several crossing sites by which the Federals might try to outflank the Fredericksburg defenders.

The two armies were now in place—Lee's 78,000 men facing Burnside's 118,000. It would be the only time in the Civil War that so many armed men confronted each other on a battlefield. And between the two behemoths huddled the star-crossed little town.

Anticipating the attack, Confederate commanders advised the people of Fredericksburg to leave, and an exodus of civilians commenced. "The evacuation of the place by the distressed women and helpless men was a painful sight," Longstreet wrote. "Many were almost destitute and had nowhere to go, but, yielding to the cruel necessities of war, they collected their portable effects and turned their back on the town. Many were forced to seek shelter in the woods and brave the icy November nights to escape the approaching assault."

As Burnside watched the steady swelling of Confederate forces across the river, his pontoons finally arrived—too late, he realized. A head-on advance through Fredericksburg now seemed out of the question, and the Union commander began to mull other possibilities.

Toward the end of November, he met on two occasions with Lincoln and Halleck and apparently won their approval for a new plan of attack. He then called his grand division commanders together and told them that he would cross the river not at Fredericksburg but at Skinker's Neck, more than 12 miles downstream, a place recommended by his engineers.

But this plan fell through almost immediately. When Federal gunboats summoned from Port Royal arrived at Skinker's Neck, they were driven away by Confederates batteries onshore. To make matters worse, Union observers aloft in hydrogen balloons spotted two of Jackson's divisions encamped around Port Royal and Skinker's Neck.

The presence of thousands of Rebel troops near the intended crossing site convinced Burnside that Lee had somehow divined his strategy. It also led him to believe, however, that Lee had divided his army between Fredericksburg and the downriver crossing sites. If this were true, Burnside reasoned, then the Rebel commander must have weakened his Fredericksburg defenses to strengthen his downriver position.

It now made sense to Burnside to revert to the original plan—a strike at Fredericksburg. He would throw everything he had across the river, drive a wedge between the separated Confederate forces, and destroy Longstreet's corps before Jackson could come up to reinforce him.

Having arrived at this conclusion, Burnside

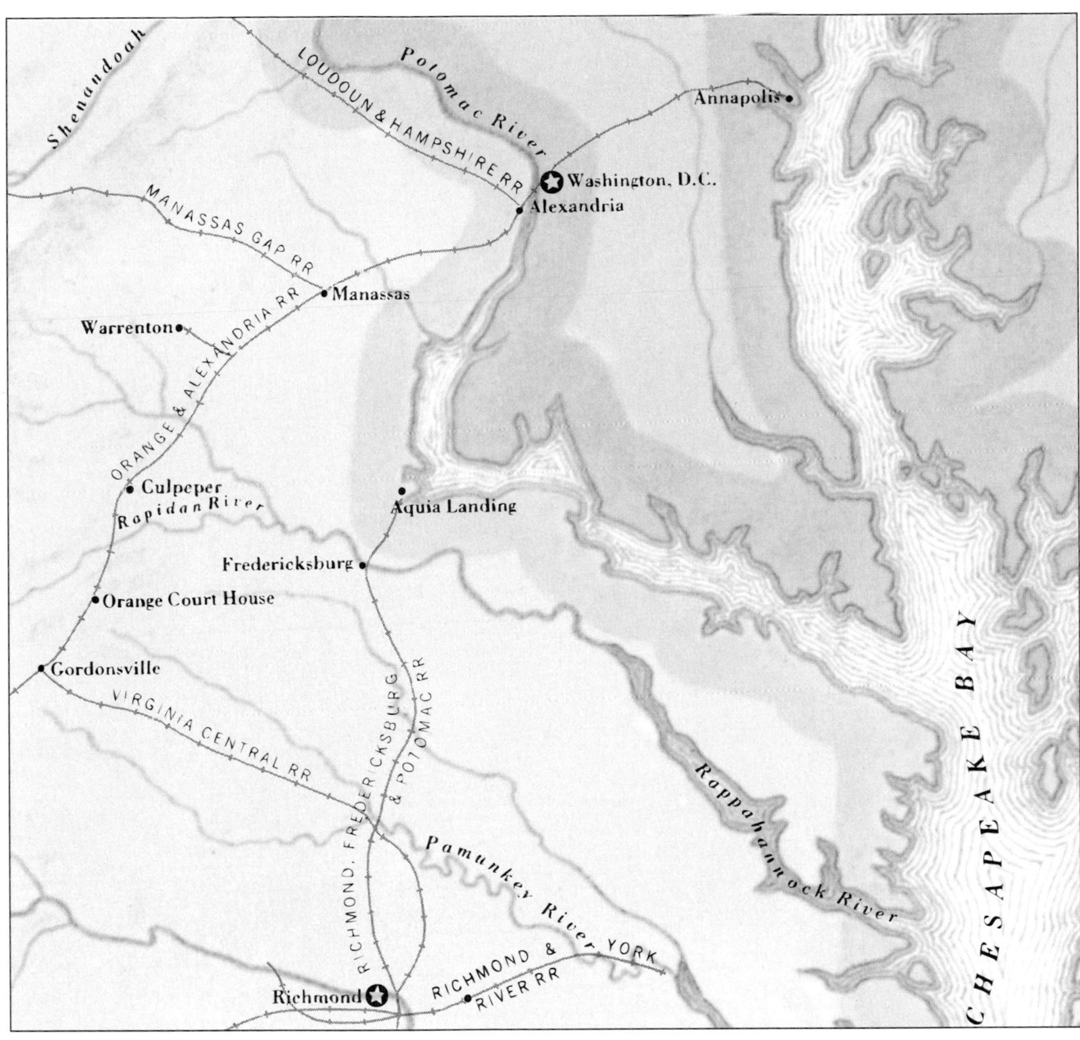

By the latter half of 1862 the Rappahannock had become the de facto boundary between Union and Confederate forces. Lee's army maintained a continuous line of pickets and outposts along the river from north of Culpeper to the point downstream from Fredericksburg where the Rappahannock was no longer fordable. The Army of the Potomac depended on proximity to its two principal supply lines: the Orange & Alexandria Railroad and the Potomac River.

nonetheless remained uncertain about it and sought reassurance from his commanders. None was forthcoming. Most of his officers opposed the plan, and some were outspoken in their opposition. When Burnside asked the opinion of Colonel Rush C. Hawkins, commanding a IX Corps brigade, that officer replied with remarkable prescience: "If you make the attack as contemplated, it will be the greatest slaughter of the war; there isn't infantry enough in our whole army to carry those heights if they are well defended." Just as candid was Lieutenant Colonel Joseph H. Taylor, who told Burnside bleakly: "The carrying out of your plan will be murder, not warfare."

His officers could clearly discern what Burnside refused to recognize—that the Confederates here could not be surprised. The Federals would have to build their pontoon bridges under the watchful eyes of the enemy—indeed, under heavy fire. Then the narrow columns that crossed over would have to tussle with skirmishers before they ever got to the main Rebel line. Lee would have plenty of time to summon reinforcements to the point of attack, wherever it happened to be.

Yet Burnside insisted that he held the advantage. "Oh! I know where Lee's forces are, and I expect to surprise him," he declared. "I expect to cross and occupy the hills before Lee can bring anything serious to meet me."

The crossing would commence in the early-morning hours of December 11. On the bitter-cold evening of December 10 a Federal band marched down to the riverbank opposite the town and, as the men of both armies listened, played "Yankee Doodle," "Hail Columbia," and other familiar tunes. Then, after a pause, the band struck up "Dixie," and cheers and laughter erupted on both sides of the Rappahannock. It was a last interlude before the slaughter.

CHRONOLOGY

1862	
November 7	*Burnside assumes command of the Army of the Potomac*
November 15	*Federals begin march toward Fredericksburg*
November 17-20	*Union forces consolidate east of the town*
November 18-19	*Longstreet departs Culpeper for Fredericksburg*
November 23	*Lee orders Jackson to Fredericksburg; Longstreet in place on heights west of town*
November 24-27	*Delayed arrival of Federal pontoons*
December 1-3	*Jackson arrives and deploys downriver*
December 4	*Engagement at Skinker's Neck*
December 9-10	*Burnside formulates attack plans*
December 11	*Federals bridge Rappahannock and occupy Fredericksburg*
December 12	*Franklin's and Sumner's grand divisions concentrate west of the river; Jackson moves into position south of town*
December 13	*Battle of Fredericksburg*
December 15-16	*Federals withdraw back across the Rappahannock*
1863	
January 20-24	*The "Mud March"*
January 25	*Burnside relieved of command*

ORDER OF BATTLE

ARMY OF NORTHERN VIRGINIA (Confederate)

Lee 78,000 men

First Corps Longstreet

McLaws' Division
Kershaw's Brigade
Barksdale's Brigade
Cobb's Brigade
Semmes' Brigade

Pickett's Division
Garnett's Brigade
Kemper's Brigade
Armistead's Brigade
Jenkins' Brigade
Corse's Brigade

R. H. Anderson's Division
Wilcox's Brigade
Featherston's Brigade
Mahone's Brigade
Wright's Brigade
Perry's Brigade

Hood's Division
Law's Brigade
G. T. Anderson's Brigade
Robertson's Brigade
Benning's Brigade

Ransom's Division
Ransom's Brigade
Cooke's Brigade

Second Corps Jackson

Early's Division
Atkinson's Brigade
Hoke's Brigade
Walker's Brigade
Hays' Brigade

D. H. Hill's Division
Rodes' Brigade
Doles' Brigade
Colquitt's Brigade
Iverson's Brigade
Grimes' Brigade

A. P. Hill's Division
Brockenbrough's Brigade
Gregg's Brigade
Thomas' Brigade
Lane's Brigade
Archer's Brigade
Pender's Brigade

Taliaferro's Division
Paxton's Brigade
J. R. Jones' Brigade
Warren's Brigade
Pendleton's Brigade

Cavalry Stuart

Hampton's Brigade
W. H. F. Lee's Brigade
F. Lee's Brigade
W. E. Jones' Brigade

ARMY OF THE POTOMAC (Federal)

Burnside 118,000 men

Left Grand Division Franklin

I Corps Reynolds

1st Division Doubleday
Phelps' Brigade
Gavin's Brigade
Rogers' Brigade
Meredith's Brigade

2d Division Gibbon
Root's Brigade
Lyle's Brigade
Taylor's Brigade

3d Division Meade
Sinclair's Brigade
Magilton's Brigade
Jackson's Brigade

VI Corps Smith

1st Division Brooks
Torbert's Brigade
Cake's Brigade
Russell's Brigade

2d Division Howe
Pratt's Brigade
Whiting's Brigade
Vinton's Brigade

3d Division Newton
Cochrane's Brigade
Devens' Brigade
Rowley's Brigade

Cavalry Brigade Bayard

Center Grand Division Hooker

III Corps Stoneman

1st Division Birney
Robinson's Brigade
Ward's Brigade
Berry's Brigade

2d Division Sickles
Carr's Brigade
Hall's Brigade
Revere's Brigade

3d Division Whipple
Platt's Brigade
Carroll's Brigade

V Corps Butterfield

1st Division Griffin
Barnes' Brigade
Sweitzer's Brigade
Stockton's Brigade

2d Division Sykes
Buchanan's Brigade
Andrews' Brigade
Warren's Brigade

3d Division Humphreys
Tyler's Brigade
Allabach's Brigade

Cavalry Brigade Averell

Right Grand Division Sumner

II Corps Couch

1st Division Hancock
Caldwell's Brigade
Meagher's Brigade
Zook's Brigade

2d Division Howard
Sully's Brigade
Owen's Brigade
Hall's Brigade

3d Division French
Kimball's Brigade
Palmer's Brigade
Andrews' Brigade

IX Corps Willcox

1st Division Burns
Poe's Brigade
Christ's Brigade
Leasure's Brigade

2d Division Sturgis
Nagle's Brigade
Ferrero's Brigade

3d Division Getty
Hawkins' Brigade
Harland's Brigade

Cavalry Division Pleasonton

"We shall doubtless move tomorrow or next day at farthest. The line of march will be to Fredericksburg (this is a secret)."

Major General Edwin V. Sumner, flanked by some of his staff, poses for one of Mathew Brady's photographers on November 13, 1862, at a hotel in Warrenton, Virginia. Sumner had just been appointed commander of one of the Army of the Potomac's three grand divisions that two days later would lead the march on Fredericksburg. At far right stands Lieutenant Colonel William W. Teall, Sumner's son-in-law and his chief commissary officer. Next to Teall is Sumner's topographical engineer, Lieutenant Alonzo H. Cushing. To Cushing's right is Sumner's son Sam, a cavalry officer serving as an aide-de-camp. Captain William G. "Win" Jones, a Sumner family friend, stands at the far left.

LIEUTENANT COLONEL WILLIAM W. TEALL

STAFF, MAJOR GENERAL EDWIN V. SUMNER

In these letters to his wife, Teall brings news of her father, General Sumner, and her brother Sam, summarizes the intrigues behind yet another reorganization of the Army of the Potomac, and commits a common breach of military security by naming the first objective of the upcoming campaign. The army's restructuring seemed a boon to her 65-year-old father, but a month later his grand division would be severely repulsed at Fredericksburg. Sumner died of illness in March 1863, while Teall served as an officer in the Subsistence Department until he resigned in February 1864.

Hd Qrs Army of the Potomac
Warrenton, Va
Wednesday, Nov. 12, 1862

This is another beautiful day my dear wife, & I will take a spare moment to drop you a line. Sam took quarters with me again last night & enjoys as much as I do the comfortable room which the ladies of the house so kindly appropriated to my use. Many calls have been made today by the different officers located in & around the town & Genl Halleck & Meigs have arrived from Washington to consult on the plans for the future movement of the Army. Yr father has been sent for by Genl Burnside & he is now at his head qrs. They will remain till tomorrow & it is pretty certain the plans marked out at Washington do not receive the cordial approbation of Genl Burnside & his advisers here. This of course you will not mention. It is by no means certain that Genl Burnside will hold command if forced to depart from the plans he deems essential to the safety of the Army. Hooker & his friends doubtless would be delighted to have him retire in hopes of securing the command himself. Whatever may occur yr father will not surrender his. It has been definitely settled at Washington to divide the Army into 3 divisions to be commanded by yr father, Franklin, & Hooker. This will give yr father an Army of over 40,000 men & Genl B. has told him to make his selection of corps & position. He will not retire even if in the future arrangements Hooker should succeed to the command of the grand army in the field. This he has fully decided on. . . .

Ambrose E. Burnside reluctantly accepted leadership of the Army of the Potomac largely at the urging of other officers who were intent on blocking the rise of the scheming General Joseph Hooker. He manfully took responsibility for the Fredericksburg disaster and performed useful service in a number of lesser commands through the rest of the war. Enjoying his greatest success after the war, he was thrice elected governor of Rhode Island and was subsequently a U.S. senator until his death in 1881.

Same as above
Nov. 13, 1862

Another beautiful day my dear wife & as matters were at rather a standstill just now I determined to accept Win's invitation to accompany him back to his camp & accordingly left about 11 & reached Genl Stoneman's HdQrs about 1. in company with Capt Cushing of yr fathers staff. Whilst there Col Brown of the 101st N.Y. came to see me & after a lunch Genl Stoneman & Win came back with us. Just as we were about returning I heard the first rebel firing of any consequence saw the smoke & the flash of the cannon in front of Genl Sturges' Command. I must say there was some excitement in it.

Genl Hallack & Meiggs returned to Washington this morning & the plan of movements & assignment of Division Commanders, all perfectly agreed on & entirely harmonious. Yr Father is next in rank to Genl Burnside & assumes Command of his old Corps the 2d & Genl Reynold's. Genl Hooker next in rank, takes his Corps & Genl Heintzleman's, & Franklin his own & Genl Wilcox's or Burnsides old Corps. Your father has the right wing & we shall doubtless move tomorrow or next day at farthest. The line of march will be to Fredericksburg (this is a secret) which we shall reach probably in 2 days after we start by forced marches. We shall be nearest the enemy & no telling how soon we may encounter them. Brady's photographic operator has just been here to sketch yr father & his staff & for the first time I have been placed on canvass in uniform. Win was also in it with us. No letters yet from home. I hope you are all well. How happy should I be could I see all tonight.

MAJOR GENERAL AMBROSE P. HILL

Division Commander, Second Corps

Unaware of Burnside's plans for a winter offensive, Hill expected to remain encamped with his command around Winchester until the spring. The fiery Hill chafed under Jackson's strict command, and this letter to Jeb Stuart reflects his chagrin that his "Light Division" never received proper credit for its critical role in the battles of the preceding campaigns.

Hd Qrs, Opequon
Nov. 14th [1862]
My dear Stuart

Many thanks for your kindness in sending me the letter—It found me with only one arm useful—the other swollen—big as old Sacketts leg—the Yanks are quiet here now—Maj White has been stirring them up considerably of late, some four hundred prisoners in the last ten days—he is a trump, and one of the best cavalry officers we have. . . . I suppose I am to vegetate here all the winter under that crazy old Presbyterian fool—I am like the porcupine all bristles, and all sticking out too, so I know we shall have a smash up before long. I dont like the complexion here—I think a fatal error has been committed, providing the Yanks have the sense to take advantage of it, which they dont often do, for they sometimes miss the peach when held to their lips. . . . The Almighty will get tired of helping Jackson after a while, and then he'll get the d—ndest thrashing—and the shoe pinches, for I shall get my share and probably all the blame, for the people will never blame Stonewall for any disaster. Good by

Yours—
Hill

LIEUTENANT ALEXANDER C. JONES

3d Arkansas Infantry, Cooke's Brigade

The constant campaigning of 1862 had strained the Confederacy's ability to supply its troops, many of whom had to face the onset of winter without warm clothing. Jones and his comrades, far from home, were fortunate to receive badly needed goods from their brigade mates in the 30th Virginia. Promoted to captain in 1863, Jones suffered a severe wound in his right arm at the Wilderness on May 6, 1864. He later returned to duty and was paroled at Appomattox.

The 3d Arkansas Regiment of Infantry was the sole representative of our State in the Army of Virginia for nearly two years. We were brigaded with the 30th Virginia (from Fredericksburg and vicinity) and the 27th and 36th North Carolina. The Virginia and Arkansas soldiers became better acquainted and more intimate than the other regiments; indeed, we became very social and friendly.

Shortly after the awful fatigues and marches of the first Maryland campaign, culminating in the bloody battle of Sharpsburg, the troops were camped somewhere between Shepherdstown and Winchester. We were sorely in need of clothing and shoes, and there was not a blanket in the command, while the frosty nights of that cold climate pinched severely. At that time the 30th Virginia received a considerable supply of shoes and blankets from their friends and relatives at Fredericksburg, about eighty miles distant. When these supplies arrived, we of the 3d Arkansas were surprised to receive a message from the headquarters of the 30th, requesting that we send a detail to receive our

This marksmanship medal was presented to the best shot among members of the Fredericksburg Greys, a militia unit organized shortly before the war. In 1861 the Greys became Company B of the 30th Virginia Infantry, and the following year they fought in defense of their native soil against the onslaught of Burnside's troops.

share of these good things. Colonel Manning called a meeting of the officers, and we passed some resolutions warmly thanking the Virginians for their generous offer, but declining to accept on the ground that the donors of those goods intended them for the relief of their own kin. The reply came back immediately and in the strongest terms: "We are brothers fighting in the same cause, and, besides, you are a long distance from home, and it is impossible for your friends to help you. We insist upon it that we divide." And they did.

LIEUTENANT JAMES P. SMITH

STAFF, LIEUTENANT GENERAL THOMAS J. JACKSON

Jackson's staff had expected Lee to bring their corps across the Blue Ridge to attack the Federals near Warrenton or to leave it in Winchester until spring. Hence, they were caught off guard when orders came to move quickly to a position on the Rappahannock River—though their commander seemed to take the new plan in stride.

That evening as the night came on and the snow fell, a courier arrived, spattered with mud and mounted on a wearied, snow-covered horse, and bearing a sealed letter. Thinking it a dispatch from some cavalry picket on our front, I opened it and was surprised to find it a letter signed, "Robert E. Lee." In a few minutes Jackson came from his room, quite erect and aroused. "Who opened this letter, young gentlemen?" On my feet at once, I replied: "I opened it, general, supposing it to be a dispatch from some cavalry command." He said, "Captain Smith, you and Colonel Pendleton come into my room." There we discovered that General Lee, after giving reasons for taking a defensive line on the Rappahannock, instead of the North Anna river, had instructed Jackson to move his command, not east over Ashby's Gap, but south on the Valley turnpike, and, crossing the Blue Ridge, to

Normally attired in a "faded, semi-military coat" with a battered cap tugged down over his eyes, Stonewall Jackson surprised his troops in late November when he appeared in a smart new suit given to him by Jeb Stuart. This portrait is based on a photograph of Jackson taken that month in Winchester. Although he posed for the photograph in his old uniform, the artist chose to portray him in his new attire.

Englishman Frank Vizetelly, the only "special artist" accompanying the Rebels, produced these scenes for the Illustrated London News. Below, Confederates mill around near Fredericksburg's waterfront while keeping an eye on Yankee pickets, visible in the tree line along the Rappahannock's far bank. The bottom right sketch shows a view of the town from the Federal side of the river. At bottom left, Rebel cavalrymen are entertained by a black camp attendant.

40—JAN. 10, 1863 THE ILLUSTRATED LONDON NEWS JAN. 10, 1863—41

THE CIVIL WAR IN AMERICA.

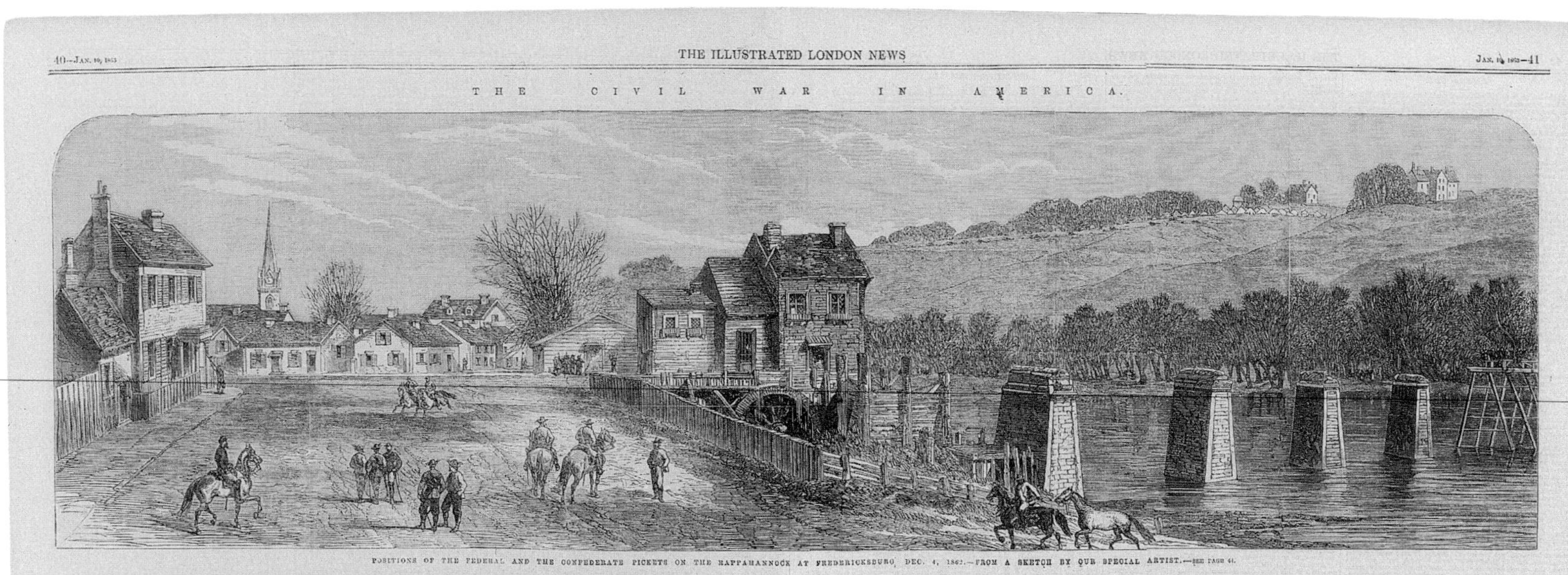

POSITIONS OF THE FEDERAL AND THE CONFEDERATE PICKETS ON THE RAPPAHANNOCK AT FREDERICKSBURG, DEC. 4, 1862.—FROM A SKETCH BY OUR SPECIAL ARTIST.—SEE PAGE 41.

NIGHT AMUSEMENTS IN THE CONFEDERATE CAMP.—FROM A SKETCH BY OUR SPECIAL ARTIST.—SEE PAGE 41.

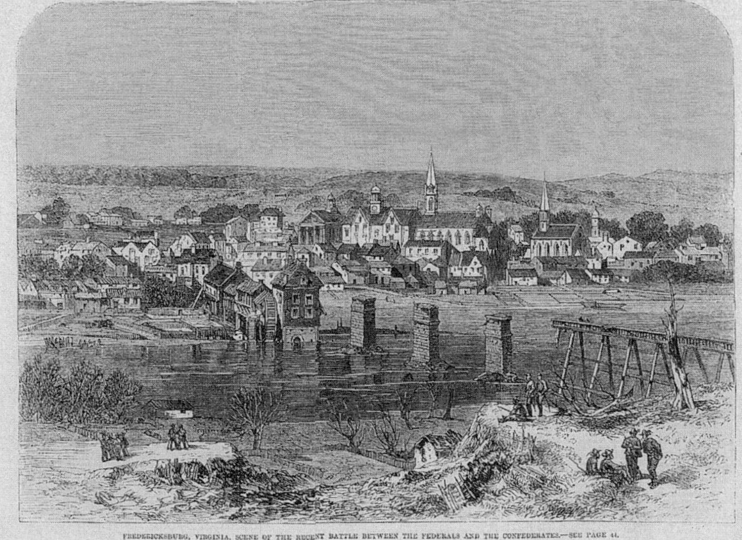

FREDERICKSBURG, VIRGINIA, SCENE OF THE RECENT BATTLE BETWEEN THE FEDERALS AND THE CONFEDERATES.—SEE PAGE 41.

"Young gentlemen, this is no longer the headquarters of the Army of the Valley, but of the Second Corps of the Army of Northern Virginia."

march by Orange to Fredericksburg. So our stay for the winter in Winchester was for one night only, and on the morning of November 20, the town woke up to a great disappointment, for Stonewall Jackson and all of his command had gone at daylight.

The general and his whole cavalcade visited the field of the battle of Kernstown, going over in detail the operations of the engagement, the general commending the service there of the Rockbridge Artillery. Going up the valley from Kernstown, by Middletown, and Strasburg, he turned east at New Market and over the Massanutton Gap, crossed the Luray Valley, and went up into Fisher's Gap of the Blue Ridge. Early on the clear, cold morning of November 25, the staff came out of their tents quite on the top of the mountain, at Fisher's Gap, and looked west over the Valley and the mountains, as Spotswood and his knights had gazed westward at Swift Run Gap, and then east far and away over the plains of Madison and Orange. There was a little delay in our gathering at the out-of-door breakfast table. When at length the general came, to our surprise in a new uniform and sword, he blushed and smiled, saying, "Young gentlemen, this is no longer the headquarters of the Army of the Valley, but of the Second Corps of the Army of Northern Virginia." He had taken the occasion on the mountain top to announce the new title of his command, and to appear in new and elegant uniform. When he was next seen by large bodies of his troops, on the lines from Fredericksburg to Hamilton's Crossing, he was not recognized for some time.

CAPTAIN JAMES C. NISBET

21ST GEORGIA INFANTRY, HOKE'S BRIGADE

The quest of Nisbet's regiment for some of the local apple brandy while they marched out of the Valley entailed certain risks: The troops first ignored General Jubal Early's orders denying them access to the liquor, then boldly displayed their drink-induced high spirits to the usually stern and puritanical Stonewall Jackson.

On November 21st we bade the valley girls goodbye, promising to come back; and commenced our march down the valley. We proceeded through Winchester to New Market, where the head of the column turned towards the Blue Ridge on to Columbia Bridge which spans the eastern branch of the Shenandoah and thence to Luray Court House.

When our pike road leading across the Blue Ridge turned up the Hawks-bill Valley, our boys struck a lively gait. Captain A. S. Hamilton was commanding the regiment. We were halted for a ten minutes rest, as was customary with Jackson's Corps, after marching two miles. My company requested me to make a detail to take the canteens and buy apple brandy for all that wanted it. Captain Hamilton consented; so each company made a detail. When we made the Valley Campaign in the spring our men had found Kite's still-house at the head of Hawks-bill Valley, at the foot of the mountain. When the detailed men went through the big apple orchard and got to the still-house they were halt-

"In spite of orders to the contrary, we used to frequently pass our pickets, descend to the water's edge and signal to the rebels opposite."

ed by a cavalry guard, who said that General Jubal Early commanding Ewell's Division had forbidden Kite selling brandy to his men. This being reported the regiment led by Captain Hamilton broke ranks and went over there. Captain Hamilton asked the lieutenant of the guard if General Early got any brandy as he passed? He answered: "Yes, he had his canteen filled and the keg behind his ambulance." Captain Hamilton said: "Then we will buy what we want," and told old mate Kite to use certain men to draw the liquor and to receive the money. When we had bought what we wanted other regiments were served as they arrived.

The pike road leading across the Blue Ridge to Madison Court House winds up the mountain by easy grade. It was a cool November afternoon, the brandy warmed the boys up and made them hilarious. They sang corn-shucking songs. One of my men, Riley Thurman, who had a remarkably fine voice, led. The whole brigade joined in the chorus, which they could do well, as the leading regiment was often close to the rear of the brigade, on account of the windings of the road.

General Jackson caught up with us, and in trying to pass on was caught in the jam and had to listen to some very *risque* couplets. The austere Presbyterian elder could not hide his amusement at the cheek of the fellow leading. He did not seem to be worried that his twenty thousand veterans felt happy and light hearted. . . .

. . . The inhabitants of this favored region through which we passed were worthy of their inheritance. The devotion of all to the Southern cause was wonderful. No oppression, no destitution, could abate their zeal! The women sent husbands, sons and lovers to battle as smilingly as to a marriage feast. With the Virginian, patriotism was stronger even than the ties of blood. Through all the towns we passed, and along the pikes, we were greeted with enthusiasm. They met us at their doors and gates with the best of food and words of encouragement; mid smiles and tears, they waved Confederate flags brought forth from their hiding places. It was ever thus with these noble women. Although insulted and plundered by the invader, they never faltered in their loyalty to old Virginia and the South.

PRIVATE EUGENE A. CORY

4th New York Infantry, Andrews' Brigade

Elements of the II Corps were the first units of the Army of the Potomac to reach the Rappahannock River across from Fredericksburg. These troops, among them the 4th New York, quickly established picket posts along the river, where they could keep watch on the Confederates. As often happened when there was no fighting, such locations soon provided the opportunity for spontaneous exchanges of food, clothing, and equipment between the well-supplied Yankees and the more hard-pressed Rebels.

Our first picket duty on this line, was upon the river bank, about one-half mile in front of our camp, and about two miles above Falmouth. The river at this point was full of rocks and fordable, with banks low, immediately at the edge of the river, but rising into quite a high hill a short way back. The pickets were stationed upon the hills overlooking the river, and in spite of orders to the contrary, we used to frequently pass our pickets, descend to the water's edge and signal to the rebels opposite, who, if I recollect rightly, belonged to the Fourth Georgia and Eighth Alabama regiments. Upon seeing our signals, they would at once prepare for business by loading themselves with cloth haversacks of tobacco, and holding them above their heads,

With the Rappahannock in the background, a sergeant from the 11th Alabama trades tobacco to soldiers of the 57th New York in exchange for a copy of the New York Herald. Arthur Lumley, who sketched this encounter for the New York Illustrated News, noted that the exchanges were soon stopped by the inflexible Major N. Garron Throop of the 57th, who approaches on horseback at the upper right to arrest the hapless Rebel. Throop (inset) died on January 12, 1863, of a wound received at Fredericksburg.

plunge into the icy cold water, and make their way across to our side, sometimes passing from rock to rock, and sometimes up to their breasts in water. Two generally came over at a time, and as soon as they arrived barter would commence, and in a few minutes the tobacco would be exchanged for overcoats, shoes, blankets, coffee and sugar, or any of the numerous articles plentiful with us, but scarce with them, when they would at once return, both parties being satisfied with their bargains. . . . On arriving in camp I had the good fortune to find among a number of comrades who had been absent from the regiment since the battle of Antietam, and just arrived from hospitals, one who had two overcoats and no tobacco; another trade was soon made, and three pounds of rebel tobacco exchanged for a better overcoat than I had sold for ten pounds. This was a piece of good fortune which did not always happen, for many a man famished for tobacco, traded away a blanket, or overcoat, which he could not replace for weeks. I once asked one of these rebel traders if they wore the overcoats which they were always anxious to purchase. He replied, "No, indeed, they were too fine for them to wear"; that they sold readily in Richmond to civilians for $100 each.

LIEUTENANT JOSIAH M. FAVILL
57TH NEW YORK INFANTRY, ZOOK'S BRIGADE

By November 20, the date of Favill's account, more than 100,000 Union troops were posted in and around Falmouth, turning the town into an armed camp governed by military law. Unable to cross the river without the proper bridging materials, they watched their foes constructing earthworks on the heights behind Fredericksburg, contemplating the doleful implications. Favill survived the conflict and was eventually brevetted a lieutenant colonel for "gallant and meritorious service."

On taking command of Falmouth, we made a list of the inhabitants, showing their age, occupation, sex, etc.

There is so much illicit communication with the enemy, that a strict surveillance is necessary, even over the women, whom we have more than once found performing the office of spies. Sentinels are posted at every street corner, and the patrol goes the rounds every hour both night and day.

The Fifty-seventh is for the time being the provost guard, and both officers and men are delighted at their good fortune. As most of the best houses were deserted when we arrived, the officers found no difficulty in securing good quarters. The difference between a good house, even if it is empty, and an ordinary shelter tent, late in November, is immense, and the officers fully appreciate it. . . .

Headquarters are in a vacant house on the southeastern corner of the principal street, opposite the lonely looking little brick church. We use the front room for an office, while the rear room does duty as a dining room, and sleeping quarters for the staff. The colonel, as becomes the dignity of the commandant, sleeps alone up stairs. The house is empty, save for the office desks and folding chairs, but when the various colored blankets are spread on the floor, around the room at night, ready for use, it looks quite luxurious. . . .

The enemy occupy the range of hills opposite, and are working night and day to make them impregnable. Apparently there are a series of hills running parallel to the river, or nearly so, in rear of each other, and the camps of Lee's army are wholly sheltered in the intervening valleys. No better position for defense could be found, and Lee must thank his stars Burnside did not establish himself on that

HAULING TEAMS OUT OF THE MUD, AN EVERY DAY SCENE ON THE ROAD FROM AQUIA CREEK, TO THE HEADQUARTERS OF THE ARMY OF THE POTOMAC BEFORE FREDERICKSBURG.—SKETCHED BY OUR SPECIAL ARTIST, ARTHUR LUMLEY. See page 115.

The angry crack of a Union teamster's whip has little effect on the exhausted and foundering horses of a Federal supply train stuck in the mud while en route to the Army of the Potomac from its supply base on Aquia Creek. Drenched by heavy downpours, roads such as this helped delay the arrival of the pontoon bridges at Falmouth and negated the surprise Burnside had achieved by his rapid movement to the east bank of the Rappahannock River.

side when he had a chance to do so almost unopposed. It is strange how constantly we fall short in our endeavors at the very moment when we might succeed. Something is missing; this time, it was the pontoon train that failed us just at the critical point in the campaign.

"It is strange how constantly we fall short in our endeavors at the very moment when we might succeed."

Atop pontoon boats like the ungainly-looking vessel pictured at right, troops placed anchoring beams followed by a series of tightly fitting planks to form a temporary bridge. Practiced Federal engineers could turn a train of pontoons (above) into a working bridge in short order, provided there was no enemy opposition. Such structures were strong enough to support the passage of horse-drawn wagons and artillery, as well as infantry columns. These bridges were indispensable to the Army of the Potomac throughout the war in spanning Virginia's rivers.

LIEUTENANT COLONEL E. PORTER ALEXANDER

ARTILLERY BATTALION COMMANDER, FIRST CORPS

Reaching the outskirts of Fredericksburg on November 19, Longstreet's men quickly began to fortify the hills, although not, as Alexander recounts, without some controversy. Alexander reportedly boasted to Longstreet that fire from his guns could cover the "ground as [well as] a fine tooth comb."

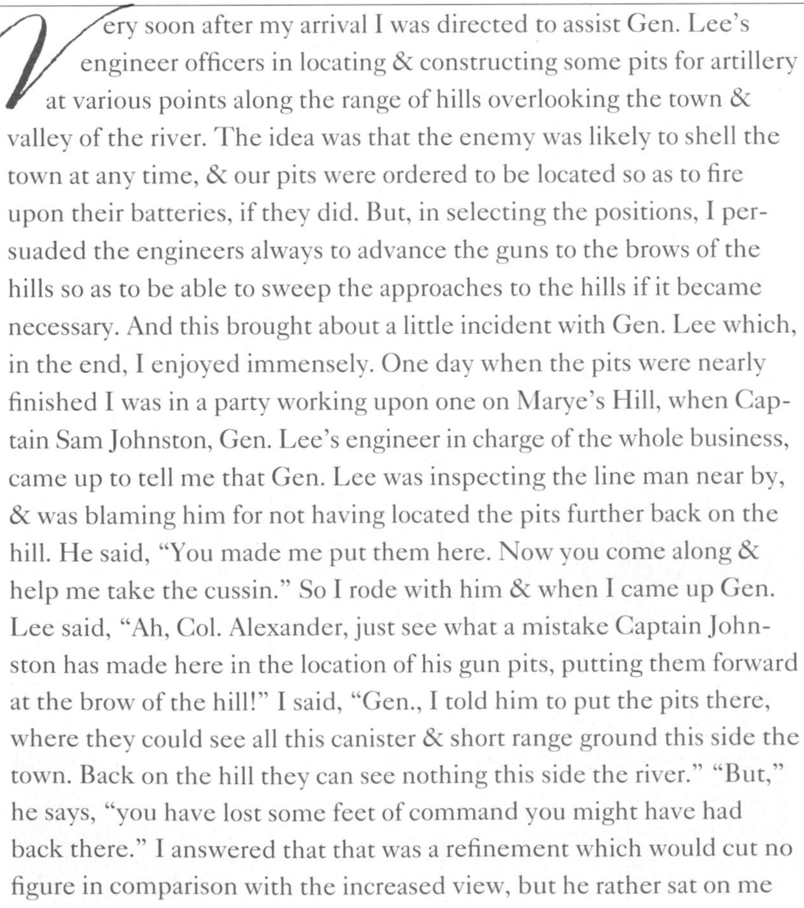

Very soon after my arrival I was directed to assist Gen. Lee's engineer officers in locating & constructing some pits for artillery at various points along the range of hills overlooking the town & valley of the river. The idea was that the enemy was likely to shell the town at any time, & our pits were ordered to be located so as to fire upon their batteries, if they did. But, in selecting the positions, I persuaded the engineers always to advance the guns to the brows of the hills so as to be able to sweep the approaches to the hills if it became necessary. And this brought about a little incident with Gen. Lee which, in the end, I enjoyed immensely. One day when the pits were nearly finished I was in a party working upon one on Marye's Hill, when Captain Sam Johnston, Gen. Lee's engineer in charge of the whole business, came up to tell me that Gen. Lee was inspecting the line man near by, & was blaming him for not having located the pits further back on the hill. He said, "You made me put them here. Now you come along & help me take the cussin." So I rode with him & when I came up Gen. Lee said, "Ah, Col. Alexander, just see what a mistake Captain Johnston has made here in the location of his gun pits, putting them forward at the brow of the hill!" I said, "Gen., I told him to put the pits there, where they could see all this canister & short range ground this side the town. Back on the hill they can see nothing this side the river." "But," he says, "you have lost some feet of command you might have had back there." I answered that that was a refinement which would cut no figure in comparison with the increased view, but he rather sat on me & had the last word, though I knew I was right & did not give it up.

Well, when the battle came on, Burnside's most powerful effort was made at that exact point, & the guns there never fired a shot at their distant view, but thousands of rounds into infantry swarming over the canister & short range ground, & contributed greatly to the enemy's bloody repulse. And a few evenings afterward, visiting Gen. Lee's camp, I took the opportunity, when the general was near enough to hear, to say loudly to Johnston, "Sam, it was a mighty good thing those guns about Marye's were located on the brows of the hills when the Yankees charged them!" I was half afraid the general might think me impertinent, though I could not resist the temptation to have one little dig at him. But he took it in silence & never let on that he was listening to us.

COLONEL JAMES D. NANCE

3D SOUTH CAROLINA INFANTRY, KERSHAW'S BRIGADE

In this letter to his sister, dated November 30, Nance expressed his disapproval of fraternization and his naive assumption that his soldiers agreed. He then described the plight of the local women, many of whom were fleeing the Yankees. Wounded at Fredericksburg, Nance was later killed in action at the Wilderness.

Since I last wrote I have been on another tour of picket duty in the city of Fredericksburg. This time I had the extreme outpost. My line of pickets ran immediately along the south bank of the river—the enemy's immediately along the opposite bank. There we stood, walked and talked, eyeing each other, but nothing more. No firing at, or conversation between, the pickets are allowed. Theirs often endeavor to betray or provoke some of ours into a conversation, but, I believe, seldom succeed. It is a wise regulation, for many reasons, that our men are not allowed to talk with them. They deserve, except in official intercourse, to be treated with the greatest contempt. . . . I missed an opportunity of crossing the river yesterday under flag of truce. There was the wife of a Yankee Surgeon to be sent over the ferry within my command; but, unfortunately, when she came, I was absent at some other point of the line, and it devolved upon my Lieut. at the Ferry to gallant the Yankee woman across the river as well as the lines. That was the only incident connected with my tour of duty in the city, if I except an interview with two ladies in the streets, who accosted me with an imploring air to have them sent out of the city. One of them was a very fair damsel who impressed me very favorably; the other, though by no means a handsome, yet a very cute, dame. Military affairs are very much the same as when I last wrote; but the city is more deserted and the female inhabitants take fresh panics occasionally that lead to further depopulation. There are doubtless many cases of suffering and trial with these good women. Although I have not seen it, I understand many of these ladies have camped in the woods and crowded together in mean houses in the vicinity of the city to escape the danger which threatens the city and its indwellers. Army wagons and ambulances have at different times been employed in hauling away the people and their effects. Notwithstanding all this preparation, it seems to me that the city is likely to suffer, if at all, only incidentally. There will be no direct attack upon the city, although if there is to be a fight in the vicinity of it, it may suffer as did the little village of Sharpsburg, Md., at Antietam. I should be sorry to see Fredericksburg suffer. No more loyal town honors Virginia, and in times of peace, I imagine, no people in her borders are more hospitable and virtuous.

A family of Fredericksburg refugees huddling around a fire bids farewell to a departing soldier before they retire for the evening to a crude bower of sticks and boughs. Certain that the town would be shelled, Robert E. Lee himself urged people to leave for the comparative safety of the countryside. Many heeded his warning, contributing to what a Confederate cavalryman called the "pitiable sight . . . [of] old men, women and children . . . shivering in the cold."

"It makes me so angry to think about those persons at home who are always harping about Onward to Richmond when they do not know what they are talking about."

LIEUTENANT CURTIS C. POLLACK

48th Pennsylvania Infantry, Nagle's Brigade

By early December, when Pollack wrote this letter to his mother, the stress and anxiety caused by conflicting orders and civilian questioning of Burnside's inactivity, aggravated by the miserable winter weather, was wearing down the morale of the Army of the Potomac. Pollack, a resident of Pottsville, Pennsylvania, lived through the Fredericksburg debacle but was mortally wounded in June 1864 at Petersburg.

We have received several very conflicting orders within the last few days. Yesterday morning we had an order from Gen. Sturgis to set aside the drills for two days to enable the men to fix up comfortable quarters for themselves. That looked very much like winter quarters, but the General told me we would be likely to stay but a week or two longer. However the order to cook rations looks very much like a move, and you must not be much surprised to hear of the Army of the Potomac crossing the river. It is very cold lately, and if we have to do much more marching this winter we will freeze to death, because it is as much as we can do to keep warm now, and we have a very comfortable fire place. I only hope Burnside knows what is good for his army and not move this winter. I would like nothing better than to see Richmond fall but I do not think winter the time to do it. If we would have to march, and we only can carry one blanket, how do you suppose we would get along with 3 on a march and we have six here. It is almost impossible, let those persons at home say what they may. No doubt they sleep warm and comfortable enough in their feather beds while the poor soldier is nearly froze and has to get up two or three times a night to walk around and keep warm. You may think it strange what I say, but it makes me so angry to think about those persons at home who are always harping about Onward to Richmond when they do not know what they are talking about.

Previously a neat, well-kept town of some 5,000 inhabitants, Fredericksburg had already suffered some damage in the first year and a half of the war. But artillery fire from both armies during this battle, particularly the Union bombardment of December 11, caused widespread destruction. Before the shelling, Alfred R. Waud drew this view of the city for Harper's Weekly from a vantage point across the river in Falmouth. Beyond the town, on the horizon to the far right, rises the soon-to-be-infamous Marye's Heights.

In the days before the battle, Yankees and Rebels gathered on the remains of the Richmond, Fredericksburg & Potomac Railroad bridge to exchange catcalls and proffer trade items across the Rappahannock. In one such exchange a German immigrant in Union blue bragged that Burnside's forces numbered in the "dousand[s]." "Oh," a Confederate replied, "bring them along . . . we reckoned you had an army!"

PRIVATE WILLIAM MCCARTER

116TH PENNSYLVANIA INFANTRY, MEAGHER'S BRIGADE

McCarter, an immigrant from Ireland, described eloquently and in great detail the Army of the Potomac's excited preparations for the battle to come on the morrow. McCarter sustained four wounds during his brigade's assault on Marye's Heights. Discharged on May 12, 1863, he suffered from his injuries until his death in 1911.

At noon, marching orders for the next day were issued to the troops. They well knew their destination. Each man was to be furnished with three days cooked rations and 80 rounds of ammunition—40 rounds to fill his cartridge box and 40 rounds for his pockets. Now comes the tug of war, I thought. . . .

During the entire day, the greatest activity prevailed in every camp. —Orderlies, on horseback, dashing to and fro, delivering dispatches to commanding officers.—Infantry regiments, and brigades, marching from one point to another, visible for a short time, and then disappearing from view behind some distant hill, or down in some dark valley skirted by dense woods.—Heavy siege guns (as a reserve) rumbling along, drawn by 4 or 6 splendid horses to each gun, and cavalry regiments taking up the various positions assigned them on this side of the river ready for an advance at any moment in the passage of the Rappahannock, if ordered to do so. Many of the "Boys" were also engaged in cleaning their fire arms, and putting them in extra trim for expected use on the morrow. During the afternoon, hundreds of bullocks stopped many a well directed rifle ball and fell to the ground dead and bleeding there to be operated on by the regimental butcher, who upon finishing the job, turned the cut-up carcase over to the Commissary of each regiment, who, in turn, distributed to each company of the regiment its portion for the 3 days rations ordered. In the evening a thousand blazing camp fires behind the Stafford Hills, and spreading over a large tract of country north of that range of little mountains, lighted up the skies, as well as the thick dark and gloomy woods in which most of our camps were situated. The scene was a lively one.—every man seemed to be busy at something for the coming storm of battle. Here, might be seen a group of the Boys around a fire, talking, laughing and joking as they attended to the boiling of huge chunks of "salt horse" (cured beef) and fresh beef in the large iron pots suspended over nearly every fire. There, in the best of spirits and good humor sat several others, cooking pork, by sticking a lump of it on a long branch of a tree and holding the meat over, or in the blaze till done. In another place could be seen men sitting or standing till their little tin cups of boiling coffee were ready for use, while hosts of others, covered over with canteens were constantly arriving with fresh water from some neighboring spring or brook and others were departing for it. Here a man was seated patching his coat or pants, sewing on a button, or cobbling his shoes. Over yonder, another was removing some of Virginia's red mud from his uniform, while not a few in every direction could be observed brightening up buttons, breastplates, muskets, bayonets and sabres. Officers congregated in groups here and there, near a camp fire, under a tree, or seated on a pile of boxes or barrels, discussed the chief topic of the day.—the anticipated struggle of the morrow. Every body seemed to enjoy the situation, and the near prospect of having, as some termed it, "another heavy brush with the Johnnys." . . .

No roll of the drum or sound of the bugle told that the hour to retire for the night had arrived. Oh, no. The work of the morrow seemed to have taken full possession of the minds of every man wearing the blue, from the highest officer down to the little drummer boy. The desire for sleep had fled as well as everything else not connected with the coming struggle. The night being clear and very cold, favored the preparations going on and pointed to the morn as one well suited for the march of troops, inasmuch as the ground, which, for a few days before had been soft and damp, would then have become comparatively hard & dry by freezing.

"If tomorrow night finds me dead remember me kindly as a soldier who meant to do his whole duty."

COLONEL SAMUEL ZOOK

BRIGADE COMMANDER, II CORPS

In a bitter mood on the evening of December 10, Zook, in this letter to a friend, predicted the impending Federal disaster after scathingly recounting the operational blunders that set the stage for it. Although Zook survived Fredericksburg and even gained the general's star he so coveted, he later fell fatally wounded at Gettysburg on July 2, 1863.

Tomorrow we commence the crossing of the Rappahannock & will be sure to have a fearful fight—In fact I expect we will be licked, for we have allowed the rebs nearly four weeks to erect batteries &c. to slaughter us by thousands in consequence of the infernal inefficiency of the Quarter Master Genl & his subordinates. If we had had the pontoons promised when we arrived here we could have the hills on the other side of the river without cost[ing] over 50 men—Now it will cost at least ten thousand if not more.

I expect to be sacrificed tomorrow. I should not care a cent about it, if I could have rec'd a Brig. Genl, but your Shinolas, Busteeds & Browns who never saw a fight must be promoted & such as I am who are fools enough to do the fighting are left to die Cols. after as many years as they please to stand it, & fate does not cut them off short of it. . . .

. . . If tomorrow night finds me dead remember me kindly as a soldier who meant to do his whole duty.

A Day of Slaughter

Before dawn on December 11, men of the 50th New York Engineers began laying pontoon bridges across the Rappahannock opposite Fredericksburg. On the far bank, hidden in rifle pits and basements and behind walls of riverfront buildings, the men of William Barksdale's Mississippi brigade waited for enough light to find targets.

Burnside's belated offensive had finally begun. As soon as the bridges were finished, the troops of Edwin Sumner's grand division were to race over them, march through the town, and attack Lee's Confederates on the ridge beyond. About a mile to the south, William Franklin's grand division would cross the river and sweep over a broad plain, hit the Rebel right wing, and, with Sumner's command, force Longstreet's corps off the heights. Joseph Hooker's grand division would remain in reserve, ready to add its weight when the enemy began to give way.

Viewed from the southern end of Marye's Heights, the broad open ground lying west of Fredericksburg offered the 40,000 Federals who crossed it scant cover from the lethal rain of bullet and shell sent their way from the Rebel line on December 13.

As a mist lifted and the forms of the engineers emerged in the pale light, the Mississippians in the town opened fire, killing and wounding a number of the bridge builders and driving the rest back.

All morning the Rebels turned away attempts to advance the bridges. At about noon the frustrated Federals brought every available artillery piece—150 guns—to bear on the hapless town to suppress the sniping and for the next two hours fired 5,000 shells into Fredericksburg. The bombardment wrecked buildings and started fires but failed to dislodge the defenders, who merely found abundant new firing positions in the rubble.

Not until about 2:30 did the exasperated Federals hit on a solution—an amphibious attack. Using the pontoons as assault boats, teams of infantry volunteers stormed the far bank, gained a toehold, and gradually pried Barksdale's men out of their lairs. The Rebels withdrew and joined the main Confederate body at the foot of the ridge, while the town was occupied by four Union brigades.

To the south, Franklin's advance was stymied by confusion. His engineers had managed to lay two bridges that morning, but a series of contradictory orders from Burnside held the troops back. Only the following morning did Franklin march his entire force across the Rappahannock and deploy it on the open ground west of the river.

That same day, December 12, Sumner's troops continued to pour into Fredericksburg as Burnside pondered his next move. With time on their hands, the soldiers began looting the town, moving through the deserted homes, taking what they could carry and smashing the rest. Federal commanders tried to stop the wanton destruction, but mostly in vain.

The Federal delays gave Lee plenty of time to prepare. Eyeing Franklin's corps spreading out on the plain, he first summoned two and then all four of Jackson's divisions from downriver, intending to deploy them along the ridge below Longstreet to extend and strengthen the Confederate right.

Later on December 12 Burnside rode to Franklin's headquarters to discuss with him a change of strategy. Having lost all chance of striking a divided Rebel force, Burnside now wanted Franklin's grand division to make the main attack by surging around the Confederate right flank and threatening the enemy's rear. After this opening attack had made headway, Burnside would unleash Sumner against Lee's left, a classic one-two combination.

But the written orders Burnside issued early the morning of December 13 did not—according to Franklin—square with his understanding of the battle plan agreed upon the previous day. To compound matters, neither Burnside nor Franklin had a grasp of the geography of the area. The result would be calamitous.

Burnside ordered Franklin to attack by crossing the railroad that paralleled the river, marching via the "Richmond road." This road, however, did not cross the railroad but ran alongside it. Burnside actually had a turnoff from the Richmond road in mind, but in wishing to put Franklin on this road he was doubly mistaken, because this route would have positioned Franklin short of the end of the Rebel line. Franklin, in the event, would complete the tragedy of errors by making his turn sooner, on an obscure farm road.

As a morning fog lifted, the Federal troops moved to the attack and soon had to pay the price of their commanders' ignorance and confusion. Instead of moving far enough south to go around Jackson, they turned directly into the teeth of two of his divisions.

Leading the Federals was George G. Meade's division, supported on the right by John Gibbon's. No sooner had Meade's troops got under way than shells began to fall into their ranks, stalling their attack for more than a half-hour.

Finally Meade's men pressed on up the slope and found themselves pouring through a gap in the Confederate lines, briefly driving back the Rebels in their front and on both flanks. But Confederate reinforcements turned the tide, and soon Meade's formations, along with Gibbon's, were put to rout. Franklin's Federals were back where they started—having lost 4,830 men. Jackson's losses were also severe—3,415—but he had held his ground.

Farther north, the Confederates looking down on Fredericksburg from their ridge held an impregnable defensive position. Artillery atop the rise dominated the broad plain rolling out toward the town, and along the base of the heights ran a sunken road protected by a stone wall that provided perfect cover for Rebel riflemen.

To assail the heights, the Federals would have to advance from the town and cross a canal spanned by three narrow bridges, two of them no more than planks, under the very muzzles of the Confederate guns. Beyond the canal a low bluff offered some cover, and 350 yards farther up the slope there was a slight incline where a man could escape rifle fire by hugging the earth. Otherwise, there was no protection at all.

It fell to William H. French's division of the II Corps to lead the attack. At midmorning a brigade commanded by Nathan Kimball stepped from the cover of the town and immediately came under murderous artillery fire. The survivors nevertheless crossed the canal bridges and trudged up the muddy slope.

Waiting for them behind the stone wall were the troops of Thomas R. R. Cobb's Georgia brigade, supported by a regiment of North Carolinians. When Kimball's Yankees approached within 125 yards of the wall, a sheet of orange flame flashed from behind the stone wall. Another Confederate volley followed, then another.

Hundreds of Federals fell. Most of the survivors reeled back and dropped down behind the incline. Another of French's brigades went up the slope, only to be mowed down. A third came on and met the same fate. French's division had been shot to pieces.

Despite the slaughter, Burnside could think of no better tactic than to pour more formations into the holocaust of Rebel fire. All afternoon the procession continued: Winfield S. Hancock's three brigades were repelled one after another with horrible losses, as were the divisions of Oliver O. Howard and Samuel D. Sturgis.

As the butchery continued, Hooker met with Burnside and argued that further attempts to take Marye's Heights would be a "useless waste of life." But Burnside stubbornly insisted that Hooker throw his grand division into the fray.

Hooker did as ordered, but when his lead brigade met the same fate as the others, he called a halt. Seven Federal divisions had been committed, at a cost of 7,000 casualties. The Confederates on the heights lost only 1,200 men. Not a single Federal soldier reached the stone wall.

After driving Confederate defenders away from the western bank of the Rappahannock, Federal engineers rapidly finished laying six bridges: a pair at the northern end of town for use by the II Corps, a single "middle" bridge used primarily by the IX Corps, and a cluster of three spans downstream at a bend in the river, employed by the I and VI corps. By morning on December 12, Sumner's grand division had taken up positions in and around Fredericksburg, while Franklin's two corps had spread out across the plain to the south. These deployments finally convinced Lee that Burnside intended to launch a frontal attack. Longstreet's men had been dug in and ready on the heights west of town since the last days of November, and Burnside's continued dithering through December 12 gave Lee time to bring up Jackson's corps to extend and strengthen the Confederate right. By the morning of December 13, both armies were poised for battle, but the Rebels, even though outnumbered, enjoyed both an exceptionally strong position and the far simpler objective: Repel the enemy.

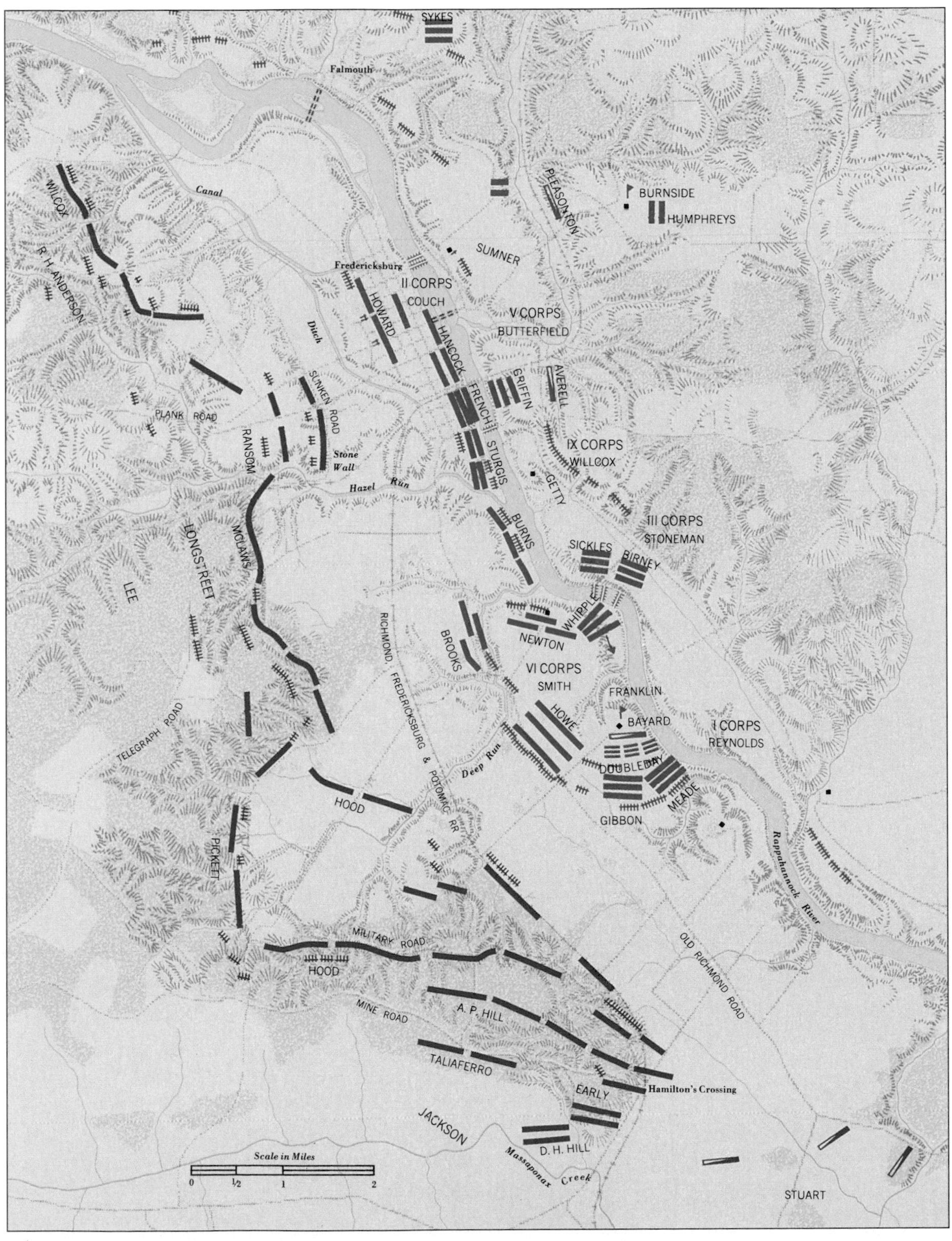

"Over 100,000 infantry were visible, standing apparently in great solid squares upon the hilltops, for a space of three miles."

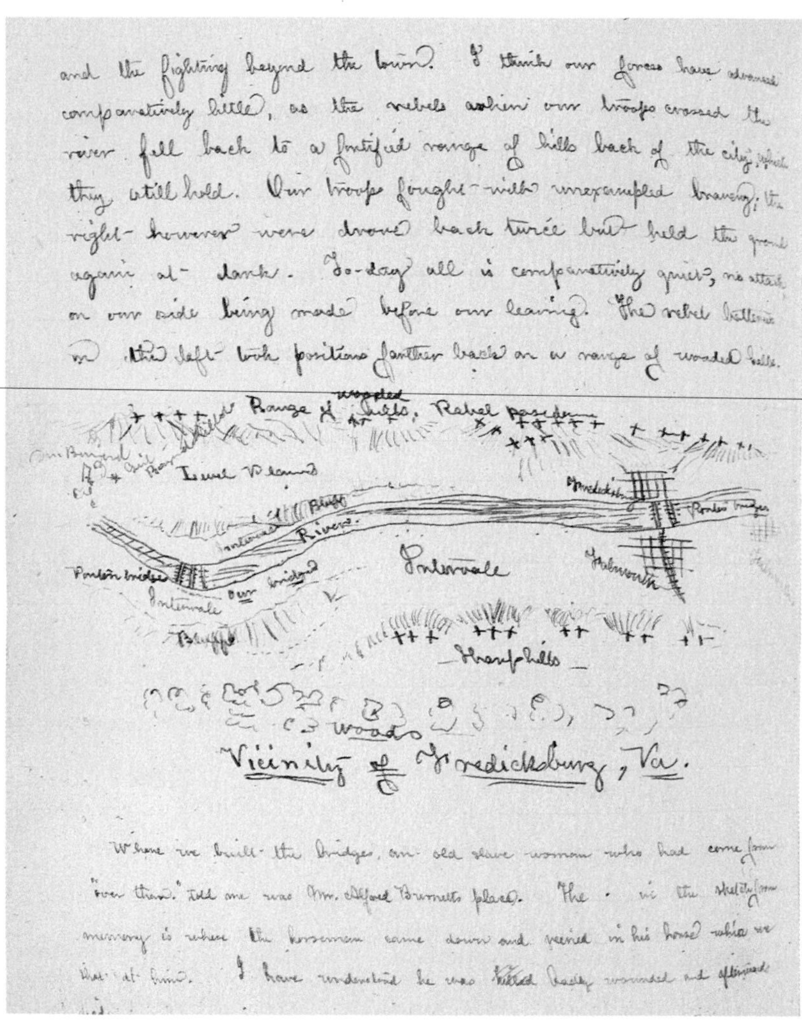

and the fighting beyond the town. I think our forces have advanced comparatively little, as the rebels when our troops crossed the river fell back to a fortified range of hills back of the city, which they still hold. Our troops fought with unexampled bravery; the right however were drove back twice but held the ground again at dark. To-day all is comparatively quiet, no attack on our side being made before our leaving. The rebel batteries on the left took positions farther back on a range of wooded hills.

Where we built the bridges, an old slave woman who had come from "over there" told me was Mr. Alfred Burnett's place. The · in the sketch from memory is where the horseman came down and peered in his house when we shot at him. I have understood he was killed badly wounded and afterwards died.

This page from the journal of Private Gilbert W. Thompson of the U.S. Engineer Battalion shows the setting of the action on December 11, including the positions of the Federal pontoon bridges. Thompson's battalion and the 15th New York Engineers laid the less contested bridges south of town, depicted on the left; the 50th New York came under heavier fire working on the spans directly opposite the town.

SERGEANT THOMAS J. OWEN

50th New York Engineers, Engineer Brigade

Formerly a New York farmer, Owen stood next to his captain, Augustus S. Perkins, while bridging the Rappahannock under fire and witnessed Perkins' death. A few days later Owen accompanied the captain's body home to Athens, Pennsylvania, for burial. Promoted to lieutenant in 1864, Owen finished the war with a detachment of engineers in the Shenandoah Valley and later moved to Wisconsin.

Our Company, with three others from our regiment, had been detailed to lay two pontoon bridges across the Rappahannock at this point. The material for the bridges had all been taken down the dug road to the little plat at the margin of the river; one bridge was built about half way across the river, and the other one just begun. We were in the act of unloading a pontoon boat by sliding it off the hind end of a wagon that had been backed up close to the water. Captain Perkins was helping us, and was pulling on a small rope attached to the boat; and just as it slid off the wagon, the enemy opened a volley on us. Then the air was full of "bees" and all was confusion for a little while. The firing continued, and men, horses and mules fell killed and wounded.

Daylight soon came, and so did the ambulance men with their stretchers, picking up the dead and wounded. There lay the Captain. He had been instantly killed. I helped lay him on a stretcher, and they carried him back up the hill he had come down so full of life such a short time before, amid the roar of a hundred pieces of artillery, that were now belching forth a shower of shot and shell over our heads, on the city and the enemy beyond.

Unarmed field engineer troops attempting to bridge the Rappahannock River opposite the north end of Fredericksburg take heavy fire from Confederate marksmen on the morning of December 11. This Alfred R. Waud sketch captures the Yankees' predicament of having to work out in the open as Barksdale's Mississippians pick them off from the opposite shore. "The infantry supporting us on the flanks were at long range, and could do little damage to the enemy," complained Major Ira Spaulding of the 50th New York Engineers. The bridge builders' efforts cost them 59 killed and wounded.

LIEUTENANT COLONEL E. PORTER ALEXANDER

Artillery Battalion Commander, First Corps

Alexander began the war as captain of engineers and quickly ascended to chief ordnance officer of the Army of Northern Virginia. At Fredericksburg the 27-year-old served as General Longstreet's artillery chief, taking charge of the deployment of the First Corps cannon on the heights overlooking the town. Alexander's candid 1,200-page memoir, completed at the turn of the century, includes this account of the futile attempt of Union artillery to dislodge Barksdale's brigade.

At last, near noon, Burnside out of all patience with the delay, thought to crush out the sharpshooters with one tremendous blow. He already had about 170 guns in position extending from Falmouth, above, to nearly two miles below Fredericksburg. He ordered that every gun within range should be turned upon the town & should throw fifty shells into it as fast as they could do it. Then I think was presented the most impressive exhibition of military force, by all odds, which I ever witnessed. The whole Federal army had broken up their camps, packed their wagons & moved out on the hills, ready to cross the river as soon as the bridges were completed. Over 100,000 infantry were visible, standing apparently in great solid squares upon the hilltops, for a space of three miles, scattered all over the slopes were endless parks of ambulances, ordnance, commissary, quartermaster & regimental white-topped wagons, also parked in close squares & rectangles, & very impressive in the sense of order & system which they conveyed. And still more impressive to military eyes though less conspicuous & showy were the dark colored parks of batteries of artillery scattered here & there among them. Then, in front, was the three mile line of angry blazing guns firing through white clouds

THE BOMBARDMENT OF FREDERICKSBURG, DECEMBER 11, 1862.

In an effort to drive the Confederates out of Fredericksburg, Federal artillerists bombard the town from Stafford Heights across the river. Approximately 150 cannon homed in on the city, pounding it with 5,000 projectiles in a two-hour span. Although many buildings were reduced to rubble, the Mississippi brigade, joined by 100 or so Floridians, stubbornly clung to their positions within the town. By 2:30 p.m. Union artillery chief Henry J. Hunt admitted to General Burnside that his guns had failed to dislodge the Rebels.

of smoke & almost shaking the earth with their roar. Over & in the town the white winkings of the bursting shells reminded one of a countless swarm of fire-flies. Several buildings were set on fire, & their black smoke rose in remarkably slender, straight, & tall columns for two hundred feet, perhaps, before they began to spread horizontally & unite in a great black canopy. And over the whole scene there hung, high in the air, above the rear of the Federal lines, two immense black, captive balloons, like two great spirits of the air attendant on the coming struggle.

To all this cannonade not one of our guns replied with a single shot! We were saving every single round of ammunition we had for the infantry struggle which we knew would come. I had come forward to Marye's Hill to watch events & I sat there quietly & took it all in. And I could not but laugh out heartily, at times, to catch in the roar of the Federal guns the faint drowned pop of a musket which told that Barksdale's men were still in their rifle pits & still defiant. The contrast in the noises the two parties were making was very ludicrous.

Although bound by strong Southern ties, Brigadier General Daniel P. Woodbury spurned promises of higher rank in the Rebel army to remain loyal to the Union, taking charge of the Army of the Potomac's Volunteer Engineer Brigade. Woodbury agonized over his men's inability to bridge the Rappahannock early on December 11, complaining that "the majority seemed to think their task a hopeless one." He died of yellow fever at Key West, Florida, in August 1864.

FRANCIS BERNARD
Resident of Fredericksburg

After enduring the Federal artillery storm, the citizens remaining in Fredericksburg on December 11 were ordered to evacuate the contested town. The Bernard family fled to Danville the following spring. Francis, a child in 1862, vividly recalled the harrowing scenes decades later "as if they had only happened yesterday."

What a scene met our eyes when we left the house after the shelling. Our pretty garden was strewn with cannon balls and pieces of broken shells, limbs knocked off the trees and the grape arbor a perfect wreck. The house had been damaged considerably, several large holes torn through it, both in front and back. While we were deploring the damage that had been done Lieutenant Eustace returned in breathless haste to say that he had just heard an order from General Lee read on Commerce street, saying that the women and children must leave town, as he would destroy it with shell that night sooner than let it fall into the hands of the enemy, who were rapidly crossing the river on pontoon bridges. They urged my mother to take her children and fly at once from the town. After resisting until the men, in despair, were almost ready to drag her from her dangerous situation, she finally consented to leave. The wildest confusion now reigned, the servants wringing their hands and declaring they could not go without their "chists," which they all managed to get somehow and put upon their heads, but the men insisted so that we had only time to save our lives, that they would not even let my mother go back into the house to get her purse or a single valuable.

So we started just as we were; my wrapping, I remember, was an old

The effects of the Union artillery barrage are readily apparent in this view of shattered Fredericksburg buildings, captured by a Mathew Brady photographer in May 1864. This perspective looks northeast toward the intersection of Hanover and Liberty Streets on the western edge of town.

This unpublished sketch by artist Frank Vizetelly provides a panoramic view of Fredericksburg and its surroundings during the Federal bombardment on December 11. In the left f ground, partially wooded on its western slope, is the prominent high ground known as Marye's Heights. Two days later Confederate infantry and artillery superbly positioned o the opposite side of the heights would slaughter wave after wave of Federals sent marching out against them from the city beyond. As was typical for sketches intended for rerender

ewspaper engravings, the artist included numerous explanatory notes for use by the newspaper's engravers and editors. Some of the highlights pointed out by Vizetelly include distant rows of Union guns shelling the city, marked by the smoke rising from their barrels, and the masses of Federal troops arrayed on Stafford Heights. In the foreground a el column marches past on its way to take up position on Marye's Heights to support a battery of the Washington Artillery, already dug in and visible through a break in the trees.

This fragment of a Yankee shell destroyed the bed of Fredericksburg resident John Elder, who fortunately was away with friends when his house was struck.

ironing blanket, with a large hole burnt in the middle. I never did find out whether Aunt B—— ever got her clothes on, for she stalked ahead of us, wrapped in a pure white counterpane, a tall, ghostly-looking figure, who seemed to glide with incredible rapidity over the frozen ground. . . .

We plodded along under the heavy cross-fire, balls falling right and left of us. We [left] the town by way of the old "Plank Road," with batteries of Confederates on both sides. The ground was rough and broken up by the tramping of soldiers and the heavy wagons and artillery that had passed over it, so that it was difficult and tiresome to walk, and the sun got quite warm by this time and the snow was melting rapidly, the mud was simply indescribable. . . .

When we got about two miles from town we overtook many other refugees; some were camping by the way and others were pressing on, some to country houses which were hospitably thrown open to wanderers from home, and others to "Salam Church," about three miles from Fredericksburg, where there was a large encampment. . . .

. . . All was bustle and confusion. I suppose there were several hundred refugees there. Some were cooking outside in genuine gypsy fashion, and those who were infirm or sick were trying to get some rest in the cold, bare church. The leafless trees, through which the winter wind sobbed mournfully, the scattered groups seen through the smoke of numerous fires, and the road, upon which passed constantly back and forth ambulances and wagons full of wounded soldiers, presented a gloomy and saddening spectacle.

PRIVATE JAMES M. DINKINS

18th Mississippi Infantry, Barksdale's Brigade

A farmer and mechanic from Canton, Mississippi, Dinkins left behind his wife and home in June 1861 and saw his first action at Manassas and Balls Bluff. After marching and fighting through the first 11 months of 1862, Dinkins and his comrades were forced to endure the artillery storm that rained down upon them in the homes and streets of Fredericksburg.

Suddenly, as it was unexpected, the flash of these guns, followed by the explosions, hurled at the same instant . . . iron into the city. The shells exploded in and over the town, creating the greatest consternation among the people. The bombardment was kept up for over an hour, and no tongue or pen can describe the dreadful scene. . . . Tons of iron were hurled against the place, and nothing in war can exceed the horror of that hour. The deafening roar of cannon and bursting shells, falling walls and chimneys, brick and timbers flying through the air, houses set on fire, the smoke adding to the already heavy fog, the bursting of flames through the housetops, made a scene which has no parallel in history. It was appalling and indescribable, a condition which would paralyze the stoutest heart, and one from which not a man in Barksdale Brigade had the slightest hope of escaping.

An 18-year-old student at the outbreak of the war, William W. Durr enrolled in Company D of the 13th Mississippi. He was killed in Fredericksburg on December 11. When Barksdale's brigade finally withdrew back to the heights, Durr's body was most likely left in the town, eventually falling into Union hands. The final notation in the young man's service record assessed him as "a true patriot and a brave and uncomplaining soldier."

"About half an hour after the bombardment had ceased, the fog cleared away, leaving a picture which riveted every eye and sickened every heart."

During that hail of iron and brick, I believe I can say that there was not a square yard in the city which was not struck by a missile of some kind. Under cover of the bombardment, Burnside undertook to renew his efforts to complete the bridges, but the matchless men of Barksdale's Brigade, acting under the immortal Lieutenant Colonel Fiser, concealed in their pits along the river bank, poured a volley first and then a concentrated fire on the workmen and drove back all who survived their deadly aim. During this time the flames were blazing from every quarter, and ladies and children were forced to flee from their cellars to escape death by fire, even at the risk of being stricken down by shells and bricks.

The horror of the occasion was heightened by the veil of fog, which obscured all objects 50 yards distant. About half an hour after the bom-

This battle flag was carried by the 17th Mississippi Infantry, another of Barksdale's regiments that contested the Union efforts to bridge the Rappahannock. Faintly visible in the upper portion is the name of the 17th's first commander, Colonel William D. Holder, who was absent while recovering from a wound received at Malvern Hill in July 1862. The Allen C. Redwood sketch at right depicts Mississippi troops taking aim at the Yankee engineers from behind houses and trees.

BARKSDALE'S MISSISSIPPIANS OPPOSING THE LAYING OF THE PONTOON-BRIDGES.

bardment had ceased, the fog cleared away, leaving a picture which riveted every eye and sickened every heart. Mansions that for years had been the scene of a boundless hospitality and domestic comfort, lay in ruins and smoldering ashes. Blackened walls and wrecked gardens were all that were left of numerous happy homes. The memory of those scenes will be hard to efface.

Defeated at every turn, the Federal commander abandoned his bridges for the time and began to cross in boats. He directed a destructive rifle fire against the Mississippians along the river bank, and also against those in the city. Colonel Fiser continued to dispute this passage, and many of the boats were forced to return to remove their dead and get others to take their places.

After a large force had been landed above and below, Colonel Fiser was ordered to rejoin the brigade in the city. The enemy soon formed line and dashed at the Mississippians, determined to drive them from their rifle pits and other places of shelter. . . .

Barksdale's Brigade watched them from their hiding places and awaited their near approach. Suddenly, when within about 75 yards of our line, as if by common impulse, a volley rang out from the rifle pits on the cold air, which sounded almost like one gun, and hundreds fell dead in their tracks. The front line of the enemy, paralyzed and dismayed by the shock, fell back in confusion. In the meantime the Mississippians were firing on them as they ran. It was a dreadful slaughter, which might have been considered a retaliation for the dreadful bombardment of two hours before. Quickly the second line advanced, firing as they came, and was met by a deadly aim from the Confederates. The column halted in front of Barksdale's men, when the third line rushed to their support and charged headlong into the city.

Whole companies of Barksdale's men were concealed in cellars, where they remained even after the enemy had passed, and emerging, fired into the rear of the Federal line from behind corners of houses and stone walls. The Mississippians began to retire slowly, fighting as they retreated. It was a grand sight which was witnessed by both armies. Hundreds of brave officers and men fell ere they could reach the city.

PRIVATE JOSIAH F. MURPHEY

20TH MASSACHUSETTS INFANTRY, HALL'S BRIGADE

One month shy of his 20th birthday, Murphey "saw the elephant" at Fredericksburg when his brigade was ordered to clear the town of Confederates. Although he received a wound that impaired his vision, Murphey completed his term of service in July 1864. He returned to Nantucket, where he spent the remaining 67 years of his life.

This kind of work continued at intervals throughout the whole day and we were no nearer crossing than in the morning and something had to be done. Burnside called for volunteers to charge over in pontoon boats and drive the rebel sharpshooters from the bank of the river and our brigade commander [Colonel Norman Hall] offered the services of our brigade. Col. Hall said, "my soldiers are ready to cross the river in the boats and drive out the Confederates." Permission was granted and it was planned that the boats would be ready on the shore and the troops at a given signal should rush down to the bank of the river, jump into the boats and pull quickly across, [and] charge up the bank on the other side. It was a desperate game. . . .

After getting into the boat two men sat down at the oars; one was Thomas Russell of this town, the other man I do not remember, but he pulled Russell right around and headed the boat upstream. Lieut. Leander F. Alley said to me, "Murphey, take that oar," which I did and we soon had the boat across on the other side where she grounded a few feet from the shore. We jumped out and waded to the land. The other boats had got there first, had charged up the bank, [and had] driven out the rebel sharpshooters and taken with the wounded about twenty prisoners, who were brought back in the first boats that returned after we got across and before the pontoon bridge was finished. But now that the sharpshooters were driven away from the bank our engineers soon had the bridge completed and the troops in reserve

"Where men fell and left a vacant place other men stepped into their places and although death stared us in the face there was not a man who faltered."

were beginning to move across it. We lay under the bank of the city and as soon as the troops began to cross we were ordered forward. Our company formed in two platoons of about thirty men each at the lowest end of a street called Farquier street and began our advance up the street. As soon as we came in sight of the rebels who were concealed in every house and behind every fence they opened a terrible fire on us at short range and our men began dropping at every point, those struck in the vital parts dropping without a sound, but those wounded otherwise would cry out with pain as they fell or limped to the rear. But despite the terrible fire we pressed on up the street. Where men fell and left a vacant place other men stepped into their places and although death stared us in the face there was not a man who faltered. Our chief company officer Capt. H. L. Abbott said "hold your fire, boys, until you see something to fire at."

We had now arrived at the corner of a cross street called Caroline street and I, being on the left flank of the company, turned to look down the street to see if anything could be seen to fire at and bringing my gun to the ready at the same time. At that moment I felt a sharp stinging pain on the right side of my face and presto, I knew no more.

When I came to I was lying on the ground where I had fallen, and the company had advanced a short distance up the street. The balls were still flying thick around me and I realized I was wounded. I clapped my hand to my face to stop the flow of blood but it was no use. It flowed between my fingers and down onto my clothing and filled me full. I got up rather faint, and a feeling of madness came over me, and a word in your ear gentle reader and let it go no further, I swore; I cursed the whole southern confederacy from Virginia to the gulf of Mexico; but on a second thought I realized it was war and banished such thoughts from my mind and made my way across the river.

HARPER'S WEEKLY.
A JOURNAL OF CIVILIZATION.

Vol. VI.—No. 313.] NEW YORK, SATURDAY, DECEMBER 27, 1862. [SINGLE COPIES SIX CENTS. $2 50 PER YEAR IN ADVANCE.

Entered according to Act of Congress, in the Year 1862, by Harper & Brothers, in the Clerk's Office of the District Court for the Southern District of New York.

THE ATTACK ON FREDERICKSBURG—THE FORLORN HOPE SCALING THE HILL.—[See Page [illegible].]

Massachussetts and Michigan soldiers from Colonel Norman J. Hall's II Corps brigade leap from pontoon boats and charge up the riverbank to force Barksdale's Rebel brigade from Fredericksburg in this front page illustration. The caption bestowed Hall's men with the title of Forlorn Hope, a British military term referring to the first volunteers to attack a fortified enemy position.

Shown here in the gray militia uniform he wore as a member of the Richardson Light Guard before the war, Robert S. Beckwith donned Union blue when he enlisted in the 20th Massachusetts, soon earning a lieutenant's commission. As a member of Hall's brigade, he participated in the storming of the town late on the afternoon of December 11. Shot down in front of Marye's Heights two days later, Beckworth died from his wound on New Year's Eve.

PRIVATE SIMEON H. GUILFORD

127TH PENNSYLVANIA INFANTRY, HALL'S BRIGADE

Hall's was the first of four Union brigades to enter and occupy Fredericksburg on the evening of December 11. It was joined by Colonel Joshua T. Owen's and Brigadier General Alfred Sully's brigades from General Oliver O. Howard's division. Colonel Rush C. Hawkins' IX Corps brigade crossed the river into town later that night. Guilford, a member of a nine-months regiment, recounted the first action he and his comrades had witnessed since entering the war four months earlier.

The distance from the bridges to the rebel entrenchments on the hills behind the town had been carefully calculated, and the guns accurately sighted now opened a terrible fire upon the troops on the bridge. Captain Fox, of the 127th, was struck by a fragment of shell as soon as he reached the foot of the bluff, and died soon afterward. It was the first time the 127th had been under fire, and by a natural impulse they dodged when they heard a shell screeching over their

From the river's eastern bank, English-born artist Alfred R. Waud sketched a column of Yankees from Hawkins' brigade passing over the Rappahannock across the so-called middle bridge to enter the southern end of Fredericksburg on the night of December 11. In the distance, fires in the center of town illuminate the riverfront and the ruins of the railroad bridge. Waud, hired by Harper's Weekly early in 1862, eventually became one of the war's premier "special artists," doggedly accompanying the Army of the Potomac on most of its campaigns.

heads. General Howard with his staff occupied a prominent position on the bluff as we descended to cross. As he saw the boys dodging he called out, "Don't dodge, boys, they can't hit you." A moment later a shell passed close to the head of the General and he dodged. "Don't dodge, General," cried one of the boys. "Oh," said he in reply, "it's natural."

One of the regiments about to cross (the 129th Pennsylvania, it is said) came marching toward the river with its band at the head. As the regiment filed down the ravine, the band took a position on the bluff, and as a means of encouraging the troops struck up the popular air of "Bully for you."

General Sam Sturgis, who had already crossed with his division, saw the band from across the river and heard the music. "Where does that band belong?" he asked in his rough way. Nobody answered. "They'll knock the miserable stuffing out of those fellows in less than two minutes," said he. Hardly had he spoken when a shell came screeching through the air and landed near that band on the North bank. The music stopped suddenly and the musicians rapidly distributed themselves in different directions.

Although he earned a certain renown before the war as an Indian fighter, Samuel D. Sturgis, commanding a IX Corps division, was better known for his colorful vocabulary than his military prowess. His most famous remark, "I don't care for John Pope one pinch of owl dung," targeted the loser at Second Manassas. Routed at Brice's Cross Roads by Nathan Bedford Forrest in June 1864, Sturgis finished the war "awaiting orders."

SERGEANT S. MILLETT THOMPSON

13th New Hampshire Infantry, Hawkins' Brigade

Mustered into service in September 1862, Thompson's regiment witnessed the effects of war for the first time when they entered Fredericksburg on the night of December 11. Seven months later Thompson won a lieutenant's commission from the governor of New Hampshire. During an assault on enemy works around Petersburg on June 15, 1864, he was badly wounded in his left ankle. While convalescing with the aid of crutches he fell and reinjured the ankle, leading to his discharge in October.

Soon, at 6.20 p.m., the long line of our whole Brigade, defiling to the left from our place of bivouac . . . moves in a dead silence slowly over the hills where an hour or two before we had double-quicked, then on down the steep river bank, and across the ponton bridge muffled with earth and straw, and thrown across the river near the lower end of the city . . . as we follow the crooked road, and we enter the battered, torn, crushed and burning city, no one opposing. . . . We cross with a slow route-step, every man cautioned to move as quietly as possible, pass up a steep paved way, turn to the left down the street, and about 8 p.m. deploy in line of battle along Caroline street, also called Main street, and is the second street up from the river. . . . Guards are quickly stationed, and Companies E and B are sent at once as pickets to the rear of the city and along Hazel Run. While these pickets are taking their positions along Hazel Run, the "Taps" are being sounded in the Union Army, and less loudly in the Confederate Army also. With the exception of one or two men in each company who had recently served as guards, the Thirteenth entered the city with unloaded muskets, and loaded them after halting in Caroline street; and about 9 p.m., after standing there a long time in line of battle under arms, the Thirteenth stacks arms along the west side of Caroline street, and bivouacs on the west sidewalk, the side towards the enemy. Other troops similarly occupy the east side. The night is very dark, the streets are filled with the débris of the shattered city and clouds of smoke from the burning buildings, while bummers turn to forbidden pillage. Many houses are entered, blinds closed, fires kindled in stoves and fireplaces, and hot coffee is drank, in the proud deserted halls . . . to our own comfort and to the good health of the house-owners—just now absent because of Gen. Burnside's cast-iron hail-storm. The city seems much like a city in the early hours of the morning before the inhabitants are astir. . . .

. . . As we cross the city on entering, there lies on the sidewalk as he fell, his gun still held in his hand, a Confederate First Sergeant in a new, clean, Confederate dress uniform, with the regulation chevrons and insignia on the sleeve. His cap held by a loose throat-strap is still on his head, and merely tilted back from a handsome forehead, which alone remains of the whole front part of his head. He was probably instantly killed by a shell or shot, and lies a ghastly object seen in the dim light of a distant fire. Sergt. Chas. F. Chapman of E is the first to see him, and taking First Sergeant Charles M. Kittredge of B and the writer by the arm, Chapman calls out: "Here—see what you First Sergeants are all coming to!" This was the first body of a man killed in the war, that any of us had seen.

MAJOR FRANCIS E. PIERCE

108th New York Infantry, Palmer's Brigade

After serving as a captain for a month, Pierce received a field promotion to major at Antietam, and three months after witnessing the sacking of Fredericksburg described here he was promoted to lieutenant colonel. Pierce was shot in the temple at Morton's Ford on February 6, 1864, but was back in action during the Wilderness campaign, where he was wounded again. He returned to duty six weeks later near Petersburg and was given a succession of temporary brigade commands in the II Corps.

During the day our brigade (14 Conn.108 N.Y.130 Penn.) laid in Caroline St. Our batteries from the east side of the river opened on the rebs some, firing right over us, but elicited only feeble replies from the rebs. Their pieces seemed too small and most of them struck in the city, 3 of them near us, one near enough to click the top branches of a small peach tree at the bottom of which Col. Powers, Lt. Porter and myself were sitting. We were in danger all day of course—at any moment a shell *might* burst right there—very uncomfortable position on the whole. 3 or 4 dead rebs were lying around promiscuously and acted with their ghastly gaping death wounds as monitors of what might be in store for us. Troops crossing all day long. Fredericsburgh given up to pillage and destruction. Boys came into our place *loaded*

Loath to besmirch the Union cause, Leslie's Illustrated Newspaper refused to publish this sketch by Arthur Lumley of Federal troops looting Fredericksburg on the night of December 12. "This night the city was in the wildest confusion," scribbled the disgusted artist on the back of his drawing, "houses burned down furniture scattered in streets men pillaging in all directions." Lumley assessed the orgy of destruction as "a fit scene for the French Revolution and a disgrace to the Union army. This is the view of what I saw."

with *silver* pitchers, silver spoons, silver lamps and castors etc. Great three-story brick houses furnished magnificently were broken into and their contents scattered over the floors and trampled on by the muddy feet of the soldiers. Splendid alabaster vases and pieces of statuary were thrown at 6 & 700 dollar mirrors. Closets of the very finest china ware were broken into and their contents smashed onto the floor and stamped to pieces. Finest cut glass war goblets were hurled at nice plate glass windows, beautifully embroidered window curtains torn down, rosewood pianos piled in the street and burned or soldiers would get on top of them and dance and kick the keyboard and internal machinery all to pieces. Little table ornaments kicking in every direction—wine cellars broken into and the soldiers drinking all they could and then opening the faucets and let the rest run out. Boys go to a barrel of flour and take a pailful and use enough to make one batch of pancakes and then pour the rest in the street—everything turned upside down. The soldiers seemed to delight in destroying everything. Libraries worth thousands of dollars were overhauled and thrown on the floor and in the streets. . . . It was so throughout the whole city and from its appearance very many wealthy families must have inhabited it.

> "It was curious to observe these men upon the eve of a tremendous battle rid themselves of all anxiety by plunging into this boistrous sport."

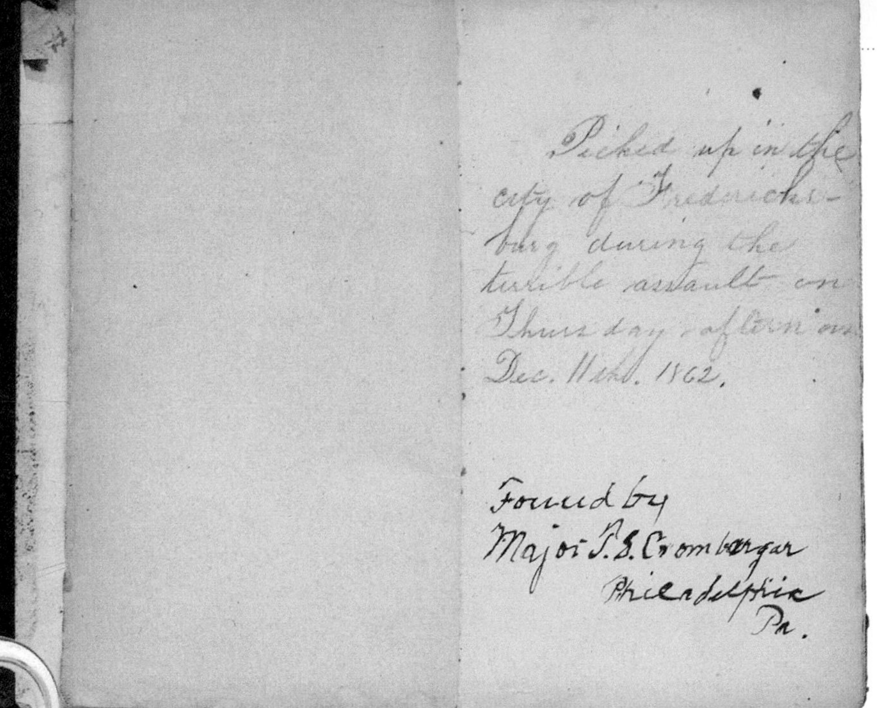

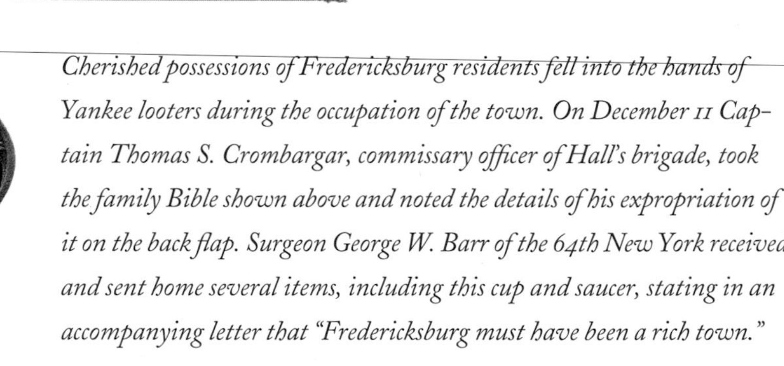

Cherished possessions of Fredericksburg residents fell into the hands of Yankee looters during the occupation of the town. On December 11 Captain Thomas S. Crombargar, commissary officer of Hall's brigade, took the family Bible shown above and noted the details of his expropriation of it on the back flap. Surgeon George W. Barr of the 64th New York received and sent home several items, including this cup and saucer, stating in an accompanying letter that "Fredericksburg must have been a rich town."

LIEUTENANT JOSIAH M. FAVILL

57TH NEW YORK INFANTRY, ZOOK'S BRIGADE

Although II Corps commander General Darius N. Couch made an effort to stop the wholesale looting of Fredericksburg, it had little effect. Lieutenant Favill not only observed the hands-off approach many officers took to the bacchanalian atmosphere that pervaded the town but even expressed an indulgent attitude toward it. Favill, officially the adjutant of the 57th New York, was serving at this time as an aide-de-camp to Colonel Samuel K. Zook, the brigade commander.

Early this morning, . . . our division . . . marched up the cut and filed off into the principal street to the right. Here we stacked arms and the men were dismissed. They immediately made a dash for the houses, and ransacked them from cellar to garret. Very soon the streets were filled with a motley crowd of men, some of them dressed in women's clothes, others with tall silk hats, curiously conspicuous where nothing but caps are worn; many brought out sofas, chairs, etc., which were planted in the middle of the street, and the men proceeded to take their ease. Some carried pictures; one man had a fine stuffed alligator, and most of them had something. It was curious to observe these men upon the eve of a tremendous battle rid themselves of all anxiety by plunging into this boistrous sport. No attempt was made by the officers to interfere, and thus their minds were distracted, until summoned to fall in to storm the heights.

ROBERTA CARY CORBIN

Married into a prominent and wealthy family, Mrs. Corbin was the mistress of Moss Neck, an imposing 1,600-acre plantation located 10 miles southeast of Fredericksburg. She presided over the estate while her husband, Private Richard Corbin, was away on duty with the 9th Virginia Cavalry. Her five-year-old daughter, Jane, and unmarried sister-in-law, Catherine, also occupied the manor.

On the 12th of December, 1862, our quiet country neighborhood had been startled by many rumors afloat of a coming battle. Early that morning my husband's sister and I started off on an inspection tour. We were eager to see and hear all that we could. There was with us at the time a young lad, Willie Roberts; and as we had only two riding horses, I took Willie upon my pony behind me as our cavalier escort. Zephyr was small in stature, but fully equal to the double weight. Thus we set out, a miniature cavalcade, Zephyr and Flirt, Kate's pony, shaking their heads and making the dust fly.

We rode to Belle Hill, the home of my husband's father, Maj. James Parke Corbin, and there we spent the day, hearing accounts of troops moving up from Port Royal and from Guinea Station to Fredericksburg. Toward twilight we returned to Moss Neck, meeting many Southern soldiers on the way—not an uncommon occurrence at this time—to whom we gave a nod and a smile. However, as we drew nearer home uniforms became more numerous, and presently a fine-looking officer, cap in hand, stepped forward and said in a courteous tone: "Ladies, you are about to meet several regiments. Indeed, a whole division is just now coming." While he was speaking we saw opening ranks before us and long lines of soldiers, who stood aside to leave the road clear. Thus we made a triumphal entry between ranks of infantry who were quite surprised at two ladies passing escorted in such a novel fashion.

Most embarrassed were we and most respectful were the soldiers as we ran the gauntlet; yet when we got through and drew near the house we found that the whole place was occupied by troops. So dense were they that we were compelled to dismount and to creep in through the back way into our own house. "All strategy is fair in war." Yard, stable lot, and all the place had become one moving mass of soldiers—on foot, on horseback, with wagons, ambulances, and artillery pieces—all moving as nearly as possible in a bee line, removing obstacles, fences, etc., and making short cuts through the fields.

That night we did not go to bed. The troops were moving all night long, and the tramp, tramp, tramp of the marching men and the heavy rolling of the wagons and artillery drove away all thought of sleep.

Patterned after an English country residence, the Moss Neck manor house spanned 250 feet from wing to wing on high ground two miles east of the Rappahannock. The estate, pictured here after the war, was used by Stonewall Jackson and his staff as their winter headquarters beginning on December 16.

MAJOR GENERAL JOHN B. HOOD

Division Commander, First Corps

Shortly before the battle Hood had a brief but prophetic exchange with Stonewall Jackson. Jackson was dead within five months, while Hood indeed became "badly shattered"—first at Gettysburg, where his arm was mangled, then at Chickamauga, where a wounded leg required amputation. He survived the war but died of yellow fever in 1879.

On the 11th of December, 1863, General Burnside having completed all necessary preparation, began to lay pontoons above and below the railroad bridge which had been destroyed. That entire day and night he consumed in crossing his forces to the southern bank of the river, under cover of, at least, one hundred pieces of artillery. During the 12th he formed his line below and above Deep Run, whilst upon the range of hills overlooking the valley, Lee's forces lay in readiness to receive the attack. General Jackson had, meantime, moved up to form line on our right, and that day, if I remember correctly, as we were riding together in direction of General Lee's headquarters, the conversation turned upon the future, and he asked me if I expected to live to see the end of the war. I replied that I did not know, but was inclined to think I would survive; at the same time, I considered it most likely I would be badly shattered before the termination of the struggle. I naturally addressed him the same question, and, without hesitation, he answered that he did not expect to live through to the close of the contest. Moreover, that he could not say that he desired to do so. With this sad turn in the conversation, the subject dropped. Often since have I thought upon these words, spoken casually by each of us, and which seem to have contained the prophecy of his untimely death and of my own fate.

COLONEL ZENAS R. BLISS

7th Rhode Island Infantry, Nagle's Brigade

Facing his baptism of fire, Bliss (above, left) recalled the last hours before the fight, including one of the stranger prebattle rituals. After Fredericksburg, Bliss saw little action, serving mostly as an inspector and administrator, but in 1898 he was awarded the Medal of Honor for his performance in this battle. Standing with him is Major Jacob Babbit, mortally wounded on December 13.

There was very little firing done during the afternoon and night, and the men laid in the streets, and I took a bed I found in a vacant house, and my Field and Staff Officers occupied the bed and room with me. It was a terribly dark night. The fog which had existed several days was as thick as ever, and there was a drizzling rain, and as there were of course no lights in the streets, it was almost impossible to get about from one house to another.

Just at dark, Captain Mighels, Adjt. General for General Sturgis, came

Rebel pickets in this sketch attributed to Alfred Waud lie sprawled where they fell near the bank of the Rappahannock, struck down during the brief but sharp fight contesting the Federal crossing downriver from Fredericksburg on December 11. Most likely drawn the next day, the sketch also shows, in the background, Union batteries firing away from Stafford Heights and the pontoon bridges used by Franklin's grand division.

to me and asked me, if I did not want to ride out to the grave of [Mary] Washington. I told him yes, and we mounted our horses and started. It had gotten quite dark, by the time we reached the edge of town, going towards the grave yard.

As we rode along we heard someone call us from behind, and asked us where we were going. We told them, and they said, "Well you had better come back. I am the last of our pickets, and the Rebels are right ahead of you," and we turned, and rode back. Why we were not fired upon was a mystery, and as a matter of fact we were within fifty yards of the enemies' lines.

Mighels remained with me that night, and he and I slept in the bed. He got a chicken's head, that had recently been cut off, and drew a sort of horseshoe on the wall over the back of the bed, and put around it cabalistic signs and figures, saying he was going to "hoodoo us." After it was drawn, he went through with some absurd performances, and pronounced the charm complete, and that we would pass through the battle unscathed. He slept on the back side of the bed next to the hoodoo; I next; Page next; Babbitt next; then Sayles; the Doctors, and the Chaplain.

After going through his incantations, we were soon asleep, and sleeping as soundly as far as I know, as we ever did, though we all knew well, that there was to be a terrible battle in the morning, and that probably some of us would pass in our checks. . . .

During the evening some of the Zouaves found a place nearly opposite our house where a lot of bacon and flour had been "cached." They got lights in some way and commenced digging up the provisions. The Rebels must have seen the lights, for while the Zouaves were digging up the provisions, and congratulating themselves on their find, a shell was dropped, and exploded right in the midst of them, and several were wounded.

The part of the street in front of our house had been burned and several chimneys were left standing, and I cautioned my men to keep away from them, and not to put their blankets for the night where they could be hurt by the falling bricks and stones. I think my men followed my advice, but others were less careful, and during the night one or more chimneys fell, killing or wounding several.

Federal I Corps Attack

At 8:30 a.m. on December 13, elements of William Franklin's grand division began to deploy across the plain south of Fredericksburg to attack Stonewall Jackson's lines in the hills beyond. In the Federal vanguard was George Meade's division, supported on the right by John Gibbon's and on the left by Abner Doubleday's.

Meade's three brigades of Pennsylvanians had barely gotten started when the march was abruptly halted by Confederate artillery fire from a lone Rebel gun dodging from place to place on the plain well forward of Rebel lines under the daring command of Major John Pelham. The rest of Jackson's artillery remained silent; outgunned, they waited for the enemy infantry. The massed Federal cannon on the plain probed for Pelham, who withdrew after frustrating the Yankee advance for nearly an hour. Franklin's batteries also poured their shells into Jackson's main position, but their targets were obscured by the wooded slope.

About noon, Meade and Gibbon had their men moving again, while Doubleday remained in position to guard the left flank against Rebel cavalry. As the blue ranks advanced, the Confederate gunners readied their pieces. Then, when the Federals were within about 800 yards, Jackson's massed artillery unleashed a firestorm. Federal artillery replied by sighting in on the Rebel batteries, and for nearly an hour a furious duel ensued, until Jackson's guns were largely suppressed. Meade judged the time right and once more sent his line rolling forward.

By 1:00 p.m., Meade's lead units had charged past a railroad embankment and were clawing their way uphill through a thick patch of woods. Without knowing it, they had headed right through a breach in the Confederate line—a 600-yard gap left unmanned because Rebel division commander A. P. Hill thought the area to be impassable.

The defenders paid for this misconception. Rolling through the gap, Meade's men drove deep into the Confederate lines, then veered north and south, hitting Rebel brigades under Generals James H. Lane and James J. Archer in the flanks and forcing them back. Some of the Pennsylvania regiments charged straight ahead, up the slope across Military road, and swarmed into the position held by the South Carolinians of Brigadier General Maxcy Gregg's brigade.

Gregg had assumed that the woods to his front were occupied by fellow Confederates. His men were resting, their arms stacked, when the Pennsylvanians charged into them. Believing that the attackers must be friendly troops, Gregg rode among his men imploring them not to shoot. A prominent target in his general's uniform, he was soon knocked from his horse by a Yankee bullet, mortally wounded. Meade's men swept over his command.

But the Yankees' almost inadvertent success had run its course. Regiments from reserve Rebel divisions commanded by Brigadier Generals Jubal A. Early and William B. Taliaferro rushed through the woods and crashed into the Pennsylvanians, blunting their momentum. Braced up by the arrival of help, Archer's and Lane's men rallied and formed new lines facing the Federals that had penetrated the gap.

Now the Pennsylvanians found themselves nearly surrounded—and without support. Gibbon, attacking to the north, had failed to penetrate the Confederate line along the railroad embankment. General Franklin, little inclined to support any renewal of the assault, still had some 20,000 men uncommitted during Meade's attack but declined to send reinforcements.

To make matters worse, Meade's troops were running low on ammunition. More than one-quarter of the men in his division now lay dead or wounded, and more Rebel reinforcements were coming up. Meade's men, then Gibbon's, began to yield their hard-won ground and were soon driven back over the railroad embankment and out onto the plain.

As the Federals retreated toward the Rappahannock, Colonel Edmund N. Atkinson launched a counterattack with his brigade of Georgians that succeeded in sweeping up whole companies of lagging Yankees. The Rebel charge was finally stopped by Federal artillery and the infantry of General David B. Birney's division, which had come up to cover Meade's retreat.

Meade and many of his senior officers were convinced that with reinforcements they could have prevailed against Jackson's Rebels, but General Franklin, disheartened by the sacrifice and frustrated by Burnside's failure to provide clear objectives, did not renew the attack.

After an hour-long artillery duel, two divisions of the Federal I Corps attacked the deepest part of Jackson's position. Meade's Pennsylvanians exploited a gap and breached A. P. Hill's line, but swift counterstrokes by a half-dozen Confederate brigades drove the unsupported Federals back to their starting point. Birney's division of the III Corps moved up to stop the Rebel surge, and by 2:00 p.m., fighting sputtered to a halt.

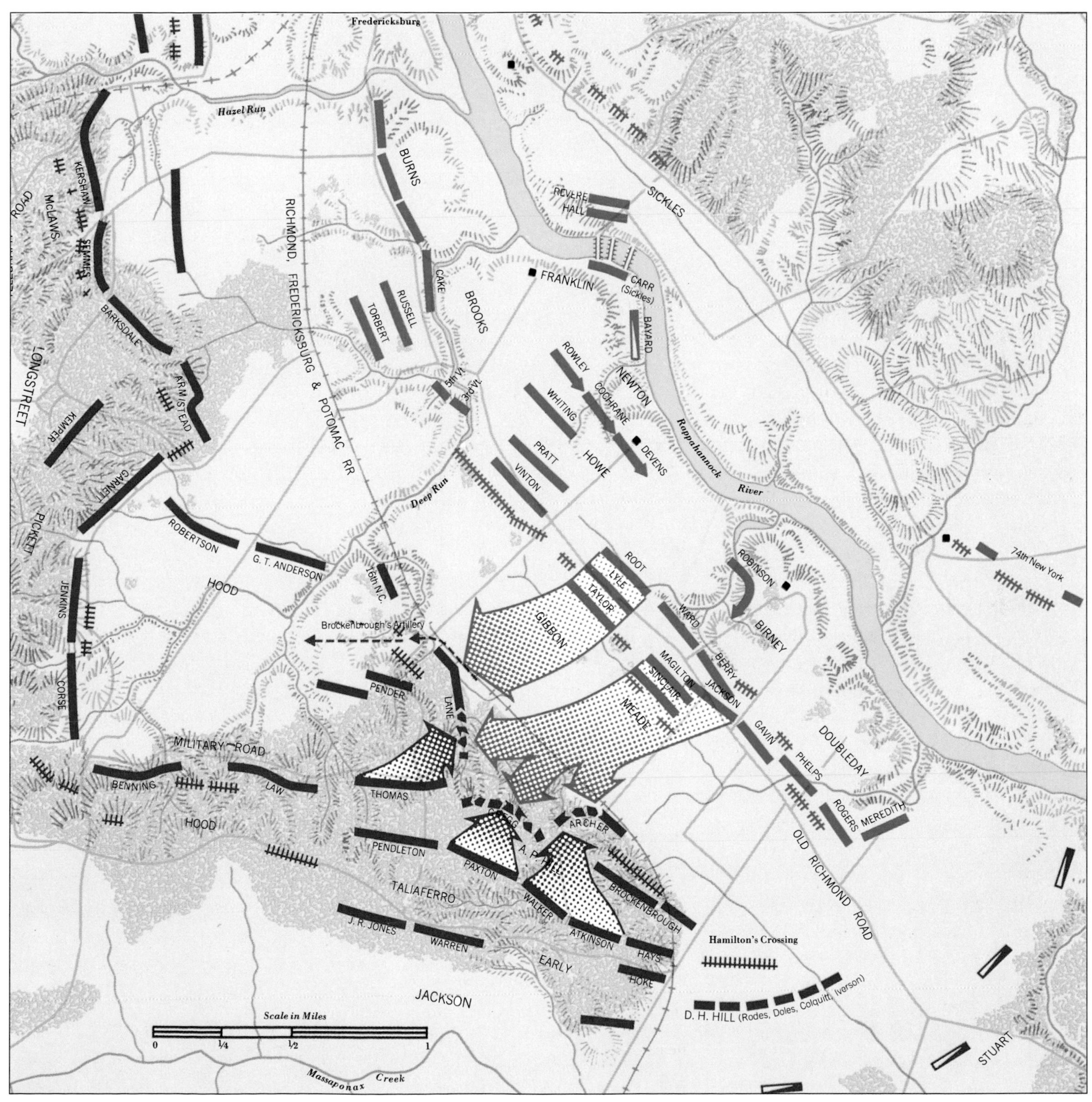
Fredericksburg
Hazel Run
BURNS
RICHMOND, FREDERICKSBURG & POTOMAC RR
ROAD
KERSHAW
McLAWS
SEMMES
BARKSDALE
LONGSTREET
ARMISTEAD
KEMPER
GARNETT
PICKETT
JENKINS
CORSE
REVERE
HALL
SICKLES
FRANKLIN
CARR (Sickles)
BAYARD
CAKE
BROOKS
RUSSELL
TORBERT
5th Vt.
3rd Vt.
ROWLEY
WHITING
COCHRANE
NEWTON
DEVENS
HOWE
PRATT
VINTON
Rappahannock
River
Deep Run
ROBERTSON
G. T. ANDERSON
HOOD
16th N.C.
ROOT
LYLE
TAYLOR
GIBBON
WARD
ROBINSON
BIRNEY
74th New York
Brockenbrough's Artillery
PENDER
LANE
MAGILTON
SINCLAIR
BERRY
JACKSON
MEADE
GAVIN
PHELPS
DOUBLEDAY
ROGERS
MEREDITH
MILITARY ROAD
BENNING
LAW
THOMAS
HOOD
GREGG
A. P.
ARCHER
PENDLETON
PAXTON
TALIAFERRO
WALKER
BROCKENBROUGH
OLD RICHMOND ROAD
J. R. JONES
WARREN
ATKINSON
HAYS
EARLY
HOKE
Hamilton's Crossing
JACKSON
D. H. HILL (Rodes, Doles, Colquitt, Iverson)
Scale in Miles
0
1/4
1/2
1
STUART
Massaponax
Creek

PRIVATE GEORGE W. SHREVE

Henry's (Virginia) Battery, Stuart Horse Artillery

Using the cover of heavy fog and cedar shrubs, Major John Pelham fired the first shots of the contest when he opened up with a single 12-pounder gun on the massed ranks of the Federal I Corps less than 400 yards away. Shreve, a member of the gun crew, had enlisted under Pelham during the Peninsula campaign at Yorktown, on April 15, 1862. He served as a gunner until captured and paroled in the Shenandoah Valley in April 1865.

The 13th of December opened with a dense fog enveloping the whole field. A part of our Battery crept slowly from Hamilton's Crossing down into the plain, toward the river, until we came to a cross hedge row, of cedar, behind which we noiselessly formed "In Battery."

Beyond the hedge, we could hear the Federal Infantry (Franklin's Corps) maneouvering; distinguishing a medley of voices, but could not see them. Evidently they were only a few hundred yards distant. The fog commenced to lift between nine and ten o'clock, and exposed to our view as we peered through, the hedge, a grand spectacle of marshalled soldiery, in readiness for the fray, spread out in vast proportions, on the level plain, in our immediate front. With alertness, and yet fearing annihilation at their hands, in such close range, of their infantry, we commenced firing. The unexpected presence of our guns so close to them, seemed to paralyze them, and throw them into disorder. Instead of rushing for us, and overwhelming us with their numbers, they were evidently afraid of us, judging no doubt, that we had a strong force concealed behind the hedge. We were far in advance of any supports, either of cavalry or infantry. Our fire must have been very effective, and gave them a wholesome fear of us. Immediately after our first fire, and while in the act of loading the second charge, we received the fire of their artillery, showing how ready their guns were for action. No. 1 in my detachment that morning, was "Hammond," who joined us in Maryland during our recent campaign there; as he stepped in with sponge staff to swab out after the first fire, a shell from the enemy's gun, cut him down, and he had time only to say "tell Mother I die bravely." We continued firing for about twenty minutes, when we were commanded to cease, and to lie flat on the ground. While in this position, a shot struck squarely the head of one of our men, and decapitated him, as he lay prone on the ground. The rain of shot and shell upon us was terrific, both from their Field Batteries at close range, and also from their big guns on the north bank of the river, but being concealed by the hedge, the enemy's gunners shot too high and so we escaped. We resumed firing after a short rest, but were soon ordered to "limber to the rear," and we fell back under the cover of our guns, which opened from the hill in our rear, and left, as the enemy began to advance.

John Pelham, known for his bravery, earned further accolades at Fredericksburg during the morning hours of December 13. Robert E. Lee was so impressed with the Alabamian that he specifically mentioned the "gallant Pelham" in one of his Fredericksburg battle reports. Lee and his countrymen would soon have to grieve over Pelham, mortally wounded on March 17, 1863, during the Battle of Kelly's Ford.

"A shell from the enemy's gun, cut him down, and he had time only to say 'tell Mother I die bravely.'"

Hd Qrs Army Potomac
Dec 13th 5:55 a.m.

Maj Genl Franklin
Comm'g Left Gr Division
Army Potomac

Genl Hardie will carry this dispatch to you, and remain with you during the day – The Genl Commanding directs that you keep your whole command in position for a rapid movement down the old Richmond road – and you will send out at once a Division at least to pass below Smithfield to seize if possible the height near Capt. Hamiltons on this side of the Massaponax taking care to keep it well supported and its line of retreat open – He has ordered another column of a Division or more to be moved from Genl Sumners Command up the Plank Road to its intersection with the Telegraph road where they will divide with a view to seizing the heights on both of these roads – holding these two heights with the height near Capt Hamilton will he hopes compel the Enemy to evacuate the whole ridge between these points – He makes these moves by columns distant from each

Burnside sent this order, taken down by his chief of staff, John G. Parke, to General William Franklin (above) outlining the movements of his grand division. The wording Burnside used in the directive, however, was so tentative and imprecise that it left Franklin confused. By nature a cautious man, Franklin accordingly delayed the expected assault by his command yet made no effort to contact his commander in order to clarify Burnside's intentions. Largely because of his poor showing in this battle, he was relieved of command in January 1863.

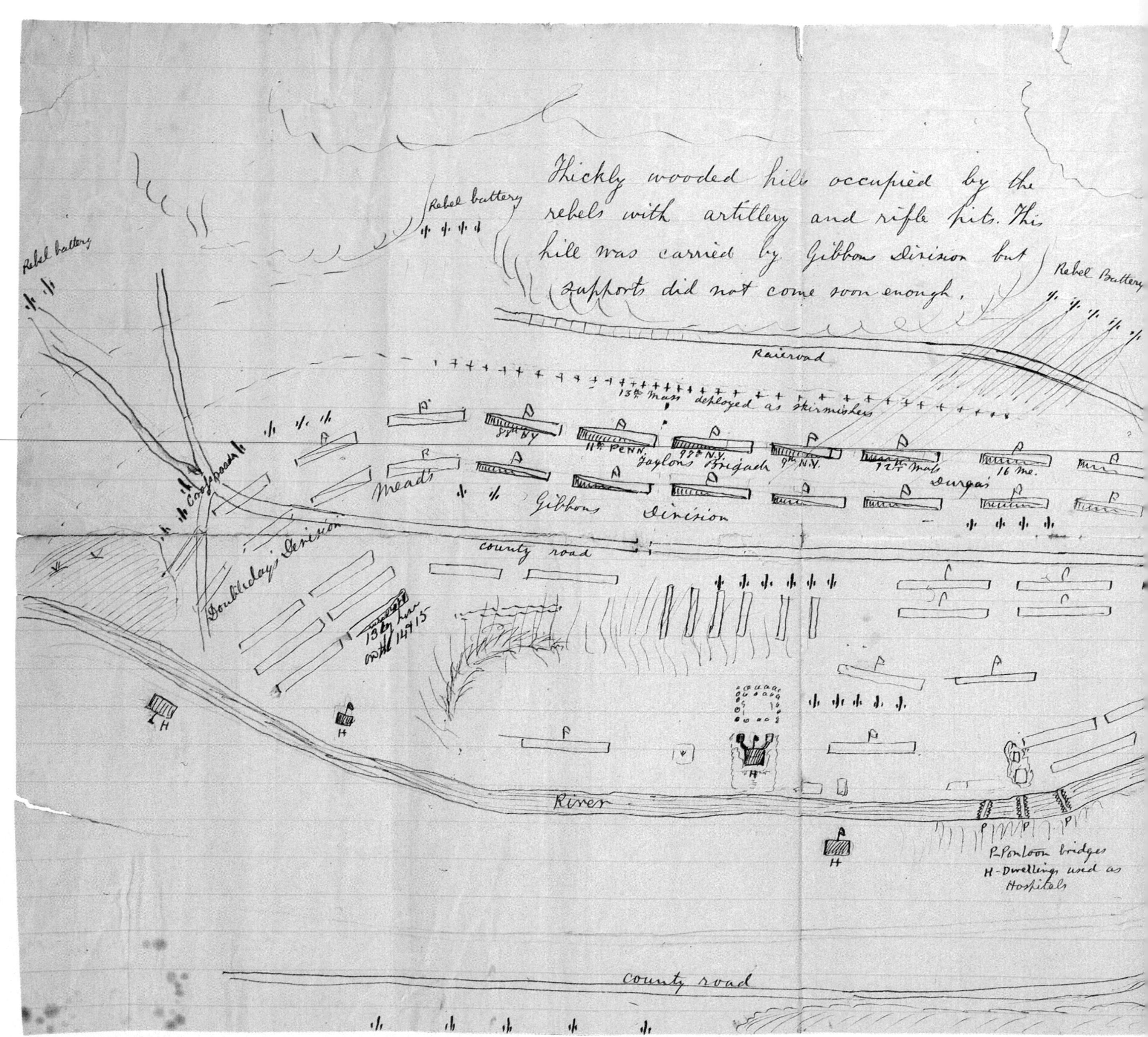
Thickly wooded hill occupied by the rebels with artillery and rifle pits. This hill was carried by Gibbons division but supports did not come soon enough.
Rebel battery
Rebel battery
Rebel Battery
Railroad
13th Mass deployed as skirmishers
11th Penn.
97th N.Y.
9th N.Y.
Taylors Brigade
12th Mass
16 Me.
Meads
Gibbons division
Cross roads
Doubleday's Division
county road
River
P-Pontoon bridges
H-Dwellings used as Hospitals
county road

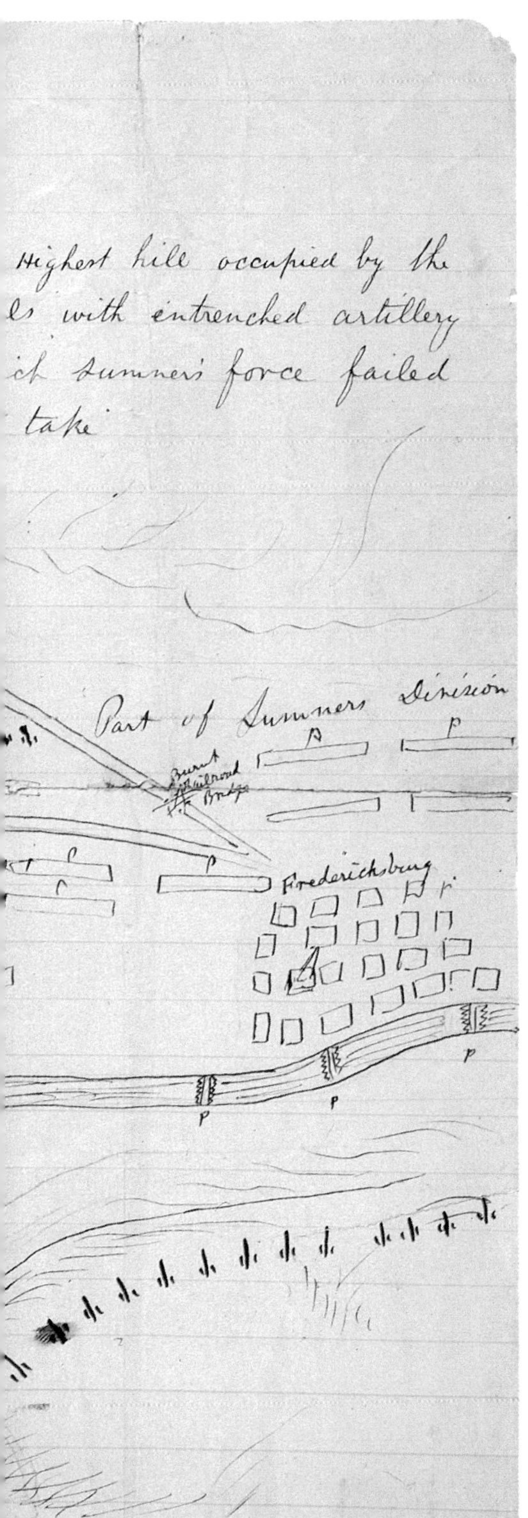

This identification badge was worn by Private John B. Curtis of the 13th Massachusetts, which formed the skirmish line for Gibbon's division. A Vermont native, Curtis enlisted with the 13th while working in Boston. Captured at Gettysburg, he was later exchanged and mustered out in 1864 with the rank of corporal.

Another soldier in the 13th Massachusetts, George Brigham, drew this overview of the Union attack on the Confederate left flank. Although Brigham greatly exaggerated the deployment of his regiment and division, his sketch still contains a wealth of detail: Running across the lower third of the drawing is the Rappahannock River, spanned by six pontoon bridges—slightly out of place. The large "winged" building next to the Rappahannock, near the map's center, is the Bernard house—Franklin's headquarters. The Richmond Stage road is denoted as a "country road," and on this thoroughfare at the left edge of the paper is marked the position of Pelham's bedeviling "Rebel Battery." Although crudely drawn, the lines emanating from the muzzles of the Confederate cannons on the right of the "thickly wooded hills" graphically illustrate the commanding field of fire enjoyed by Jackson's men.

"I had no time to notice who remained standing, being naturally engaged in pressing down hard, bearing on and flattening out that I might not interfere with any of the flying iron."

CORPORAL BATES ALEXANDER

7TH PENNSYLVANIA RESERVES, MAGILTON'S BRIGADE

Born in Campbelltown, Pennsylvania, Alexander, a machinist in civilian life, recounts the effect of Pelham's fire on the exposed ranks of his brigade on the morning of December 13. Shortly before his three-year enlistment was due to expire in June 1864, Alexander was captured at the Wilderness. He was exchanged after surviving incarceration at Andersonville and received a medical discharge on February 27, 1865.

When thus standing in line a cannon boomed out on our left, at close range, seemingly on the Bowling Green road, a shot whizzed high in the air passing over our heads from left to right along the line. Naturally supposing, from the position, 'twas one of our own batteries, we thought our gunners had had too much "commisary" this morning, and so remarked. Another report, then a third, each time the missile coming lower in the air, when they discovered 'twas the enemy. The order was given "down." when from the force of the custom we fell forward face downward, i.e., I suppose the whole line did so, excepting the field and some of the line officers, as I had no time to notice who remained standing, being naturally engaged in pressing down hard, bearing on and flattening out that I might not interfere with any of the flying iron, but courteously (?) allow right of way. This single gun, as subsequently learned, was commanded by Major Pelham. . . . He soon got the range when his shells exploded low overhead and on the flanks of some regiments. The field officers of the Seventh were dismounted close in our rear. A large fragment of shell with force somewhat spent (I saw it fall) struck Adjutant Harvey's horse, tearing down a triangular piece of hide from its side which hung down some fifteen inches. The animal remained quietly in place as though it, too, deemed this part of the program. I could now see some of the happenings, for after Major Pelham had introduced himself, got range, &c., we suddenly became familiar with his manner and were encouraged to a certain extent to raise our heads and look about while he amused himself. Moving his gun slightly to his left he planted at least two solid shot, or unexploded shells, in the prostrate ranks immediately on our front. One fellow was buried by his comrades in about five minutes after being killed.

Off December 13th 1862
To. Gen Burnside
Two batteries playing upon Reynolds advance in rear of his first line cause him to desist the advance; they are on the Bowling Green road near the river they must be silenced before he can advance heavy firing in our front
James A. Hardie
Brig Gen Vol
Recd per Signal Tel
10.10 A.M

Brigadier General James A. Hardie, Burnside's liaison with Franklin's grand division, sent this message to his chief explaining the havoc caused by Pelham's barrage and the resultant delay in the Yankee attack. Both armies often referred to the Richmond Stage road as the "Bowling Green Road" in their dispatches.

CAPTAIN DAVID G. MCINTOSH

PEE DEE (SOUTH CAROLINA) ARTILLERY, A. P. HILL'S DIVISION

Outmatched, McIntosh and the other artillerymen of Jackson's corps endured the Federal shelling while holding their fire for the Federal infantry. Promoted the following spring, McIntosh performed distinguished service as an artillery battalion commander until the end of the war.

Early on the morning of the 13th, General Jackson rode along the front and by our guns. A. P. Hill and Colonel Walker his Chief of Artillery did the same thing. We were cautioned to keep ourselves concealed as much as possible, and ordered on no account to reply to artillery fire, or engage in artillery duels: That our fire must be reserved to use upon infantry and then not until the enemy had reached a given point. Our expectations were excited all the more from the fact that a heavy fog hung over the plain concealing it from our view.

But though we could not see through the fog, there was no lack of ominous sounds to indicate what was going on. The heavy rumble of artillery and ordnance wagons, the bugle calls, and the noise of many bands of music filled the air, and we knew full well what it all meant. When the mist lifted about ten o'clock, a gorgeous panorama was spread out before us. Our preparations for the order of battle were still in progress. As far as the eye could see, back towards the river, and stretching up towards Fredericksburg, the vast plain was filled with

Infantrymen of Colonel John M. Brockenbrough's Virginia brigade, posted near Hamilton's Crossing, await the assault of Franklin's Federals. On the slope above them, Confederate artillerymen peer through the fog, ready for the enemy's advance. Holding the extreme right of A. P. Hill's line, the Virginians were some of the first troops to aid the units on their left being driven back by Meade's attack.

"The commanding form of the cool and intrepid Turney was laid low by a minie-ball which entered his mouth and came out at his neck."

moving masses of men, rapidly deploying and forming alignments into what appeared to be three lines of battle, and here and there large gaps in the lines being filled with artillery, while moving about and adding more life and color to the scene were squadrons of cavalry. Back of it all the Stafford Heights stood out crowned with heavy Parrotts and siege pieces, which had not waited for the mist to lift before they began throwing their heavy missiles and feeling our position. No grander military spectacle was ever presented to human view. . . .

However, before the mist had cleared away, and during the earlier hours of the morning, the heavy guns from the Stafford Heights had been engaged shelling the woods which served as a screen, making it very uncomfortable. Some of the shells were of enormous size, and tearing through the tree tops above us brought down huge limbs which was trying to the men and which frightened the horses greatly until they were taken out of reach.

When the field batteries belonging to the divisions of Meade and Gibbon opened their fire, the situation became still more trying. . . .

. . . [Then] the batteries of Birney's and Sickle's divisions were brought into play, making a total of sixty-seven guns whose fire was directed on this front. But our orders were strict to save our ammunition, not to fire until the given signal, and then at the columns of infantry. There was therefore nothing to do, but to lay still and take it. The gun redoubts offered little protection, some of the men lay flat on the ground, and some hugged the trunks of the large trees, which was all right but for the limbs which came down from above.

Stern-faced and ill-tempered Major General George G. Meade had the nickname Old Snapping Turtle. At Fredericksburg his division began well in its attack, breaching Jackson's line and taking more than 300 prisoners. Eventually driven back by heavy counterattacks, Meade maintained that he could have held the position if he had been supported by some of the 20,000 men who stood idle during the fight.

LIEUTENANT JOHN H. MOORE

7TH TENNESSEE INFANTRY, ARCHER'S BRIGADE

The headlong charge of Meade's infantry—at first unopposed—surprised the troops of Archer's and Lane's Rebel brigades, temporarily routing them. Confederate officers had to work frantically to regroup their men and prevent a potential debacle. Moore, who served with the 7th until Appomattox, and his fellow Tennesseans were commended by their colonel for returning "immediately to the front lines" and helping to force back the Federal infantry.

The extreme left of Archer's brigade and the extreme right of Thomas' brigade . . . believing they were about to be surrounded, gave way; yet their comrades on the right, unaware of the condition of affairs on the left, and seeing the enemy routed in their front, were amazed at this confusion. Their officers and men on the right were enraged at what seemed to them dastardly cowardice, and rushing toward their broken lines, officers and privates stormed at, shouted and threatened them as base cowards. Officers leveled their pistols and, with many privates, fired into these fleeing comrades and broken ranks.

Presently the true condition of affairs appears, when the victorious brigades of Franklin emerge from the woods. The line was broken to escape capture. Line and field officers rushed to and fro, wildly shouting, "Into line, into line!" and even in the face of a flanking foe, the gallant Colonel Turney, who temporarily commanded Archer's brigade, succeeded in reforming his regiments at right angles to the former line of attack. This gave a brief check to the victors. Still the infantry and artillery fire scourged the line. Rout or capture seemed inevitable. The commanding form of the cool and intrepid Turney was laid low by a minie-ball which entered his mouth and came out at his neck. His apparently lifeless form was hurredly placed on a blanket, and four of his devoted followers attempted to carry his body on this improvised litter to the rear, and beyond the reach of captors. These had not proceeded far, when a shell burst among them, and they in turn lay helpless by the side of their bleeding commander. . . . Dead I certainly thought he was, for he was literally covered with blood that oozed from a wound in the head and covered his face beyond recognition.

Working his way around to the rear of a Rebel trench with a small mixed company, Adjutant Evan M. Woodward of the 2d Pennsylvania Reserves captured more than 100 members of the 19th Georgia, along with their battle flag (left). One of the regiments of Archer's brigade that was overrun that morning, the Georgians had the unhappy distinction of being the only Confederates to lose their colors at Fredericksburg.

"Well, I hope they're not our men, for I've killed one."

CORPORAL BERRY BENSON

1st South Carolina Infantry, Gregg's Brigade

So unexpected was the fire coming at them from their front that Maxcy Gregg's men, supposing themselves to be in the second rank of the Rebel line, were hesitant to fire back. Benson survived this chaotic action unharmed but was wounded in 1863 and captured at Spotsylvania in 1864. Held at the Union prison camp at Elmira, New York, he escaped by tunneling out in October 1864 and somehow made his way back south, where he rejoined his regiment, serving until Appomattox.

Lying in the woods behind our stacked arms, we underwent a heavy shelling, a good many men being wounded, some in our company. A man belonging to Co. E. lying close to me, had his arm shattered. Capt. Haskell, out in front of us, sitting with his back to the enemy, leaning against a sapling the size of a man's arm, quietly munched a cracker.

Suddenly there began to come mixed with the shells, rifle balls. Faster and faster they came, and there was quite a stir on our right, where we could see men jumping up and seizing their guns, some beginning to fire.

We sprang to the stacks, but our officers shouted, "Let the guns alone! Lie down! Those are our men in front!"

Whish came the bullets, faster than ever. The commotion on our right increased, and far up to the right we could see our men jumping up and seizing their guns. Many were firing and loading as fast as they could, others stood irresolute, many officers in front trying to keep the men from firing.

We could stand it no longer. We all rose, and the officers then ordered us to take arms. We no sooner had them in hand than we saw men in front. Some cried, "They are Yankees!" and began firing. Others shouted: "No, they're our own men; don't shoot."

Then came the cry, "Forward!" My old schoolmate, Sergt. Pete Ransom, sprang forward on the left, heading the charge. Down the slope we went, firing, and driving whoever they were. But we did not drive far, being halted and ordered back.

All was hubbub, some saying, "They were Yankees, I tell you. I saw their blue clothes." Others said, "Couldn't be Yankees; there's a N.C. brigade out front; been there all the time."

Sergt. Mackey says: "Well, I hope they're not our men, for I've killed one." He was very pale, and plainly in great trouble lest he had killed one of our own men, for of the killing he was positive.

Then to know, a few men were sent down to the front to look at the dead. They soon returned with the good news that it was the enemy. Mackey's man they found dead just where he had said.

On the right, the trouble had been worse. The enemy through a gap between two brigades in our front had advanced in a line oblique to ours, striking our right first, which received the brunt of the meeting. When they first advanced, Gen. Gregg, being quite certain it was the first line of battle falling back, rode in front of his men commanding them to cease firing. And thereby he lost his life, for the enemy came quickly upon him and he was shot from his horse by a single soldier, receiving a wound from which he died. How it was that the line which was in our front got out of position, exposing us to surprise, I don't think was ever clearly explained.

During the battle—just after our charge while we were down in the woods in a state of considerable excitement—a rabbit jumped up and ran here and there among the men, seemingly frightened out of its wits. And no wonder, for in all directions it heard the rattle of small arms, and the roar of artillery and bursting of shells. In its imagination no doubt it was the last grand hunt of the world, a very Judgment Day. Finally the poor creature jumped up on a stump just in front of the line and squatted there, the most conspicuous position it could possibly have found.

During the confusion brought on by the Federal breakthrough, Brigadier General Maxcy Gregg, seen here in his prewar South Carolina militia uniform, ordered his men to hold their fire, thinking that the troops moving through the woods to his front were fellow Rebels. The mistake cost Gregg his life, as a Union Minié ball tore into his spine, unhorsing him and paralyzing him. He died on December 15.

CORPORAL BATES ALEXANDER

7th Pennsylvania Reserves, Magilton's Brigade

The 7th incurred 86 casualties while pressing toward the Confederate defenders. Overall, Magilton's brigade suffered the loss of 632 troops during the failed Union effort. This account, first published in an 1895 edition of the Hummelstown (Pennsylvania) Sun, confirms Stonewall Jackson's grim contention that after the initial Yankee charge the "storm" of shot produced by his gunners and infantry caused the Federals "first to halt, then to waver, and at last seek shelter by flight."

We were now under way in this ever-to-be-remembered charge, one of the most terrible pieces of work; 'twas even worse than standing in front of the famous corn field at Antietam, as we lost over three times the number here. Soon after leaving our batteries we struck a deep ditch running obliquely to our line of advance. Those on our left jumped as did each succeeding file as they came up, quickly resuming their places in line. The ditch, so to speak, passed down the line and fell to the rear causing no confusion. We were now well into the enemy's warm fire on this December day, the men inclined their heads somewhat as though moving against a driving rain. The familiar "chock," "chock" of balls stricking the line was heard constantly to right and left while men tumbled out of line in quick succession. We seemed to press in hard on the colors; twice came very near loosing my place in line. Had we been recruits half would have been forced out of ranks. We were so close together that there was little place for balls to pass between the men, we were surely shoulder to shoulder in this advance. The big men at the head of Captain Barrett's Co., being pressed by those on their left squeezed me against our "C" till I could scarcely breath. With this great pressure on both sides and a determined little fellow in my rear, Fulmer, of Annville, Pa., I went into battle this day. . . . I noticed Bennie Small [Smith] of Middletown, Pa. lying supporting himself on left elbow, shot through the right shoulder, one of "E" was shot through left shoulder. The sharp thud of a spent ball on my front below the belt caused me to quickly look and feel for a hole in overcoat, but no hole this time, though 'twas no false alarm as I felt it thump against me with some force. I had heard of men having been shot through without feeling pain for an instant, and didn't know but that—well I was pleased it ended as it did.

Soon thereafter Fulmer said, "Bates a ball went through your haversack." Holding up my left hand I said in reply, "I know it, look there."

"The familiar 'chock,' 'chock' of balls stricking the line was heard constantly to right and left while men tumbled out of line in quick succession."

Private Charles Decker of the 142d Pennsylvania Infantry, wounded during the attack, was one of 243 casualties in his regiment, the hardest hit in Meade's division. Wounded again and briefly captured, the battle-scarred veteran was detailed as a cattle herdsman until he was discharged in 1865.

Situated at the base of the wooded slope defended by the Rebels, the slightly elevated bed of the Richmond, Fredericksburg & Potomac Railroad was a crucial terrain feature during the fierce contest waged on the Union left. Charging over it during their opening attack, many blue-clad troops later sheltered here from the murderous fire that drove them back.

FRANKLIN'S MEN CHARGING ACROSS THE RAILROAD.

I had been wounded in the coat sleeves, at the wrist, ball passing through overcoat and dress coat sleeves, carrying away a bit of hide and allowing about one drop of blood to come forth in defence of flag. The spot burned as though a coal of fire had touched it. Quickly clutched my hand to see if bone was broken, another passed through the bottom of haversack, cut away the bowl of my spoon and a corner of my button brush. 'Twas full of mischief, but happily did no serious harm. . . .

Arriving at the R.R. we halted and lay against the sides of a cut about three feet in depth . . . many of us lay with backs against the bank toward the enemy while some occupied the ditches by the track and the opposite bank. A very few sat on the rails as at such times men generally try to get cover, or as low down as possible. Here we lay for a few minutes listening to the roar of Yankee and Confederate cannon as they slam into each other. . . .

The line began to move forward. I had heard no order. 'Twas said Sergt. James McCauley, brother of Major L. G. McCauley, caused the move by jumping up on the bank and calling, "wide awake, fellows, let's give em h——." The line went forward without regular order, making a grand dash for the woods along which the enemy was posted. While thus moving the Fredericksburg battery had a splendid opportunity to take us in flank on our left, which they did to a certainty, their canister buzzing among us quite lively. We didn't allow them much of this for we gained the wood about as soon as any good runners similarly situated could have done. But they killed Pete Hagey, and knocked a leg off of Wm. Gross, also Henry Dillman from Gravel Hill; color guard lost a leg and died in Richmond. We were rushing wildly for the wood to escape this flank fire. Pat Cassidy jumped a high brush heap while I close in his rear, had to pass round but gained the wood about on time with Cassidy. I could run at such times like a scared deer.

Gaining the wood, at this point somewhat open, we slackened our pace as the battery could not now reach us. A light worm or snake fence, now nearly demolished, ran along the edge of the wood. The first of the enemy's infantry that I saw was one who had been firing from a rest on the crotch or fork of a dogwood tree just high enough to allow him to take aim while kneeling. He must have had a glorious time and smiled while "working his gun" as we advanced. But the poor young soldier had been struck by a ball or small fragment of a shell just above the right eye, he lay on his back with legs still bent under. It seemed as though a bucket of blood had run out of his head. One of our men ran across to him, cut his belt, snatched it from beneath him and crammed it into his haversack with scarcely a halt. . . .

Color Corporal Reuben Schell (below) of the 7th Pennsylvania carried this battle-torn color during Meade's attack. As he rushed across the railroad tracks, a Rebel "ball" smashed into his belt buckle. Fortunately for Schell, the bullet did not penetrate his skin, although the impact knocked him down. Captured with most of his regiment at the Wilderness in 1864, Schell survived imprisonment to return home.

. . . We were advancing at a quick step, without regard to order, so far as alignment was concerned, and it seemed "we didn't care for nothing," when a discharge of musketry, such as we had never before heard, greeted our ears. It sounded as one large gun. There was a sudden halt, "about face" and forward for the Yankee rear. The tall form of Corporal Bill Cunningham of Palmyra, Pa., appeared as he very suddenly emerged from the low pines in front of my position, and the next instant the gallant boys were almost flying down the old roadway or through the bushes, some of us bore a little to the left (in retreat). Arriving at the little old fence there was no time for graceful climbing so I, for one, cleared it at a bound. Orderly Sergt. Pete Leininger, of Lebanon, Pa., must have acted likewise, as he told me he was "trailing arms" when his musket struck the fence discharging the "buck and ball" past his ear, causing him to think the enemy was at his heels. I did not notice Leininger till we were in rear of our batteries, probably too far in advance of him, as this was one of my good days for running.

Private William A. Martin (above) of the 28th North Carolina received a wound earlier in 1862 (the effect of which is visible over his eye) and had only recently returned to duty. As the troops of Gibbon's division approached, Martin, it was reported, "coolly sat on the [railroad] track, and called to his comrades to watch the Yankee colors, then he fired and down they went. This was done repeatedly." Lieutenant Charles W. Duke (left) of the 90th Pennsylvania in Gibbon's division was killed shortly after his regiment began to move toward the Rebel lines.

While Sergeant William Wells' woolen overcoat sheltered him from the cold, nothing could protect his regiment—the 16th Maine—from the deadly fire leveled at it by Lane's North Carolinians positioned behind the railroad embankment. The Rebels' accurate shooting killed or wounded 197 of the 16th's 427 soldiers. Wells was among those hit, suffering a severe leg wound that led to an amputation.

SERGEANT WILLIAM A. MCCLENDON

15TH ALABAMA INFANTRY, HOKE'S BRIGADE

McClendon and the other soldiers in his brigade were posted by Jubal Early in the second line back behind Hamilton's Crossing. The brigade rushed forward to blunt Meade's breakthrough, winning warm praise from their commander, Brigadier General Robert Hoke, in his after-battle report. McClendon served with the 15th Alabama throughout the war and eventually won a lieutenant's commission.

My brigade was . . . directly in the rear of Gen. Maxey Gregg's Brigade of South Carolinians, were attacked with such overwhelming numbers that caused them to fall back, and in General Gregg's effort to rally his men he was shot and killed almost instantly; this caused some confusion, but they never broke but kept falling back, contesting every inch of ground the advancing enemy gained. Colonel Hoke called us to attention, and ordered us to fix bayonets. A perfect stream of wounded was passing to our rear. The firing in front was of the heaviest kind. The cheers of the advancing Yankees could be plainly heard. They were following and crowding the South Carolinians with perfect joy, but poor fellows, they did not know what they were soon to meet. Capt. W. C. Oates . . . was in command of my regiment and was eager to order an advance but had to wait until Colonel Hoke ordered. When everything got right, Hoke ordered us forward, with orders not to fire until we had passed our men in front. We soon came upon them when we halted and was ordered to fire, and immediately we raised the "Rebel Yell" and rushed on to the Yankees with the bayonet. They could not stand. They were not expecting such a deadly volley. They broke and we [ran] after them down the hill to the cut in the railroad where we overhauled a goodly number of them crouched down, waving white handkerchiefs to surrender. Our troops on the right and left charged simultaneous with us, and had the same success. The railroad made a curve at this place and as far as I could see to the right and left there were Yankees and our men all mixed up together. The South Carolinians had killed and wounded a great many when they advanced upon them, and they were lying scattered about, some beyond the railroad. . . . The Yankees went to the rear in a hurry. I believe they were really anxious to get out of it.

Helping to close the gap in the Confederate line was Brigadier General Alexander R. Lawton's brigade, commanded by Colonel Edmund N. Atkinson while Lawton recovered from a wound suffered at Antietam. In the ranks of the brigade was Hillery T. Wright (above) of the 61st Georgia, who was wounded in the face, left arm, and hip. After a long convalescence, Wright returned to the ranks but ended the war as a prisoner after his capture at Winchester in September 1864.

This coat and ring belonged to Adjutant Edward P. Lawton, brother of his brigade's absent commander. Lawton was helping to lead the Georgians' crucial counterblow when he was felled by a Federal bullet. Undeterred, he limped forward until he received another wound—this one mortal—and was captured. He died in an Alexandria, Virginia, hospital, on December 26.

CAPTAIN JAMES C. NISBET

21ST GEORGIA INFANTRY, HOKE'S BRIGADE

Nisbet describes the pandemonium that erupted in the Confederate ranks as one of the shattered units of Archer's brigade fell to the rear before the Federal thrust, temporarily blocking the fields of fire of the Confederate regiments held in reserve. Momentum shifted when Hoke's and Atkinson's brigades made their hard-driving counterthrust, running over friend and foe alike to hammer the Yankees back.

The firing with small arms in our front became very heavy and kept getting nearer. The regiment was called to attention. We were standing in line awaiting orders when I saw Rebs pouring out of the woods. I ran forward and recognized my old schoolmate, Colonel Jack Hutchins, of the 19th Georgia Regiment, Archer's Brigade. He said: "Cooper, stop those men." We ordered them to form in the rear of our line.

I asked: "Jack, what's the matter?"

He answered: "We were in a riflepit and had just repulsed an attack from the front when the enemy came up on my left flank and were getting in my rear. I had to order my men to fall back. They have captured half of my regiment. The woods there are full of them."

Captain Hamilton said: "We will recapture your men and take the Yanks, too, in a few minutes." We ran down our line, ordering the 21st to pass over Rebs and Yanks and not to stop to capture or shoot until they got in the riflepit.

Just then an officer came dashing down the line crying out "second line forward!" which we did with a rush recapturing the men of the 19th Georgia, and of course their captors fell into our lines. We reached the riflepit . . . and fired into a brigade that was advancing.

After a few rounds the brigade fighting us fell back into a long, deep railroad cut. Colonel Hoke ordered a charge of the whole brigade, which he led gallantly. We went into the railroad cut, capturing many prisoners. I emptied my self-cocking Colt's, the fine weapon captured from the colonel commanding Manassas Junction, as we advanced.

I ran up in front of my men and jumped into the cut, landing on a big captain's head, ramming it down in the mud. The men piled in after us and seeing that we were outnumbered, were inclined to be rough but we stopped them as the Yanks wanted to surrender.

"Men who have been all through this war say we came in under the hottest fire they had ever seen."

LIEUTENANT EDWARD E. WILLIAMS

114TH PENNSYLVANIA INFANTRY, ROBINSON'S BRIGADE

As the spirited Rebels rolled past the railroad line, they nearly overwhelmed several Federal batteries. Brigadier General John C. Robinson's III Corps brigade double-quicked into action, rescuing the guns by delivering "a galling fire into the face of the enemy" that blunted and reversed the Confederates' momentum. Philadelphian Williams served with the 114th until badly wounded in the right leg at Chancellorsville. Disabled by this wound, he resigned from the army in February 1864.

We moved down to the river early in the morning and lay there till about 1 o'clock. Heavy fighting was going on mostly opposite to us until about 1 o'clock [when] our Brigade was ordered over. We crossed the bridge, our Regmt on the road [and] we soon got into the fire. It was dreadful to hear and see the wounded lying around us. I felt . . . at first but we were [pushed] forward double quick. I was busy keeping the men in their places the fire kept getting hotter and hotter the shot and shell fairly rained amongst us but now I dont mind it. Willie turned around and says Ned here goes my blanket and dropped it. I had mine and my gum coat and let them go to and on we went. We met Biddles men coming out all mixed up. We went on till we reached Randolph's Battery, the Rebels had got to within 20 paces of it and were just on the point of taking it when we got up. We poured in a volly and gave one yell and rushed at them. They turned tail and run and we poured it into them until they reached the woods and then we laid down in the mud and mire. . . . Men who have been all through this war say we came in under the hottest fire they had ever seen. Our Brigadier had a shell right through his horse. . . . If we had been 3 minutes later Randolphs Battery would have been gone. Willie behaved splendid just as cool and calm as if nothing was the matter. He loaded his piece while he encouraged the men. All three of us escaped without a scratch. . . . God grant that we may never go into another Battle. I dont mind it while I am in but going in and coming out is hard to bear.

This painting shows the men of the 114th Pennsylvania, clad in distinctive Zouave uniforms, charging into Atkinson's counterattacking Georgians. Their colonel, Charles H. T. Collis, waves the regimental colors to urge on his troops, while brigade commander Robinson lies trapped under his fallen mount. The 114th was accompanied by "French Mary" Tepe (above), a vivandière, or canteen carrier, who helped succor the unit's wounded and was herself struck in the heel by a bullet.

"Then it was that those men who had never seen a battle before, had never seen Confederate troops in action, raised that Confederate yell that seemed to be a part of the nature of the Confederate troops."

Captain William B. Whitaker (above) was one of 10 men in the 16th North Carolina, positioned on Jackson's far left, who were killed during his regiment's skirmishing, first with Gibbon's men and then with Colonel Alfred T. A. Torbert's New Jersey brigade. Whitaker is shown here as a first sergeant, the rank he held upon enlisting.

LIEUTENANT COLONEL HAMILTON C. JONES

57TH NORTH CAROLINA INFANTRY, LAW'S BRIGADE

About 3:00 p.m. General Evander M. Law ordered forward two green regiments, the 57th and the 54th North Carolina, to drive back two New Jersey regiments that had moved up to the railroad tracks. The Tar Heels overwhelmed the Federals and nearly made it to the Richmond Stage road before retreating. Jones, second in command of the 57th, was taken prisoner at the engagement at Rappahannock Station on November 7, 1863. He was then held in Union prisons until the end of the war.

The regiment, when it received the order, was in the woods. . . , and in order to clear the woods, owing to swamps and thickets, was compelled to go across a corduroy road out into the open. . . . As the first company cleared the woods, a battery opened on it from the Bowling Green road, yet under this fire, company after company, as it cleared the woods, went steadily into line without a falter or a sign of confusion, and the line was formed as accurately as if on parade; then at "quick step" it started for the enemy's line on the railroad. It was in full view of almost the entire Confederate army on the surrounding hills, and of a larger part of the Federal along the Bowling Green road. As it started there came a cheer from the hills. The line moved at "quick step," with arms at right-shoulder-shift. The enemy's artillery redoubled its fire, but the marksmanship was bad, and the regiment was receiving little punishment, and moved as if on parade. At about 400 yards the enemy opened with their rifles from the railroad, but the regiment had been ordered not to return the fire until the enemy broke, and so they marched in silence. Then the files began to fall out, killed or wounded sometimes from shells and sometimes from the infantry fire, but the gaps were closed up and the regiment marched steadily forward still silent. Then the bullets flew thick and the ground in the wake of the regiment began to be strewn with those brave men, thicker and thicker. Then the fire became terrific, and at about 125 yards from the railroad the order was given to "double-quick." Then it was that those men who had never seen a battle before, had never seen Confederate troops in action, raised that Confederate yell that seemed to be a part of the nature of the Confederate troops. There was a sudden dash forward into the thunder and smoke and guns, and the Fifty-seventh Regiment was at the railroad with their guns loaded, and those of the enemy who had not fled were captured then and there. The regiment had received no orders to halt at the railroad, so Colonel Godwin, in obedience to what he considered his orders, planted his colors upon the far bank of the railroad, and immediately the regiment was again in line and making towards the Bowling Green road. It was now attacked upon its flank, yet it never faltered nor hesitated until it had gone through this ordeal, a distance of nearly 200 yards, and an order from General Law to retire to the railroad. . . . The struggle had lasted in all perhaps twenty-five minutes, and in that time 250 of the Fifty-seventh Regiment were stretched dead or wounded.

Captain Alfred A. Miller of the 57th North Carolina, killed during the afternoon attack, had earlier informed his company that he did not expect to survive it. His wife died a few weeks later—of grief, according to family tradition.

Colonel William Hatch (above), commander of the 4th New Jersey, was charged with but not tried for striking two sentries who were protecting civilian property during the Peninsula campaign. At Fredericksburg on December 13 he received a leg wound while trying to rally his men to stop the advance of Law's North Carolinians. The leg was amputated but he succumbed to the wound on December 18. The unique folding hat (top) was Hatch's headgear of choice while relaxing in camp.

"It was as if 'Old Jack' had said to the Yankee Devil, 'seest thou my faithful old Stonewall battery! Do your worst and see if thou canst terrify it!'"

CAPTAIN WILLIAM T. POAGUE

ROCKBRIDGE (VIRGINIA) ARTILLERY, SECOND CORPS

Avid to shed more Yankee blood, Stonewall Jackson ordered Poague to resume firing in the hope of provoking another ill-advised Union attack on his superior position. As Poague recounts, the provocation elicited a most unwelcome response. Not engaged in the earlier action, the battery lost six killed and 10 wounded in this exchange.

We had a good opportunity to view the field, and never before had we seen as much infantry and artillery of the enemy at one time. After an hour or so General Jackson in a brand-new uniform came to where my guns were and with his glass surveyed the field for some minutes. Then he called me to him and said, "Captain do you see that battery at what appears to be the junction of two roads?" at the same time pointing to the place, which was directly in our front. I replied in affirmation and that I had for sometime noticed it firing at something away to my right. "Can't you silence that battery?", he asked. "We can try, General," I said. "Well open on it," he ordered, "and if they get too hard for you, turn your gun on their infantry and try and stampede that!" He at once turned and went off to the left.

The order amazed me, and as I thought a moment, I was confounded by its apparent absurdity. Stampede infantry after being knocked out! But it was "Old Jack's" order, exactly as he gave it,—for the words burned themselves into my memory—*never to be forgotten*. . . .

What did he mean! Well I have no trouble about the first part, but the second part puzzled one. . . .

. . . I never could understand it except as a bit of grim humor. He knew what would happen when we opened, about five minutes after he left. Such a tempest of shot and shell I never have witnessed any where during the war. It was as if "Old Jack" had said to the Yankee Devil, "seest thou my faithful old Stonewall battery! Do your worst and see if thou canst terrify it!" I don't know how many were the batteries in all that wide stretch of bottom that were turned loose on our devoted section. It was not long before Colonel Coleman came rushing right into the vortex of the storm demanding: "What does all this mean, Captain! Who ordered you to open fire?" "General Jackson himself" I replied. "Well, I take the responsibility of ordering you to stop," he stated. "Very well, Colonel," I responded, "those Yankees down there will pretty soon compel us to quit, anyway."

Just then it was that Colonel Coleman was cut down, receiving a wound that resulted in his death, some weeks afterwards. The order to cease firing was given, and the men directed to seek any cover they could find behind trees and logs. Two of the finest soldiers in the battery were killed nearly at the same moment—Lieutenant Baxter McCorkle and Private Randolph Fairfax; and Arthur Robinson of a prominent Baltimore family was mortally wounded. Lieutenant McCorkle was trying to extinguish fire in the leaves near the caissons when his side was torn open by a missile of some sort. Fairfax was struck by a fragment in the middle of the forehead, death following quickly. Several others were wounded more or less seriously.

Just after Colonel Coleman was struck Colonel Brown arrived to see about matters and while I was telling him, a piece of shell cut through my hat brim within an inch of my head, producing a sensation of much heat about my eyes and forehead. . . .

As I passed driver John Connor holding his lead horses by a strap, flat on his breast and head up against a sapling, I said: "Hello, John, that's a mighty small protection for your head." He replied: "Yes, Captain, but if there was a ground squirrel's hole near by I think I could get into it." I had it from one of our men who is good authority that a certain fellow was stretched out behind a good sized stump with his nose within twelve inches of a pile of filth, when another seeing the situation and coveting that stump for himself exclaimed, "look at that stuff near your face." "Pshaw, go away! it smells sweet as a rose," he replied, and still stuck to his stump.

SERGEANT JACOB HEFFELFINGER

7TH PENNSYLVANIA RESERVES, MAGILTON'S BRIGADE

While lying painfully wounded on the cold, damp ground, Heffelfinger—shown above on the far right with friends during more pleasant times, scrawled this deeply felt account at 4:30 detailing the disastrous results of his brigade's charge. Heffelfinger had a remarkably eventful military career: He was wounded twice, captured and exchanged no fewer than three times, and promoted to lieutenant in 1864. He commanded a company when mustered out in 1865.

The battle has raged fiercely today—The rebels ocupy an advantagous position. Our troops are on an open plain, while they occupy a ridge in our front, and are sheltered by dense woods but about 1 1/2 P.M. one part of the line made a forward movement, our division, as usual, taking the advance. This was a fearful movement. We left the field over which we advanced, thickly strewn with our dead and wounded.—We drove the rebels from their position in the rail-road cut at the edge of the woods. On entering the woods our line was thrown into confusion by a misunderstanding of orders, but our men pushed on boldly and reached the summit of the hill. During the confusion I received a shot through both legs, completely disabling me. Our men were soon after attacked by the enemy in heavy force, and being weakened by the great slaughter in our ranks while advancing and wholy without support they were driven back over me in disorder. All that we gained at so fearful a cost is lost. I am still lying where I fell.—The rebels have advanced a line over me, so that I am a prisoner.—I am now exposed to the fire of our artillery which is fearfully destructive. Death has been doing fearful work today.

As the fighting waned, Brigadier General George D. Bayard, a promising Union cavalry officer, was struck by a shell that crushed one of his hips as he stood near General Franklin's headquarters at the Bernard house. Surgeons pronounced the wound mortal, and Bayard calmly dictated his last words home. He died the next day and was buried six days later, on a date that had originally been set as his wedding day.

Marye's Heights: First Attacks

On December 13 Major General Darius N. Couch began deploying his II Corps troops for the assault on Marye's Heights, a prominent stretch opposite Fredericksburg of the long Rebel-occupied ridge. Spearheading the attack would be the men of William French's division, three brigades that had fought at Antietam's Bloody Lane three months earlier.

Confederate artillery pounded the Union soldiers as they attempted to form up in the town's streets. Private Eugene Cory of the 4th New York Infantry described the bombardment as "perfect pandemonium." General James Longstreet had 22 cannons positioned on Marye's Heights, along with several supporting batteries on the adjacent hills to the north and south, and they were all firing with devastating effect.

Longstreet's cannoneers continued to pummel the Union brigades as they emerged from the protection of Fredericksburg's buildings onto a plain that gradually sloped up to the foot of Marye's Heights. As the Rebel artillery blew holes in his tightly packed columns, Brigadier General Nathan Kimball led his brigade—the first of a day-long succession of doomed formations—across narrow bridges that spanned a canal skirting the western edge of the town.

Deploying into line of battle under cover of an incline, Kimball's regiments advanced steadily up the slope, heading toward a five-foot-high stone wall at the base of the heights. Sheltering behind the wall in a sunken road were the Rebel troops of Brigadier General Thomas R. R. Cobb's Georgia brigade. Cobb's men were supported in the rear by 7,000 infantrymen from Robert Ransom's and Joseph B. Kershaw's divisions, and on the left by the men of the 24th North Carolina, whose trenches extended the line for 250 more yards.

The 2,000 Confederates in the front line patiently awaited Kimball's approach. "Protected both from shell and small arms," wrote one of the Georgians, "we only had to watch their approach in unbroken column, until within range." When the Federals closed to within 125 yards of the wall, Cobb's men loosed a lethal volley that cut blue-clad soldiers down by the hundreds. Kimball's men bravely continued to advance but could get no closer than 40 yards from the wall. "The fire was so deadly," recalled an Indiana officer, that "battalions melted away like dry grass before the fire."

General Kimball was hobbled by a bullet in his leg and was carried to the rear. More than 500 men in his ranks were hit advancing on the wall. His survivors fell behind a slight swell in the earth, lay prone, and awaited reinforcements.

French's other two brigades followed Kimball's men into the action, only to be cut to ribbons in their turn. "Three times they reformed and came on unbroken as before," said one of Cobb's men, "but each time a deadly shower of bullets thinned their ranks, and in confusion, they broke and fled." Cobb's brigade inflicted more than 1,000 casualties in the leading Federal division within the first 30 minutes of the assault. Porter Carpenter of the 132d Pennsylvania Infantry likened the open ground in front of the wall to a slaughter pen. "I had heard of these pens before," he wrote to his father, "but I never thought of being led into one."

Like a succession of waves dashing at a rocky shore, the massed Union soldiers continued their death march across the gently sloping ground in front of the Confederate defenses. Following on the heels of French's men came the 5,000 troops of Brigadier General Winfield S. Hancock's division. Colonel Samuel Zook led the first of Hancock's three brigades toward the wall, but, according to one eyewitness, "as fast as his brigade crossed that muddy field they strewed it with their bodies."

Brigadier General Thomas F. Meagher's colorful Irish Brigade was next to enter the maelstrom. In a tragic irony of history, the 1,300 Federals, wearing green sprigs in their caps, advanced directly against a sector of the enemy line defended by the heavily Irish 24th Georgia Infantry. "What a pity. Here comes Meagher's fellows," yelled one of the Georgians. Without hesitation, the Southerners greeted their former countrymen with sheets of musket fire. Meagher's men surged to within a stone's throw of the wall, but the Irish Brigade paid dearly for its valor—545 casualties incurred within a matter of minutes.

The Confederates behind the wall also were taking casualties. Although Cobb's entire brigade lost fewer men than some of the attacking Federal regiments, Cobb himself was one of them, mortally wounded by a shell fragment. Even though Cobb's men appeared to be holding their own despite the loss of their commander, Longstreet, taking no chances, ordered Ransom's small North Carolina division to join the Georgians on the firing line, while Kershaw's brigade was brought up as a ready reserve.

The sixth Federal brigade to assault Marye's Heights was that of Brigadier General John C. Caldwell, with its six New York, Pennsylvania, and New Hampshire regiments. Caldwell's men reached to within 40 yards of the wall—but like all the Federal troops who had gone before them, they could get no closer. Confederate musketry and artillery chewed up Caldwell's brigade, inflicting hundreds of casualties. Colonel Edward D. Hall, commander of a North Carolina brigade, recalled that the plain in front of the stone wall was "literally black with their dead and wounded."

Colonel Nelson A. Miles, commanding the 61st and 64th New York in Caldwell's charge, despaired over the slaughter in his ranks and concluded that the tactics employed on the field were preordained to fail. The Federal infantrymen had been ordered to advance in the conventional manner, stopping at intervals to load and fire. As they paused, the stationary men made easy targets for the Rebels. Miles was convinced that only a bayonet charge had a chance of succeeding—a human wave that would overwhelm the Rebel line with sheer mass and momentum.

Before he could press his case to the high command, Miles was struck down by a bullet that penetrated his throat and exited near his left ear. Bleeding profusely, he staggered rearward to the headquarters of Major General Oliver O. Howard, whose division was waiting behind Hancock's to march off to the slaughter. Miles managed to present his argument to Howard before fainting from loss of blood. "He was determined either to be killed or promoted," remembered Howard.

By the time II Corps commander General Couch was coming to his own conclusion that only a bayonet charge might break the Confederate line, he was faced with the realization that it was too late for French's or Hancock's bloodied divisions to make the attempt. When he climbed to the steeple of the Fredericksburg courthouse to get a view of the battle-

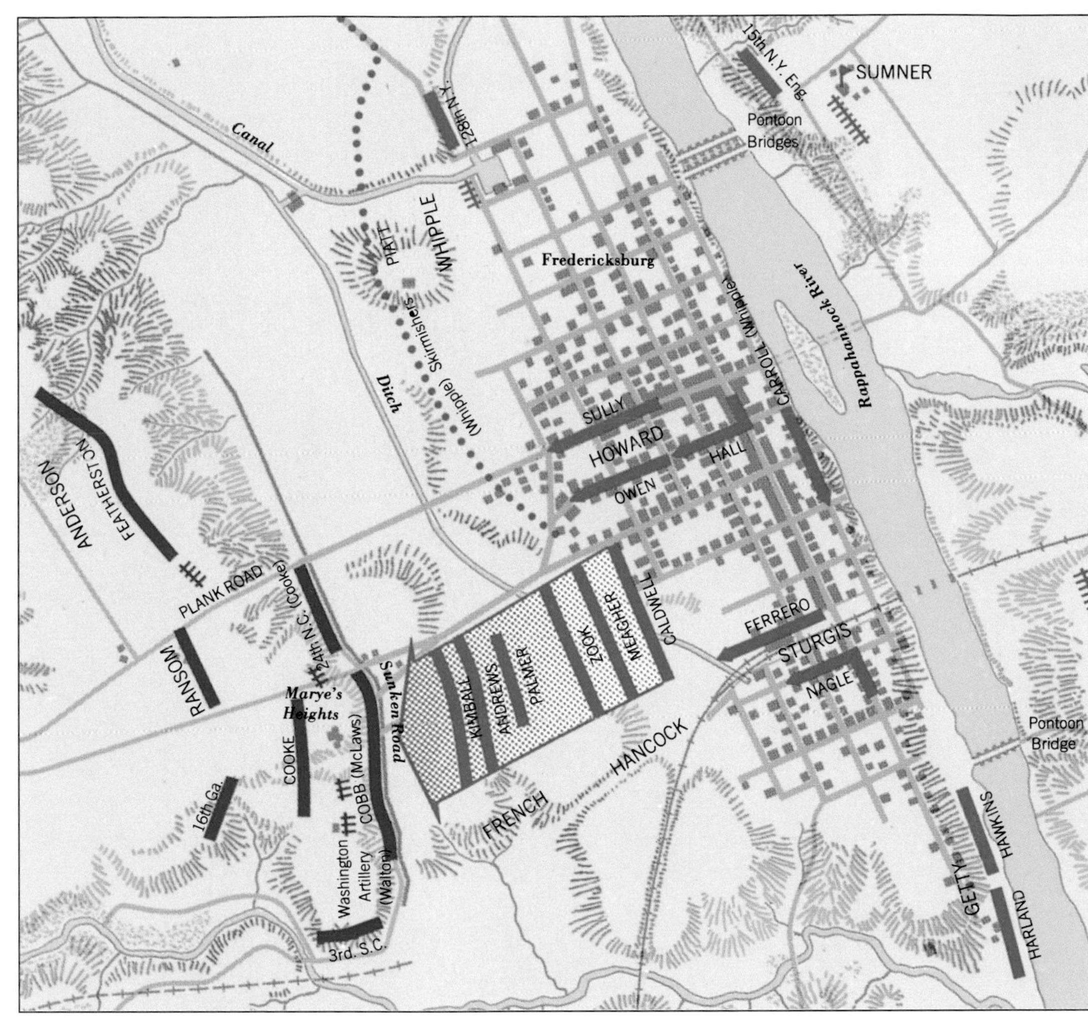

About noon the Federal II Corps, spearheaded by French's division, launched an attack on Longstreet's position on Marye's Heights. Advancing in the open, the leading brigades were driven to ground, first by cannon fire from the Washington Artillery and then by volleys from Cobb's Georgians sheltered behind a stone wall. Hancock's three brigades, coming up behind French, were likewise mauled and pinned down behind scant cover.

field, Couch was stricken by the sight of the carnage. "Oh! Great God!" he exclaimed. "See how our men, our poor fellows are falling!" Hancock lost 42 percent of his infantry—2,000 casualties to add to French's 1,100. "It is only murder now," said Couch.

On a nearby hill, Robert E. Lee observed the same panorama, but without having to countenance the wholesale slaughter of his own army. Taking in the soul-stirring grandeur of the orderly blue masses, the almost inconceivable valor of their hopeless but unwavering advance, and the triumphant efficiency of his Confederate men-at-arms, Lee told his officers, "It is well that war is so terrible, otherwise we should become too fond of it."

CHAPLAIN JOHN H. W. STUCKENBERG

145TH PENNSYLVANIA INFANTRY, CALDWELL'S BRIGADE

Stuckenberg immigrated to the United States as a child but returned to his German homeland to study theology. In September 1862 the young minister was overseeing three congregations in Erie, Pennsylvania, when he was named chaplain of the 145th, one of the regiments that advanced on Marye's Heights in the early afternoon.

We arose early the next morning—the 13th—so as to be ready for any orders that might be given. After breakfast Capt Reynolds and Lt Clay were with us. It seemed to us that we had never been in better spirits. Our conversation was lively and humorous. Had we but known what was before us! I thought of battle, of wounds, of death—and neglected not my Bible nor my prayers. But that the close of the day would find us in such different spirits and our regt in such a different condition—of this we had no idea. It was the morning so bright, so beautiful, so peaceful in nature, of the terrible battle of Fredericksburg. One of those present with us that morning, who was cheerful and happy was to be a corpse before night—Lt Clay—and another one equally happy was to be severely wounded—Col Brown—and all were to be worn and depressed by the awful sights we were to witness.

About 10 A.M. we were formed in line of battle two squares further back from the river, directly in front of the Catholic church, the theatre and Lt Maury's house. Skirmishers were sent out. The shells came sweeping down the streets—one striking a corner house diagonally

across from me. I saw distinctly a shell or a piece of railroad iron coming down the same street, twirling round and round as it went. When men came to these streets they hurried across them, lest the deathly missiles should strike them. Thicker and faster came the shells, around us was rattling the grape and canister, in front of us was the rattling of musketry constantly becoming quicker and louder. About noon our regiment was ordered on the field. Whilst waiting at the corner of the street to fall into the rear of the regiment many shook my hand heartily, saying "good bye Chaplain!"—the last "goodbye" that some of them uttered. They said it perhaps with pale and trembling lips, and with deep earnestness feeling that they were to pass through a terrible ordeal—their first battle. It almost completely unmannered me—so many thoughts rushing on my mind and deep emotions overwhelming my heart. How many I thought might be killed or wounded—some perhaps of my dearest friends in the regiment, some perhaps, who were not at all prepared to meet their God! But it was a time when calmness was required—and I composed myself.

In May 1864 one of Mathew Brady's photographers recorded this panoramic view looking west from the outskirts of Fredericksburg to the wooded crest of Marye's Heights, at center on the horizon. A year and a half earlier, Burnside's Federal columns had been savaged by artillery fire as they advanced up Hanover Street (right) and deployed in the open ground below the Rebel stronghold on the heights. "I can truthfully say that in that moment I gave my life up," a survivor recalled. "I do not expect ever again to face death more certainly."

Proprietor of a hotel in Erie, Hiram L. Brown went to war as an officer with the 83d Pennsylvania and in June 1862 was severely wounded at the Battle of Gaines' Mill. Six months later, as the colonel commanding the 145th Pennsylvania, Brown was shot through the lungs as he led his regiment in its charge on Marye's Heights. The burly six-footer recovered, only to be wounded again at Gettysburg. He was captured at Spotsylvania the following May and paroled three months later.

LIEUTENANT COLONEL FRANKLIN SAWYER

8TH OHIO INFANTRY, KIMBALL'S BRIGADE

A hard-drinking attorney from Norwalk, Ohio, Sawyer led his regiment in the first wave of the Federal assault on Marye's Heights. One of six regiments in Kimball's brigade—which spearheaded the advance of French's division—the 8th Ohio pushed back a Confederate skirmish line but was stopped by the heavy fire of the guns on the heights.

As soon as the mist lifted I crept stealthily along through the gardens and alleys to the last house within our lines, from which could be seen something of what we were to do. There is a deep mill race or canal taken from the rapids above town that completely surrounds the city, connecting with the river below. The bridges across this were torn up, and the canal itself was held by rebel sharp shooters. The plain beyond, to the foot of the hills, was crossed by numerous board and stone fences, while residences, shops, out buildings and gardens dotted the front and flank, and a long rifle pit led along the bank above the canal. These were held by considerable detachments of troops, and afforded them the most secure cover. It was our perilous duty to drive these forces back into their main works.

I returned to the regiment and received the final orders—was to go on foot, there being no way to get a horse over the canal, the regiment to march by the left flank until a crossing of the canal was effected, carrying rails and planks for the purpose. . . . The whole line was then to advance and carry the plain at the foot of the heights, leveling the fences as we moved forward, so as to enable a charging column to march uninterrupted by any obstructions. . . .

The Fourth Ohio and First Delaware had moved down to the rail-

"As soon as we rose over the little bank, the missiles came upon us spitefully, and the air was full of exploding shells."

road, and the left of the Eighth Regiment was at Hanover street. Just at noon Gen. Kimball came up to us, and said: "Move out now, Colonel, God bless you—good bye!" The command was given, and the column started at a double-quick. As we came to the slight fall in the street as it approaches the canal, a terrible fire from the sharp shooters and several shells struck the head of the column. Over twenty officers and men fell. Capt. Allen and Sergt. Maj. Henthorn mortally and Capt. Pierce severely wounded, but our step was not even checked, the men rushing down to the bank, routed the line of rebels in the canal and on its banks, who either ran or surrendered as prisoners. We were soon across, and took advantage of the bank beyond to form our line. I ran down to the left, found Maj. Smyth with the first Delaware, which was getting in line, Smyth believing that Col. Mason and Godman, with the Fourth Ohio, were all cut to pieces and driven back, Col. Godman being wounded.

The line was ordered forward. As soon as we rose over the little bank, the missiles came upon us spitefully, and the air was full of exploding shells. The fences had to be pushed or cut down, and there were several extremely bad bogs or holes, taking the men in half leg deep. The line, however, advanced splendidly, though the fire was constant and severe. The rebels gave way rapidly, not stopping to re-load, some surrendering after delivering their fire, as our men were now loading and firing as they moved. . . .

We advanced to a street parallel with our line along which were some fine dwellings and gardens, and this being the last line of cover we could secure, and immediately in front of a strong line of stone wall that no skirmish line could carry, our line was halted and the men directed to avoid exposing themselves as much as possible, and to get shelter behind the houses and fences.

PRIVATE WILLIAM KEPLER

4th Ohio Infantry, Kimball's Brigade

Preparing to launch his attack, Kimball deployed three regiments as skirmishers under the command of Colonel John S. Mason, who was instructed to secure the banks of the canal that traversed the approaches to Marye's Heights. Mason led his own 4th Ohio along with the 8th Ohio and 1st Delaware some 200 yards in advance of the Federal line of battle. The skirmishers gained their objective but were unable to make further headway.

Nine o'clock of December 13 had come, and with it the order to fall into line; General Franklin was already hard at it on our left; the orders were overheard, "Three regiments are to be deployed as skirmishers, followed by divisions, two hundred yards apart"; "do you hear that boys?" says one; "there is going to be some terrible hot work," says another; the men look downcast; they were willing to do their whole duty, but were perfectly satisfied that it would be a useless waste of lives unless a continuous bridge spanned the length of the drain ditch, and several divisions moved rapidly against the enemy with fixed bayonets. . . .

. . . We had been in readiness for over two hours; the pickets had been called in and were in line; Franklin's and Jackson's booming cannon had been heard during all this time, contending with each other on our left; on our front, Longstreet, as well as we, had remained quiet all morning, probably awaiting developments.

Colonel Mason, commanding the skirmishers, near noon gave the order to advance. Colonel Godman now commands: "Attention! Shoulder arms. Forward—file right—March!" Our regiment, now numbering nineteen officers and ninety-eight enlisted men, moves in the advance, rapidly out Princess Ann street, to the rear of the town, crosses the canal bridge and we are just in the very act of climbing up

"The sight is horrible and heart-rending; hundreds of the bleeding and mangled are dragging themselves from the dead and dying, are trampled upon by the thousands, many of whom in the excitement hardly knew whither they were going save to the certain slaughter."

an embankment two to three feet high, and can plainly see the rebels upon redoubts on Marye Heights move rapidly to and fro, while Godman riding coolly at our head, gives the order: "Deploy as skirmishers! By the left flank!" when there is a puff of smoke on the Heights and two men fall; immediately several more cannon belch forth fire and smoke and sixteen more fall; Peter Akum and Captain Wallace have received mortal injuries, and Godman is wounded in the thigh. The wounded are immediately laid in back of the embankment or helped to the house a few rods to our right and soon cared for by Surgeon Morrison.

Hundreds who had watched our advance and had seen the batteries open on us, and the men falling right and left, thought we had been annihilated. Shot and shell are still hurled over, to right, left and front of us, while the line in command of Major Carpenter and Captain Stewart, with the right flank of the regiment at the street and the left flank extending to the right until we join with the First Delaware; we continue on the run up the slope over the rise of ground, down the further slope, under a continued storm of missiles, which does now but little damage to our thin line; we cross a ravine, with its mud and fence, then up the Marye Heights slope, a triple line of rebel skirmishers rapidly vanishing behind a stone wall from which there now comes volley after volley from some half a dozen lines of rebels; again one after another of our boys fall; human nature cannot endure facing such a storm of bullets and not reply; we have reached the crest of the slope and open a vigorous fire.

We hug the ground for some time, hoping reinforcements would soon come to help us drive the enemy from the stone wall; General Kimball's other four regiments now come over the hill behind us on the run, closing the gaps that are made in their ranks by the storm of missiles; they reach us, drop down by our side, and open fire. . . .

Nearly an hour has passed by since the ordeal began, when the Second Brigade of our division forms at the canal and comes charging midst a terrific hurling of shot and shell; crosses the ravine, comes up the slope, drops down at the crest and joins the general fusilade against the stone wall. In like manner at intervals of less than half an hour comes brigade after brigade, doing just the same things, rush over the plain for one-third of a mile, over dead, wounded and dying, closing up the gaps, while the showers of lead and iron leave the field more difficult to cross because of the increased number of mangled remains that must not be trampled into the earth. . . .

. . . Thousands of men come over the slope and get down at the crest with us before the Heights and there remain, while on the hill and slope behind and among us the sight is horrible and heart-rending; hundreds of the bleeding and mangled are dragging themselves from the dead and dying, are trampled upon by the thousands, many of whom in the excitement hardly knew whither they were going save to the certain slaughter. Wounded men fall upon wounded; the dead upon the mangled; the baptism of fire adds more wounds and brings even death to helpless ones; as we look back the field seems covered with mortals in agony; some motionless, others are dragging themselves toward the rear; occasionally the shell or cannon ball that comes into their midst, sends arms, hands, legs and clothing into the air; on the front line there is no safety, for here men fall; our colors for a moment are down, for our noble color-bearer George B. Torrence, . . . falls, having his head blown from his body, leaving his blood and brains upon comrades and the flag. It is a baptism of fire and blood. Blood is everywhere. Overhead is a pandemonium of shrieking missiles.

LIEUTENANT WILLIAM M. OWEN

WASHINGTON (LOUISIANA) ARTILLERY, FIRST CORPS

The Confederate defenders of Marye's Heights included four companies of the Washington Artillery of New Orleans—an elite prewar militia unit whose ranks included many socially prominent Louisianans. Their nine guns played a crucial role in smashing the successive Yankee onslaughts, as battalion adjutant Owen described in his 1885 unit history.

On the Confederate side all was ready, and the shock was awaited with stubborn resolution. Last night we had spread our blankets upon the bare floor in the parlor of Marye's house, and now our breakfast was being prepared in its fireplace, and we were impatient to have it over. After hastily dispatching this light meal of bacon and corn-bread, the colonel, chief bugler, and I (the adjutant of the battalion) mounted our horses and rode out to inspect our lines. . . .

At 12 o'clock the fog had cleared, and while we were sitting in Marye's yard smoking our pipes, after a lunch of hard crackers, a courier came to Colonel Walton, bearing a dispatch from General Longstreet for General Cobb, but, for our information as well, to be read and then given to him. It was as follows: "Should General Anderson, on your left, be compelled to fall back to the second line of heights, you must conform to his movements." Descending the hill into the sunken road, I made my way through the troops, to a little house where General Cobb had his headquarters and handed him the dispatch. He read it carefully and said, "Well! if they wait for me to fall back, they will wait a long time."

Hardly had he spoken, when a brisk skirmish fire was heard in front toward the town, and looking over the stone wall we saw our skirmishers falling back, firing as they came; at the same time the head of a Federal column was seen emerging from one of the streets of the town. They came on at the double-quick, with loud cries of "Hi! Hi! Hi!" which we could distinctly hear. Their arms were carried at "right shoulder shift," and their colors were aslant the shoulders of the color-sergeants. They crossed the canal at the bridge, and getting behind the bank to the low ground to deploy, were almost concealed from our sight. It was 12:30 p.m., and it was evident that we were now going to have it hot and heavy.

The enemy, having deployed, now showed himself above the crest of the ridge and advanced in columns of brigades, and at once our guns began their deadly work with shell and solid shot. How beautifully they came on! Their bright bayonets glistening in the sunlight made the line look like a huge serpent of blue and steel. The very force of their onset leveled the broad fences bounding the small fields and gardens that interspersed the plain. We could see our shells bursting in their ranks, making great gaps; but on they came, as though they would go straight through and over us. Now we gave them canister, and that staggered them. A few more paces onward and the Georgians in the road below us rose up, and, glancing an instant along their rifle barrels, let loose a storm of lead into the faces of the advance brigade. This was too much; the column hesitated, and then, turning, took refuge behind the bank.

But another line appeared from behind the crest and advanced gallantly, and again we opened our guns upon them, and through the smoke we could discern the red breeches of the "Zouaves," and hammered away at them especially. But this advance, like the preceding one, although passing the point reached by the first column, and doing and daring all that brave men could do, recoiled under our canister and the bullets of the infantry in the road, and fell back in great confusion. Spotting the fields in our front, we could detect little patches of blue—the dead and wounded of the Federal infantry who had fallen facing the very muzzles of our guns.

"We could see our shells bursting in their ranks, making great gaps; but on they came, as though they would go straight through and over us."

An engraving by Confederate veteran Allen C. Redwood depicts Louisianans of the Washington Artillery battalion manning their cannon during the Federal assault on Marye's Heights. "Again and again did their heavy masses come forth from the town. They fell by thousands, under the judicious, steady, and unerring fire of my guns," reported the battalion's commander, Colonel J. B. Walton. The battalion's own loss was light—three killed and 22 wounded.

PRIVATE BENJAMIN BORTON

24TH NEW JERSEY INFANTRY, KIMBALL'S BRIGADE

Borton's unit was one of a dozen regiments, recruited for a nine-month term, that New Jersey sent off to war in September 1862. Barely trained, and without ever having fired a shot in anger, Borton and his comrades in the 24th were ordered to advance across the open fields and carry the Rebel position on Marye's Heights. Halfway across the field their unit formation was broken by Rebel volleys, and the survivors halted to return fire from the cover of a board fence.

As far as we could see in either direction stood a continuous line of soldiers in readiness to start to the field of action. Mounted officers and orderlies were continually passing back and forth along the lines, while some of the regimental officers and privates, tired of standing in the ranks, dropped out and sought a seat upon the curb or a near-by door step. Among those who had taken a resting place was a surgeon, upon whose face I noticed was depicted an intense feeling of sadness. Perhaps he could not help it, for we all knew that some of us would soon be badly wounded if not instantly killed. Yet this solemn fact did not make all men gloomy. The most lively fellows mimicked the whizzing noise of an occasional round shot or shell in its arched flight high over the housetops, or cracked jokes with their comrades. I remember seeing Comrade Gaffney pick up a large book that had been thrown away, and, after finding a place to sit down, he jestingly told us to give him our attention while he read the "law of Moses." Barney, unfortunately, had never been schooled long enough to know his letters, but feigning to be reading, he went over a nonsenical rigmarole of some sort, to which we were not inclined to listen just then. Adjutant Crowl and Sergeant Grier, perhaps to keep their courage up, tried their hand at fencing with their swords on the sidewalk.

Presently is heard the command, "Attention!" Every lounger springs to his place. We are ordered to prime. Every musket is raised and every man caps his piece. Our Colonel made some remarks, telling us to shoot low and try to wound a man in preference to killing him. Noticing a red colored scarf about my neck, he ordered me to take it off, saying it would make a good target for the enemy. The scarf disappeared. Suspense is intense. Finally, the long-expected, much-dreaded command, "Forward!" is passed from officer to officer standing at the head of their Companies. With an ominous silence akin to a funeral procession, General Kimball began the perilous march down Caroline street by leading French's First Brigade, with the Twenty-fourth and Twenty-eighth New Jersey in the center, Seventh Virginia (Union) on the right and the Fourteenth Indiana on the left. . . . I think I am telling the plain truth when I say that during that short march many of those men silently offered up to the Almighty their last prayer on earth. Our regiment was about to receive its first baptism of fire, and every one knew it.

My feelings in that trying moment cannot be described. Oh, I thought, why this shedding of blood? Why should brother take his brother's life? Under this impression, I instinctively cast a look upward to see if I could not behold a winged messenger of peace. But no; the sea of bristling bayonets moved on. Shells and solid shot from the enemy's heavy guns now came crashing through brick walls and pounded in the

Appearing older than his 40 years, Brigadier General Nathan Kimball was a Mexican War veteran and respected Indiana physician who had fought with distinction in the Shenandoah Valley and at the Battle of Antietam. While leading his brigade at Fredericksburg, Kimball was disabled by a wound in the thigh.

street about us. The first wounded man I saw was hurrying down the sidewalk with one hand pressed against a wound in his breast, inquiring for a hospital.

At the edge of the town we passed General Kimball facing us, in his saddle, who addressed his men in these words, which I never forgot:

"Cheer up, my hearties! cheer up! This is something we must all get used to. Remember, this brigade has never been whipped, and don't let it be whipped to-day."

No wild hurrah went up in response. Every face wore an expression of seriousness and dread. . . .

A minute later we realized the awful danger before us, but General Kimball's men, like Napoleon's, courageously faced it. A few steps further and we are out of the town, in the open fields, in full view of the enemy. While the brigade is coming into position, at double-quick, to assault the Confederate fortifications around Marye's Heights, the artillerymen on the summit are turning their guns upon us, and with effect. To facilitate our progress in the charge, haversacks and blankets are now thrown away. The company commanders shout sharply to their men to keep the regiments in line as they advance to the attack. Screeching like demons in the air, solid shot, shrapnel and shells from the batteries on the hills strike the ground in front of us, behind us, and cut gaps in the ranks. See there! A field officer has been struck by one of the missiles and a couple of men who have raised him to his feet are calling loudly for more help to get him off the field. As the line advances up the slope, men wounded and dead drop from the ranks.

It is not every man that can face danger like this. I saw a few so overcome by fear that they fell prostrate upon the ground as if dead. I have seen men drop upon their knees and pray loudly for deliverance, when courage and bravery, not supplication, was the duty of the moment.

Hark! There's one of my comrades, Johnny Brayerton, praying, too, perhaps for the first time in his life. It was a short one:

"Oh Lord, dear, good Lord!" he cried.

The assault of Kimball's brigade is depicted in this aerial-perspective view looking toward Marye's Heights from a point just east of the water-filled millrace. At far left skirmishers of the 4th and 8th Ohio fire from a prone position, while at center the 24th and 28th New Jersey advance through the barrage of Rebel shells to a fence line near the Stratton house. Almost two-thirds of the brigade's 520 casualties occurred in the two New Jersey regiments.

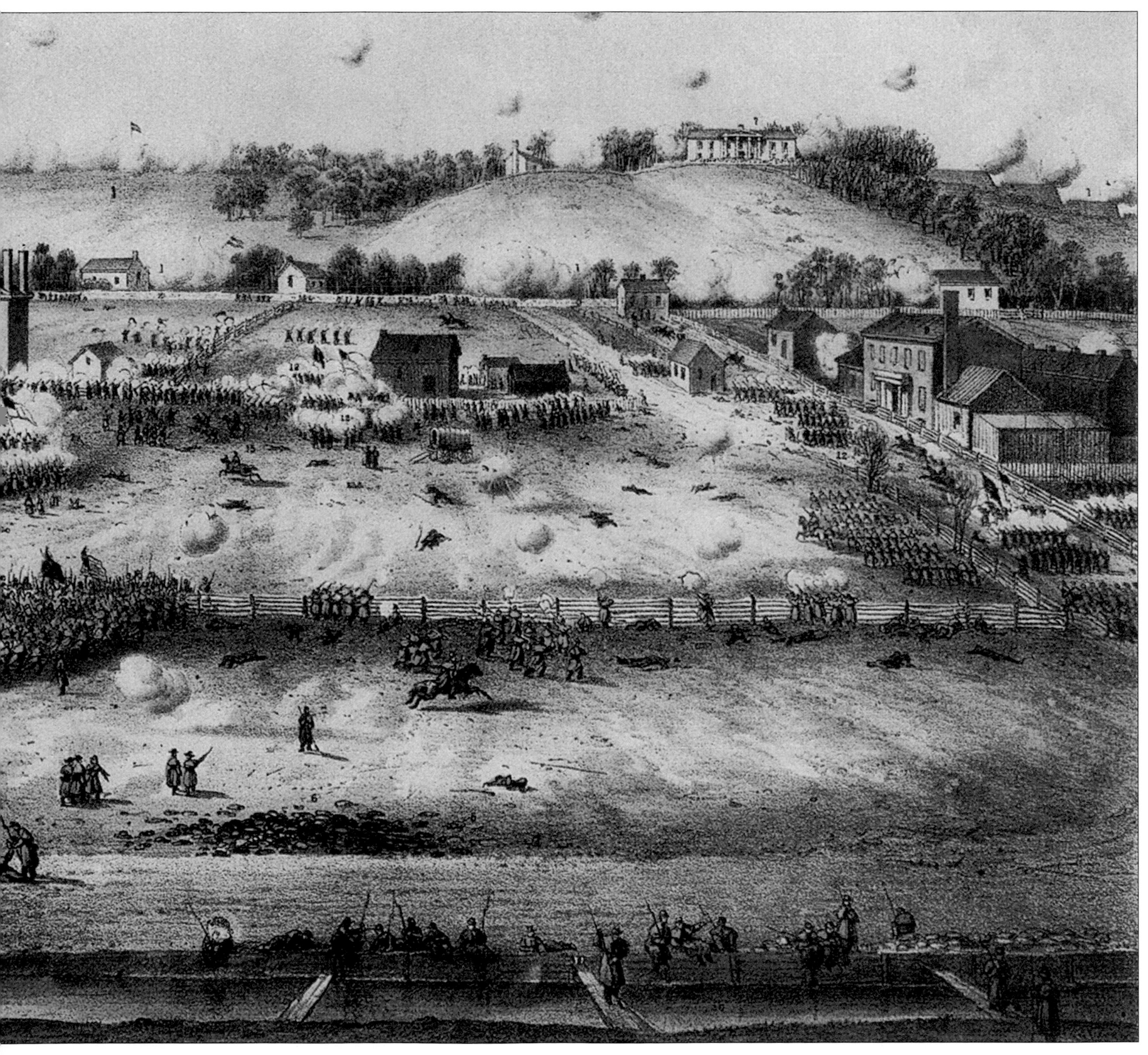

"How any man went up and back again alive is more than I can imagine."

MAJOR FRANCIS E. PIERCE

108TH NEW YORK INFANTRY, PALMER'S BRIGADE

The 108th New York, one of three regiments in Colonel Oliver Palmer's brigade, advanced in the third wave of General French's assault. Forming near Fredericksburg's railroad depot, Palmer's men marched through a deadly cross fire and deployed in line of battle 150 yards behind the shattered remnants of Kimball's and Andrews' brigades. Palmer's troops charged at a double-quick, only to meet the fate of those who had preceded them. The survivors hunkered down behind a fence and waited for reinforcements. Pierce was brevetted a brigadier general for his wartime service.

It was an awful place going up that R.R. Shell, solid shot, pieces of R.R. iron and minnie balls came down the R.R. in a perfect storm. From the place we commenced to march in line of battle up to the base of the hill on the brow of which the reb cannons were placed, it was a perfect shower of missiles warlike. Grape, cannister, shells and minnies were poured into us from the front and from the right shells were thrown into us, raking us and exploding in our ranks fearfully. We had 3 board fences to go over and through and no cover. How any man went up and back again alive is more than I can imagine. Very few men there were who did not get ball holes in their clothing and very many who did get them in some part of their clothing. I don't see how a worse place could by any means have been made. I got a ball in my blanket and another one in my cap, which made a nice scalp wound without touching the bone however. I was going along pretty well, bent down as I was somewhat protected from fire by a hill if I kept down and was about to go through the last fence. Without straightening up I just raised my head a little to find a good place to get over and through when a ball took me in the top of the cap clear back and *scratched* my head down the back side passing through my cap again near the bottom of the back of it. It tumbled me, of course, but in about 3 minutes I was up again, but it made me mad for some of my company—in fact all of them got to the hill before I did. A piece of shell took me on the inside of the left leg and makes me lame as sixty but it didn't break the skin. Well we got to the bottom of a little ridge this side of the batteries and could go no farther, it was so awful. Regiments would start and before going half the distance would come back shattered and broken—half of their men behind them. After a while we had orders to fall back which the right wing did, but the Col. and left wing being on the left of a fence which run up the hill did not hear the order and remained there until after dark. It was safer to remain than to fall back.

SERGEANT WILLIAM R. MONTGOMERY

PHILLIPS' LEGION, COBB'S BRIGADE

Anticipating an attack on the Confederate position west of Fredericksburg, on the night of December 11 Lafayette McLaws ordered three regiments of Thomas Cobb's brigade to relieve Barksdale's exhausted Mississippians in the sunken road at the base of Marye's Heights. On December 13 the full weight of the Federal onslaught fell first on Cobb's brigade but failed to breach the formidable Rebel defenses. Montgomery describes the fighting of William Phillips' Georgians, who loosed so much fire on the successive ranks of Yankees that they exhausted their supply of ammunition.

Saturday about 11 o'clock they began their advance & our brave & beloved Gen Cobb placed his Brigade behind a stone fence & pulled of[f] his hat & waving it over his head exclaimed "Get ready Boys here they come" & they did come *sure.*

We waited untill they got within about 200 yards of us & rose to our feet & poured volley after volley into their ranks which told a most deadening effect. They soon began to waver & at last broke from the *rear,* but the shouts of our brave soldiers had scarcely died away when we saw coming another column more powerful & seemingly more

The three regiments making up Palmer's brigade had lost more than 500 men in a charge on Bloody Lane at the Battle of Antietam; now, less than two months later, they sustained nearly 300 more casualties attacking another Rebel-held sunken road at Fredericksburg. The fallen included Colonel Henry I. Zinn of the 130th Pennsylvania (above) and Captain Elijah Gibbons of the 14th Connecticut (left). Brandishing his regiment's flag in one hand and his sword in the other, Zinn was shot through the head and died on the field. Captain Gibbons—a former Sunday school teacher from Middletown, Connecticut—was carried to the rear with a shattered thigh and succumbed to his wound six days later.

"Only a few rounds from our brave & well tried men was necessary to tell them that they had undertaken a work a little too hard."

determined than the first (if possible) but only a few rounds from our brave & well tried men was necessary to tell them that they had undertaken a work a little too hard. But before they had entirely left the field another column & another & still another came to their support. But our well aimed shots were more than they could stand so about night they were compelled to give up the field covered with their dead.

The whole time of the engagement our brave & gallent Gen was encouraging on his men untill a shot from the enemy's cannon gave him his mortal wound. He was on the right of our Co, only a few feet from me when wounded. Payson Ardis being one [of] our litter bearers ran to him & I shall never forget his last look as they laid him on the litter to bear him from the field. His last words to his men were—"I am only wounded Boys, hold your ground like brave men." . . .

. . . I have been in many engagements before but I never saw in my life such a slaughter.

A postwar photograph of the lane at the foot of Marye's Heights shows the four-foot-high stone wall that provided an impenetrable breastwork for the Confederates deployed behind it. The defenders increased their protection by deepening the sunken road along the wall so that only their heads and shoulders were exposed to Yankee bullets. Even so, more than 300 of Cobb's men fell, including the general, who was most likely standing behind the Stevens house (just beyond the Innis house, visible at right) when he was cut down by a shell that passed through the structure.

A brilliant lawyer, wealthy planter, and ardent secessionist, Thomas R. R. Cobb (above) was mortally wounded by a shell fragment that shattered his left thigh. He had been promoted to brigadier general a month before the battle and placed in charge of the Georgia brigade once commanded by his brother, former Georgia governor and Confederate congressman Howell Cobb.

Gold-braided kepi in hand, Irish Brigade commander Thomas F. Meagher strikes a typically dashing pose in this Brady Studio portrait. British authorities had exiled Meagher to Tasmania for his part in the failed Irish rebellion of 1848, but he escaped to the United States and became a leading figure in local Irish nationalist circles. Renowned for his powerful oratory, Meagher rallied thousands of Irish Americans to Federal service when war came. "Every blow you strike in the cause of the Union," he told the volunteers, "is aimed at the allies of England, the enemy of your land and race. Today it is for the American Republic we fight—tomorrow it will be for Ireland."

SERGEANT WILLIAM H. MCCLELAND

88TH NEW YORK INFANTRY, MEAGHER'S BRIGADE

Irish Brigade commander Thomas Meagher made an impassioned address to his soldiers before committing them to the assault, and McCleland described the event in a letter to Manhattan's Irish American newspaper. The son of Irish immigrants, McCleland was promoted to first lieutenant—the rank he wears in this photograph—in June 1863. He was killed at Gettysburg while serving as his regiment's adjutant.

About 12 o'clock we were drawn up in line, and the General gave us each a sprig of evergreen to put in our caps. We all looked gay and felt in high spirits, little dreaming, though we expected a heavy battle, that in so short a time after so many of our poor fellows would have been sent to their final doom. After the evergreen had been inserted in our caps, the General came along the line and said a few words of cheer to each regiment. Our regiment was second in line; when the General reached the colors of our regiment, he uncovered his head; General Hancock stood behind. The General said: "Officers and Soldiers of the 88th Regiment—In a few moments you will engage the enemy in a most terrible battle, which will probably decide the fate of this glorious, great and grand country—the home of your adoption." The General hesitated a moment, and then with eyes full to overflowing, through which he could hardly speak, he said: "Soldiers—This is my wife's own regiment, 'her own dear 88th,' she calls it, and I know, and have confidence, that with dear woman's smile upon you, and for woman's sake, this day you will strike a deadly blow to those wicked traitors who are now but a few hundred yards from you, and bring back to this distracted country its former prestige and glory. This may be my last speech to you, but I will be with you when the battle is the fiercest; and, if I fall, I can say I did my duty, and fell fighting in the most glorious of causes." The Regiment then gave three cheers, such as the 88th alone can give. During the delivery of this speech shells burst in and amongst us, killing a number and cutting off legs right by our side. Also during this address we heard the musketry of French's Division engaging the enemy on the outskirts of the town. Silence in the Brigade was soon broken by the orders, "Shoulder arms—right face—forward—double quick—march!"

This foot officer's sword (above) with engraved scabbard (detail shown at left) was carried by Captain John Flynn, a company commander in the 63d New York of the Irish Brigade. Although suffering from malaria and pneumonia contracted earlier during the Peninsula campaign, Flynn took part in the brigade's charge and was one of a handful of survivors who rallied around the regimental colors afterward.

"Lay him down and cut the leg off at once,—that will ease him."

PRIVATE PHINEAS P. WHITEHOUSE

6TH NEW HAMPSHIRE INFANTRY, NAGLE'S BRIGADE

As the Irish Brigade began its fateful march through the streets of Fredericksburg to the bullet-swept plain below Marye's Heights, it passed the soldiers of Brigadier General James Nagle's IX Corps brigade, who were awaiting their own summons to battle. Whitehouse, a 20-year-old farmer, survived the fight but was severely wounded at Spotsylvania in May 1864.

To those of our number who were now about to experience their first actual engagement, the whizzing of shells over our heads and through the buildings, gave anything but an agreeable sensation. Our regiment was partially protected by a large hotel, before which we were standing, awaiting the order to advance. The Irish Brigade, wearing their sprigs of evergreen, were passing along before us, when one of the noisy messengers from the enemy burst in front of a regiment, scattering the men in every direction. A groan in one place, and a faint cry in another, told us that the iron monster had not been sent altogether in vain. Our own regiment was also occasionally visited. As I was standing in the garden, near the Colonel—now Major General Griffin—a savage looking piece of a shell struck the fence about three feet in front of my face, and not much farther from the person of our commander. The Colonel smiled and quietly remarked: "If they come no nearer than that, I dont care." Soon after this, as the shells were coming uncomfortably near, two of our men were seen to crawl through a small window in the basement of a house. The Colonel soon found it out, and called them back. They came out with a rather sheepish air, and when the Colonel asked them their names and company, could hardly hold up their heads to answer. "Pretty boys you are," said the Colonel, "to crawl in there! What would your mother say if she could see you! Watch these boys," said he, turning to an officer of their company. I was glad they did not belong to the company of which I was a member.

A self-educated lawyer and former New Hampshire state legislator, Simon G. Griffin (above) had led a company of the 2d New Hampshire at First Bull Run and commanded the 6th Regiment in campaigns on the North Carolina coast and in the Battle of Antietam. At Fredericksburg Griffin's unit lost 77 of its 264 men.

PRIVATE WILLIAM MCCARTER

116TH PENNSYLVANIA INFANTRY, MEAGHER'S BRIGADE

The 116th was a new regiment that had only joined the Irish Brigade in October but was welcomed by the veterans whose ranks had been thinned by two years of combat—General Meagher passed a canteen of whiskey down the line of the new troops. Nervously awaiting the order to advance, McCarter watched as some of the more than 900 wounded of French's division were carried back to field hospitals.

Many of the wounded of French's Division were now being carried into the town from the battle field, presenting to us, who were just about to go into it, fearful pictures of the horrors of war. . . . Whilst still in position here, one poor fellow was carried past us on a window shutter, by two soldiers. His uniform indicated the rank of Captain. His face was young and deathly white. He had been hit in the leg, above the knee, by a cannon ball, which had almost torn the limb from the body, a small thready sinue only apparently holding both together. As his comrades carried him along, the lower part of the leg, nearly severed from the body, hung over the edge of the board, dangling backwards and forward at every step taken by the bearers, an extremely sickening sight to those witnessing it. Some of our Boys seeing this, shouted to the men carrying the poor, unfortunate officer, "Lay him down and cut the leg off at once,—that will ease him." No attention, however was given to this, but as the men, with their wounded commander reached the centre of my regiment, in passing down along our line, one of the Boys there seeing the situation of the sufferer, sprung out of the ranks, with pen-knife in hand, and quick as thought, cut the thread like sinue that seemed to be the only thing then that held the two parts of the leg together. This done, the limb, from the knee down, dropped on the ground, evidently much to the satisfaction and relief of its late owner who, very faint and weak from loss of blood could only smile and nod his head as a mark, or token of thankfulness and gratitude to his thoughtful and kind benefactor.

Union soldiers—some of them walking wounded—bear a stricken comrade to safety in an on-the-spot sketch by artist Arthur Lumley. Only a fortunate few of the 5,300 Federals wounded in front of Marye's Heights were evacuated during the fighting. Most lay unattended on the field until the evening of December 14, and many perished from loss of blood or exposure in the cold night air.

of an hour. . . . [I also received] a bruise on the left shoulder from a rifle ball which was stopped in its otherwise serious effects by striking my (metallic) shoulder strap, after perforating the overcoat, and before going through the under-clothing. When sensibility returned, the battle appeared to me like a dream, until a shell burst close by, tearing up the earth and covering me with mud, fairly awaking me to a sense of reality, I looked up only to see the sun go down behind the rebel breastworks on the hill, upon no pleasing shouts of victory, no flank of the enemy turned by Sigel, no Banks, nor from the firing on the left, no ground gained by Franklin—nothing of any good obtained, while night was soon to cast its shadow upon a field of carnage and slaughter, the most frightful and terrible ever experienced, and still the bloody fight goes on.

PRIVATE WILLIAM MCCARTER

116TH PENNSYLVANIA INFANTRY, MEAGHER'S BRIGADE

With regimental formations shattered and nearly half their number dead or wounded, the soldiers of Meagher's Irish Brigade hugged the earth and fired on the Rebel defenders in the sunken road. Some Federals sheltered behind the Stratton house, while others crowded into a slight swale just to the south. But the only cover most could find were the bodies of their fallen comrades. Private McCarter recalled the ordeal in his postwar memoirs.

Bullets had been singing their little songs around my head and ears since arriving on the battle ground, piercing my uniform from head to foot, and cutting open the cartridge box by my side, yet strange to say, none of them inflicted any wound worth naming, except the two already mentioned,—one, on the left shoulder, and the other on the left ankle, neither of them, at the time causing inconvenience, or much pain. But now, for something much more serious to myself than at any time before. I had discharged 6 or 7 shots, I don't know which, up to this time, and into the ranks of Cobb's Brigade right in our front; behind the stone wall. I was getting ready to fire again, had taken the cartridge out of my cartridge box, bitten the end off it,—inserted it into the muzzle of my musket,—drew the ram-rod from its place, and had just raised my right arm over my head to send the cartridge home, or down into the musket, when a bullet struck me in the uplifted arm, close up to the shoulder, and the limb dropped powerless at my side. I knew something serious had happened to me, but at the moment did not realize that a Rebel bullet had hit me, inflicting a very serious wound. At first I thought that the man in the rear, immediately behind me in the second line, or one of the men in the front, or first line, by my side, had accidentally struck my elbow with the butt end of a musket, for my feelings then were exactly like those produced by being suddenly hit in that way, or by knocking my elbow a hard blow against a brick or stone wall. But in a very few seconds more I discovered what was the matter,—and that I actually was shot, but in what particular spot, I was yet in ignorance, although I felt it to be somewhere in the neighborhood of the shoulder. A stream of warm blood now came rushing down the inside and outside sleeve of my uniform, then down the side of my pants into my right foot shoe, till it overflowed. Next, a dizziness in the head, and partial loss of sight came over me, accompanied by violent pain in the wounded part, and then growing very faint and weak from loss of blood, I fell down, flat on my face on the ground, with my musket, which I clutched with my left hand, by my side, while my comrades, now standing over me, and near me, still in line, although few indeed, continued to blaze away at the foe. . . . My consciousness speedily returning, I suppose by the fall, I attempted to rise and make my way to the rear, or to somewhere out of the range of the enemy's fire, but I had scarce raised my head, when such a shower of bullets came around it, that brought me at once to conclude, that to move was dangerous and to rise up would be fatal. Accordingly I lowered it again, stretching my body out upon the earth, and lying as close to the ground as I possibly could, to let the enemy's bullets pass over me. No sooner had I done this, than one of my comrades, the 3d man from the head, or right of the regiment, and almost my next neighbor there, was shot dead, and fell about 2 yards in front of me, right across my body. . . . Poor fellow, he was afterwards riddled with bullets, and owing to the position of his body, it stopped many a ball that otherwise would certainly have entered my own. As it was, bullets kept constantly whizzing over me, around me, burying themselves in the ground not a foot from my head and throwing mud and dust all over my person. My situation was truly an awful one.

The regimental flag and drum shown here were carried by soldiers of the 28th Massachusetts—a unit composed largely of Irish Bostonians—which was transferred from the IX Corps to Meagher's brigade just before the Battle of Fredericksburg. "It is a substantial and splendid accession," the general wrote of the addition to his force. "It has sinew, heart and soul." Each regiment in the Irish Brigade traditionally carried a green flag—emblazoned with the sunburst, harp, and shamrocks symbolic of their homeland—alongside the Stars and Stripes. But the 28th Massachusetts was the only unit to do so in the charge on Marye's Heights. The other regiments had sent their war-torn banners home to their respective states and were awaiting the arrival of new Irish colors.

"Getting on my hands and knees, spitting the sand, stones and blood out of my mouth, I looked around. The tattered colors of my regiment, thank God! were in the van."

COLONEL EDWARD E. CROSS

5TH NEW HAMPSHIRE INFANTRY,
CALDWELL'S BRIGADE

Advancing with the third wave of Hancock's division, the 5th New Hampshire came up in the wake of Meagher's brigade. Cross, the unit's commander, had experienced a colorful career as a journalist, editor, frontiersman, duelist, and soldier of fortune in the Mexican army. Recovering from his wounds, he returned to the front and was promoted to brigade command. He was mortally wounded at Gettysburg on July 2, 1863.

I passed along the ranks and spoke to the officers and men; told them it was to be a bloody strife; to stand firm and fire low; to close on their colors and be steady. To the officers I only said that they were expected to do their duty. I then took my place at the head of my men, and we started, following the Irish Brigade. As we marched up the street the enemy opened on us with solid shot and shell, and before we had reached the open fields several men were disabled. However, my regiment kept up in fine style, and we formed line of battle on the ground selected, under heavy fire of shell, grape and canister. General Caldwell and staff and General Hancock and staff were present, the latter on horseback and cool and brave as a lion. While taking up our position it became necessary to cross a deep canal or ditch filled with water. This scattered the men some, but we came forward into line in fine style. In the meantime the Irish Brigade had formed and moved forward, but instead of charging the works of the enemy, faltered, commenced firing, and finally laid down. It soon came our turn to move forward. The regiment rose up as one man, and started forward a little ahead of the line in complete order. We were thus advancing when a shell exploded in the air, directly in front of me, and about as high as my head. A large fragment hit me on the breast; a smaller piece knocked out two of my teeth and filled my mouth with sand; another bit struck me on the forehead, making a slight wound; another bit over the eye, and still another along the back of my hand. I was knocked off my feet, and lay insensible until aroused by a violent blow on the left leg, made by a piece of shell which hit me there. Getting on my hands and knees, spitting the sand, stones and blood out of my mouth, I looked around. The tattered colors of my regiment, thank God! were in the van. I tried to get on my feet, but could not stand. I then tried to crawl, but the balls came so thick and tore up the ground so spitefully that I could not do it, besides a ball struck my sword scabbard, knocking me over. After that warning I concluded to lie still, so placing myself on my back, feet to the foe, I awaited death. The failure of the rear lines to come up, and their firing at long range, placed me between the two fires, and for more than an hour I lay in expectation of instant death or a mortal wound. I employed most of my thoughts about my regiment. When the shot came particularly strong and thick, I covered my face and counted rapidly from one to one hundred. Thus I lay while the awful battle raged.

Lieutenant Daniel K. Cross of the 5th New Hampshire served on General Caldwell's staff. He risked his life to rescue his wounded brother, Edward, from the field in front of Marye's Heights, where the colonel had been wounded.

A native of Keene, New Hampshire, Private Daniel W. Trask (above) of Colonel Cross' regiment received his second wound of the war at Fredericksburg. The following year he was again wounded at Chancellorsville.

Major Edward E. Sturtevant, a former police officer, took command of the 5th New Hampshire when Edward Cross was wounded. He was seen to fall near the stone wall, but his exact fate was never determined.

Marye's Heights: Later Attacks

As surviving remnants of French's and Hancock's divisions lay scattered among the lifeless bodies on the plain west of Fredericksburg in the early afternoon, General Burnside, refusing to accept defeat, ordered the assaults to continue.

For his part General Lee, observing the battle from a nearby hill, fretted that his line of Georgians—despite their demonstrated invulnerability thus far—might finally break under the pressure. Longstreet reassured him: "General, if you put every man on the other side of the Potomac on that field to approach me over the same line, and give me plenty of ammunition, I will kill them all before they reach my line."

Longstreet nevertheless ordered General Kershaw to move his South Carolina brigade down toward the stone wall to reinforce Cobb's and Ransom's troops. Cobb had already been carried to the rear bleeding to death, and Kershaw took command. The sunken road behind the stone wall was now so crowded with Confederate infantry that the men were lined up several ranks deep.

It fell to General Couch to renew the Federal offensive. Responding to desperate calls for reinforcements from French and Hancock, Couch committed his final II Corps division, under General Howard, to the fray. Howard deployed two of his brigades astride Hanover Street to attack to the right of the divisions that had been decimated earlier and gave the order to advance.

Some of Howard's men moved over and around the troops felled in the previous assaults. "The grass was slippery with their blood," recalled a soldier of the 19th Massachusetts. "Their ghastly lips seemed to appeal for vengeance."

But Howard's soldiers could not answer the mute appeal of their fallen comrades. Rebel troops met them with a wall of lead and kept them at bay by rotating firing lines behind the wall. The front line fired, then stepped back to begin reloading and allow the second rank to take its place, followed by a third then a fourth line to produce a nearly uninterrupted storm of musketry. Kershaw described the firepower as "the most rapid and continuous I have ever witnessed."

None of Howard's soldiers could get closer than 100 yards from the Confederate line. Putting into plain language what had been horrifyingly obvious for hours, General Howard said, "The concentrated fire of artillery and infantry was too much to carry men through."

Union troops advancing against Kershaw's right flank quickly had that truth hammered home to them. Brigadier General Samuel D. Sturgis' division from Orlando B. Willcox's IX Corps probed to the left of Couch's shredded units, but the division's two brigades stalled in their tracks, losing 1,000 men in the process. In a span of two hours, four Federal divisions had been slaughtered on the slope below Marye's Heights, with a toll of 5,000 casualties.

Whatever thoughts ran through General Burnside's mind at his headquarters east of the Rappahannock as one disastrous report followed another, he refused to be swayed from his course by the repeated and costly failures. He next ordered Joseph Hooker to take his grand division across the Rappahannock River and throw it at Kershaw's line.

Hooker complied immediately with the first half of the order, moving his divisions into Fredericksburg. But after conferring with commanders who had been through the futile bloodletting before Marye's Heights, he came to the conclusion that "it would be a useless waste of life to attack with the force at my disposal."

Even as Hooker recrossed the river to argue his point with Burnside, the massacre continued. Brigadier General Daniel Butterfield, commanding the V Corps in Hooker's grand division, sent Brigadier General Charles Griffin's division through the town to relieve Sturgis' hard-pressed troops on the left. General Willcox watched helplessly as Griffin's brigades approached the Confederate works to suffer a now familiar fate: "A line of musketry opened, and his first brigade was forced back under a severe front and enfilading storm."

While the Confederates continued to destroy division after division, Hooker found Burnside and urged him to stop the massacre. Burnside refused, insisting that the attacks continue. His orders clear, Hooker crossed the Rappahannock once more and gave Brigadier General Andrew A. Humphreys the unhappy news that it was his turn to attack. Mounted and with sword in hand, Humphreys led a brigade of his Pennsylvania troops into the hail of Confederate fire where they, too, were cut up and forced to the ground.

Humphreys now determined to attempt what several Union commanders had earlier concluded was the only chance, however slight, of success—a bayonet charge. He ordered the men of Brigadier General Erastus B. Tyler's brigade to fix bayonets on their unloaded rifles and prepare to sprint for the wall across the field littered with dead, wounded, and pinned-down soldiers.

The blood-drenched day had waned to dusk by the time Tyler's brigade was ready. General Humphreys yelled, "Officers to the front in this charge. Never mind the obstacles in the way! Charge!" Tyler's men surged forward. The Federal wounded lying on the ground called out to the Pennsylvanians to stop and reached up and grabbed at them to prevent their suicidal mission. The charging brigade became disorganized and lost momentum.

The Rebels allowed the enemy to come within 50 yards of their line. "Then," according to a Confederate who waited in the sunken road, "our quintuple line rose up from behind the stone wall and delivered their withering fire. The first line melted but the second came steadily on, over the dead and dying of the former charges, to share the same fate. Ye Gods! It is no longer a battle, it is a butchery!" Completely demoralized by the carnage in their lead ranks, Humphreys' two brigades ignored the pleas of their commanders and retired from the field, leaving another 1,000 casualties as evidence of their efforts.

Brigadier General George Sykes' division of Regular Army troops tried to cover Humphreys' retreat and immediately became caught in the Confederate storm of lead. Sykes' men flattened themselves on the ground and remained there under relentless fire from the Confederate line.

With darkness approaching, Hooker ordered one more wave of assaults. Brigadier General George W. Getty's IX Corps division became the seventh one sent against Marye's Heights. Drawing the onerous duty of leading the assault, Colonel Rush Hawkins' brigade advanced on the left, aiming for the southern end of the stone wall. For a time the Confederates had trouble detecting Hawkins' troops moving forward in the twilight, but when they did, the same deadly drama was reenacted. According to General Ransom, the Rebels' volleys sent Getty's men "actually howling, back to their beaten comrades in the town." Shortly after 5:00 p.m. it was all over.

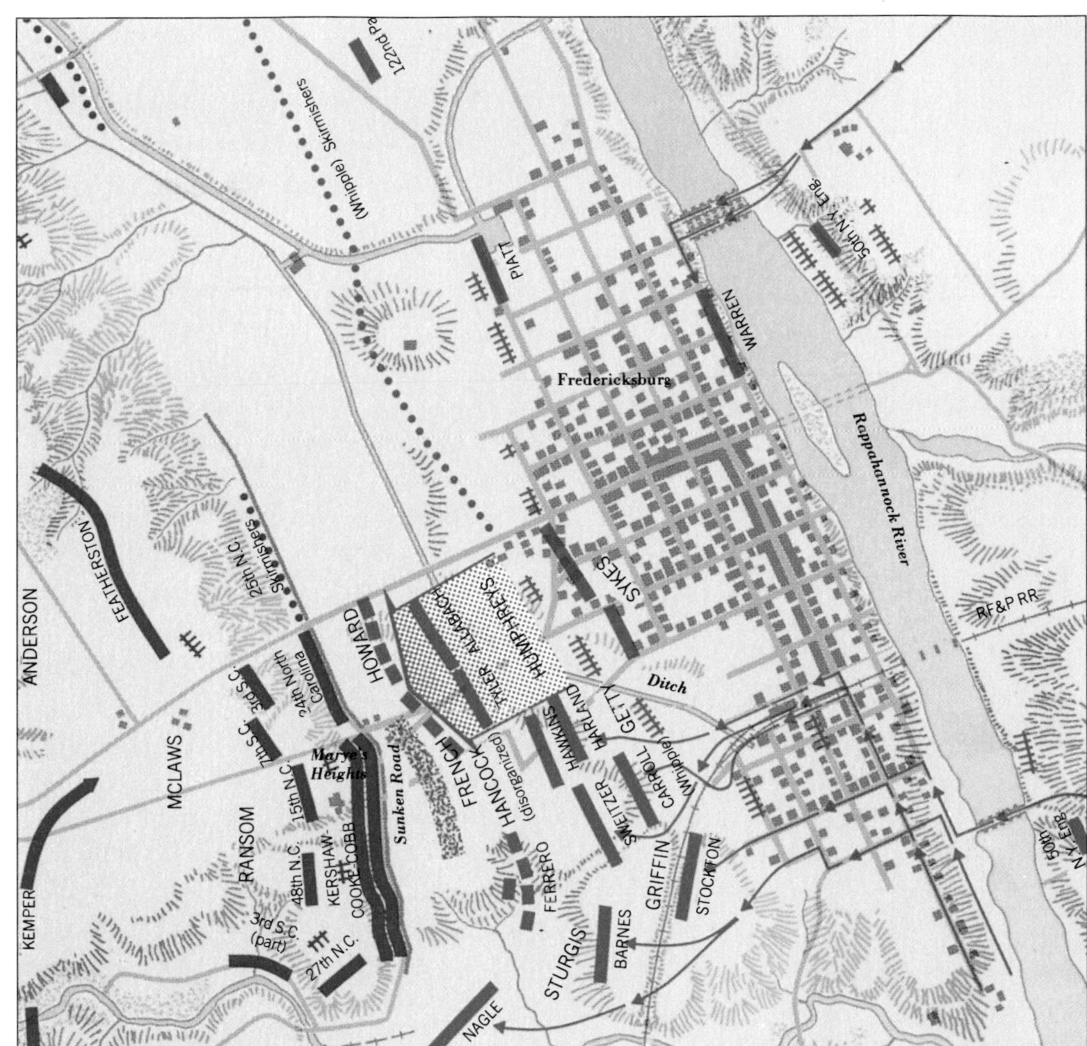

Despite the bloody repulse of two divisions, Burnside continued to feed units into the assault. Howard's division, advancing on the right, and Sturgis' IX Corps division, on the left, were the next to be thrashed by Cobb's men, who were joined by Ransom's North Carolinians and by Kershaw's brigade. As daylight faded, Burnside brought artillery forward and ordered in fresh elements from Hooker's grand division, but these attacks were equally disastrous.

General Hooker called an end to the Federal disaster, later stating acidly that he had "lost as many men as my orders required." In less than five hours, 7,000 Union soldiers had been killed or wounded in front of Marye's Heights. General Longstreet had lost only 1,700 Confederates. With the arrival of morning's light, Longstreet looked upon the killing field in front of his line. "The dead were piled sometimes three deep, and when morning broke, the spectacle we saw upon the battlefield was one of the most distressing I ever witnessed. The charges had been desperate and bloody, but utterly hopeless."

SERGEANT CHARLES C. PAIGE

11TH NEW HAMPSHIRE INFANTRY, FERRERO'S BRIGADE

After the last II Corps effort had been hammered to the ground by Rebel gunfire, Burnside ordered IX Corps commander Brigadier General Orlando B. Willcox to renew the attack. The 11th New Hampshire formed part of the first wave in this effort, which cost the regiment nearly 200 casualties, although Paige escaped injury. His luck, however, ran out at Cold Harbor on June 3, 1864, when a bullet mangled his left arm so badly that he was hospitalized for nearly a year.

At one o'clock we were ordered on to the field. We filed to the right, going up a short street. Here, our first to be wounded, Chas. Lane, was struck. Filing to the right, and obliquely, we went on to the field amid terrific musketry and shell, missiles of death. Their infantry were behind intrenchments and big cannon crowned the crest of the ridge known as St. Mary's Heights. All of these belched forth their constant fire and shells, which did terrible execution. . . .

. . . We were ordered to move right obliquely, which movement would expose our whole Regiment to a direct and yet raking fire. We were covered for a little by crossing a ravine and then we came to a board fence, or fences, for the land was divided into small farms, fields or gardens. We were ordered to lie down behind the first fence, but how the bullets and shells made havoc of that fence, and to me it was the most trying time of the day. Crash, crash, pat, pat, whiz, whiz, everything seemed going to destruction. One of my mates, lying near me, seemed in terrible mental agony, groaning and taking on. Perhaps I felt as badly as he but I kept it to myself. I felt that the hand of man or any earthly power was unable to save me, and I appealed to my Heavenly Father to save me, if it were His will.

But, soon we were ordered up and forward. "Be firm and brave boys," rang out from our Colonel. We obeyed, marching in line of battle some one-fourth of a mile, amid the terrible fire, our comrades falling as we went, until we got into our position behind a little rise of land which seemed formed for us. If we kept laid down, or very low in our posterior, we were out of the way of the solid shot and shell if they did not explode over us, which they often did. . . . When we went forward in line of battle, my position was next to the color bearer, which I did not fancy was safe; but our colors were not hit, neither was I. My position in the ranks was in the center of the Company, which I held during the afternoon, except when I crawled to some wounded or dead man to get his cartridges. . . . Capt. Patten was lying down a little to my left, feeling ill. He complimented me on my behavior. I had fifty rounds in my cartridge box, which I used. A few feet to my right a man was killed by a shell, and I crept to him and got what cartridges he had left, twenty-five. I used what Jessie Bean had after he was wounded, also got some of Manson Brickett, after which I got plenty more from reinforcements. One fellow sat down behind me who had one hundred rounds and I used more than one half of them, and then got enough from a Lieutenant to make more than two hundred which I used during the afternoon. Each time I fired, I aimed to hit some one, but I cannot affirm what the lead did.

Jessie Bean was some two feet to my left when he was hit, and others around me received wounds. Sergeant Nealey also near me, received a mortal wound through the body. After using all my cartridges, I laid down on my side and arm, and partook of the cake which I had baked in the morning. I gave some to Jessie and George Brown and it relished good.

I was some tired and my knees were wet and covered with mud, for I was on them the most of the time, except when I wished to aim at some place, which, on account of other heads, I could not reach.

I know that God was near me, and I felt no fear worth naming. When going on amid the screams, the thunder bolts, bursting of shell and whizing bullets, I felt a dread but that soon left me. I tried, no, I will not say that I tried, for it did not require much effort, to keep cool and composed in mind. . . .

. . . This was a time to try what men were made of, for all true men do not behave the same in times of danger. There is no doubt but what many shrinking, fearful men are so constitutionally made up that they cannot help acting as they sometimes do. One of my men, a Corporal, and a fellow always well made up when in camp, inclined to feel himself a little superior to some of his equals, acted cowardly. He was in my rear and hugged the ground until I felt obliged to threaten him if he did not get up and behave more manly. Another young soldier, when he fired, would not rise far enough from the ground so that his ball would go over the heads of those in front of him. I felt the whiz of his bullets, and was obliged to threaten him in severe terms.

Amid the devastation in Fredericksburg wrought by artillery fire from both sides and looting by Yankee soldiers, a column of Willcox's IX Corps, probably from Ferrero's brigade, pauses in Caroline Street on its march toward its bloody fate at the front. In the foreground of this Lumley sketch, a gaggle of infantrymen, perhaps stragglers from a II Corps regiment, lounge comfortably about on furniture dragged into the street from the surrounding buildings.

"My escape was so remarkable that it was mentioned by Gen. McLaws in his report of the battle."

PRIVATE WILLIAM M. CRUMLEY

STAFF, KERSHAW'S BRIGADE

Early in the afternoon General Joseph Kershaw's veteran South Carolinians began moving down into the sunken road—traversing one of the hottest places on the battlefield, the exposed slope of Marye's Heights—to bolster the already strong Rebel position with even more firepower. Although most of his comrades were now behind the stone wall or earthworks, courier Crumley braved the slope twice.

Just as Gen. Kershaw gave the order to the brigade to move down the hill, he ordered me to bring up the ordnance wagons. They were down some distance on the road to our camp and my orders were to bring them up to the old mill just under the hill back of our lines. I found them, hurried them forward and just as I got them in position Lieut. Deas, one of Gen. Kershaw's aides, rode up on old "Stone" (a fine sorrel horse we had captured from Gen. Stone, a Yankee general, some time before) the horse Gen. Kershaw had ridden into battle. Old Stone had a ball through his neck and Lieut. Deas was badly wounded in the leg by a piece of shell. Deas said, "General Kershaw wants another horse." It took me only a few minutes to change the saddle and bridle from old Stone to "Montgomery," a very fine grey horse of the General's that was kept with the ordnance wagons when we went into battle.

I mounted him and having heard from Deas what a fearful time the brigade had had going down the front of Marye's Heights, I decided to go round the road.

As I came round the hill and where I came to the end of the stone wall I met Capt. Mat Crumley, my brother, who was with Wofford's Brigade which had just been transferred from Jackson's command to McLaws'. We recognized each other and he stopped my horse, asking, "Where are you going?" I replied, "I am taking this horse to Gen. Kershaw." "You will be killed before you have gone fifty yards," was his cheery reply. I told him, "I am ordered to go and go I will have to or try, at least." He bade me farewell as if he never expected to see me again and started the horse with his sword as he seemed reluctant to go forward. The road on to where Gen. Cobb was wounded and which stood at the other end of the stone wall where Gen. Kershaw had his headquarters was nearly full of troops, many wounded or dead, so it was impossible for me to make much headway at speed through them. The wall was low and I was exposed from my feet up to the fire from the whole Yankee line which was behind an old fence row a little over a hundred yards from the wall. I rode through this fearful storm of minnie balls for about three hundred yards and arrived safely behind the house mentioned above.

When Gen. Kershaw was located and as soon as he saw me, he said,

"What are you doing here with Montgomery? Every horse in the brigade has been killed. Take him out at once." I explained as quickly as I could what Lieut. Deas had told me and asked him how must I get out as I could never go back by the road. His reply was, "Right over the hill." The road was cut down on the side next to the hill, so I backed Montgomery to the other side of the road so as to get a start. I drove the spurs into him. He leaped up the bank and fairly flew with me clinging to his back and flattened out like a lizard on a log. Our men in the road, many who knew me, cheered me as I rode over the hill in safety. My escape was so remarkable that it was mentioned by Gen. McLaws in his report of the battle.

Red-haired Jesse M. Pendley of Phillips' Legion, part of Cobb's Georgia brigade, poses proudly in this photograph probably taken around the time the unit was organized in August 1861 by Colonel William Phillips. Weapons such as Pendley's knife and bayonet drew no blood during the fight on December 13, as the Georgians' musket fire stopped the Yankees before they reached the Confederate line. Pendley surrendered with the other survivors of Phillips' Legion at Appomattox.

A line of Rebel infantry methodically pours rifle fire into packed Union formations in this Frank Vizetelly sketch, believed to show the northern end of the Marye's Heights position, where the 24th North Carolina occupied rifle pits supporting the Georgians and South Carolinians behind the stone wall. So effective was the musketry of McLaws' and Ransom's men that the attackers got no closer than 40 or 50 yards to their line. Farther down the position an exploding Federal shell blasts a gap in the Confederate line, soon filled by replacements from the waiting ranks kneeling at right.

COLONEL ZENAS R. BLISS

7th Rhode Island Infantry, Nagle's Brigade

As each wave of Federals quickly discovered, they were on killing ground as soon as they moved beyond the cover of Fredericksburg's buildings. Even though Nagle's brigade swung left to try to flank the stone wall, the maelstrom of artillery and small arms still inflicted 158 casualties on Bliss' regiment.

The street on which we laid was parallel to the river and nearly so to the line of battle. After awhile I received an order to move onto the plain and support General Ferrero, who was a Dancing Master from New York and had been the instructor of dancing at West Point. He was a good soldier, and was commanding at that time a Brigade,—I moved up one of the the streets perpendicular to the river, and when I got to the head of the street, I turned to the right and moved along three or four squares which brought me outside of the City, and immediately in rear of our part of the line of battle. . . .

When I ordered the men to lie down at this point, I was immediately behind a fence, and facing the enemy. They had a battery of heavy guns on our right, and had the range of us perfectly, as they were up on the heights and could see us distinctly.

The Field Officers were lying down in rear of the men, and the battery was nearly on the prolongation of the line of my Regiment. Bullets were flying from the front very thickly. I saw a man clasp his hand to his head, and saw the blood trickle through his fingers. He spoke to me, and said he was shot. I told him to cover his head with the cape of his overcoat, and remain where he was, as I thought he was pretty badly wounded. I went to the rear of the line and laid down with the rest.

I had been there but about five minutes, when a shell passed over my head, pretty close, and struck to my left and ricochetted down the street, without hitting anyone.

Colonel Sayles was about twenty feet to the right of me, and was lying on his left side and resting on his left elbow, a little diagonally, with the general line.

Major Babbitt was to my left, near the left flank of the Regiment.

I was lying on my stomach resting on both elbows. I was looking at Colonel Sayles, when a twenty pound parrot shell, or shot, struck him in the breast, and nearly cut him in two. It ricochetted and passed over my head, carrying with it a mass of blood and pieces of his lungs. One piece struck me on the cheek, another on the cap, and a third quite large piece fell between my arms, as I laid on the ground, and I scooped up the mud and covered it, as it was right under my face. I thought it was a part of his brain, as it seemed soft and pulpy. I did not know where he was hit, but I saw the upper part of his body turn nearly completely around, so that his face was partly toward me, though he was lying with his back to me.

Very soon another shell struck near me on the left, passing over my head, and Captain Rodman called to me to come up nearer the fence, that I was directly in range of the shells, and I did so. I had hardly laid down before another shell passed through the bottom board of the fence, and so near me, that I could put my hand in the hole it made in the board.

A shell from the battery struck Sergeant Major Manchester taking off his left arm. I was very glad to get the order to go to the front, when the Aide came up, and immediately gave the order. All the right side of my overcoat was covered with blood from Colonel Sayle's body.

I suppose it was about two hundred yards from our line to the extreme front of our line of battle, and the space was cut by two board fences; posts with four or five horizontal boards nailed to the posts.

We went over the first fence, but it took sometime for the men to get over, and when we came to the last fence, I told them not to attempt to get over it, but for all to take hold of the top boards and pull them off. They attempted it, but the boards were nailed on with railroad spikes and could not be pulled off. I saw a place where a shell or shot had knocked the top boards off, and I ran towards that, and just as I got to it, a man stepped in to the gap and was hit and pitched headlong over the lower boards. Another attempted to pass and he also fell. It was then my turn and I went through.

As soon as the Regiment was clear of the fence, we went on at a run, and I remember that I thought I could see a V shaped space in front of me as I ran, in which no bullets were striking, as though they had left a clear space in front of me, for my especial benefit. We were soon up

"I did not know where he was hit, but I saw the upper part of his body turn nearly completely around, so that his face was partly toward me, though he was lying with his back to me."

as far to the front as anyone had gone, and we passed over the hundreds or thousands of men lying there in line.

The fire was so deadly, and the men fell so fast, that I think those who were not hit, thought the order had been given to lie down, for without any word from us they all dropped.

The Color Sergt. Wiegant, got up and taking the colors went eight or ten paces beyond any flags and stuck the staff in the ground, farther to the front than any others had been placed.

Of course as soon as we got on the line we commenced firing, and kept it up as long as the ammunition lasted, and then fixed bayonets and remained till we were ordered off the field, after dark. The fire was terrific, and I have never heard anyone say, that they ever experienced anything like the fire there was there for so long a time.

I suppose we were about one hundred and fifty yards from a stone-wall, sunken wall, behind which Longstreet's Division of Veterans stood. This wall was a supporting wall to a cut made from a road that had passed along the foot of Maries Heights, and the faces of the hills were covered with riflepits. On top were about twenty four pieces of Artillery, which had a plunging fire on us, and we had not the slightest cover whatever.

The field over which we had attempted to cross had been cultivated and was nearly level. While we were thus exposed, the Rebels were so completely covered, that I did not see but three during the day, but the smoke and flash of the muskets were plainly visible. We remained in the same place until after dark, without doing the slightest injury to the enemy, but suffering terribly ourselves.

One thing that I noticed, that I thought very strange, and everybody spoke of the same thing, was, the rapidity with which time passed. One would think that lying there as we were, expecting to be hit every minute, and seeing our comrades falling constantly, that the time would have passed very slowly, but it went so rapidly that I was very much surprised when it began to grow dark, and could hardly believe that night had come, tho I guess everyone on the field was praying for it. . . .

Adjt. Page had sat down on the ground beside me, and Captain Winn sat on my left. Page asked me how I thought the battle was going, and I told him. I did not know, but I thought we were getting the worst of it. Just at that moment a spherical case shot, filled with bullets and slugs, exploded immediately over our heads, and very close to us, probably not more than three or four feet above us. Page was struck in the head and fell on my left arm.

Captain Winn asked if he was killed and I shook my head, as I did not want Page to hear the remark, if he were alive. He did hear it though, and raised his head and said, "Colonel, I am not dead." I told him he was all right, to cover his head with his overcoat cape, and lie still and I would have him taken off the field as soon as possible. When he raised his head I saw that his left eye was gone, and the blood was streaming from the wound. The projectile entered his left temple and knocked out his eye.

At the time the shell exploded, I was struck pretty sharply on my left wrist. I had a soldier's overcoat, and had the sleeves rolled up so that it was several thicknesses on my arm, and the bullet struck on the roll and did not break the skin. When Page raised his head I saw the bullet lying near my wrist, covered with blood, and I suppose it had passed through his head and struck me, and I picked it up and told him that was the bullet that hit him, and to keep it. He carried it home and showed it to many people as the bullet that had knocked his eye out.

"The fire was so deadly, and the men fell so fast, that I think those who were not hit, thought the order had been given to lie down."

Sometime during the afternoon of December 13 special artist Alfred Waud sketched this panoramic view of the battlefield from the vantage point of a church steeple. Most conspicuous are the lines of smoke rising from the muskets of thousands of Union infantrymen pinned down on the low ground west of Fredericksburg. On the heights beyond, more isolated clouds of smoke shroud the positions of Confederate batteries. On the top edge of the sketch Waud has included the label "Marye Mansion" to indicate the position of the prominent colonnaded building below.

LIEUTENANT WILLIAM H. S. BURGWYN

35TH NORTH CAROLINA INFANTRY, RANSOM'S BRIGADE

In this excerpt from a letter to his aunt, the 17-year-old Burgwyn relates the hazards of being exposed to Federal fire on the high ground behind the stone wall. Promoted to captain before his 18th birthday, Burgwyn was captured at the Battle of Fort Harrison in September 1864 and held until his release shortly before Appomattox.

On the morning of the 13th there was a heavy fog which cleared off about 10:00 a.m. and I thought though this was not such a sun as that of Austrilitz I hope it will prove as fortunate to us as that was to Napoleon. About 1:30 p.m. we moved through a storm of shell to a position in a ravine about sixty yards closer to our batteries to support them. While in that position though it seemed impossible for us to be hurt we lost one officer and two privates killed. We stayed there about an hour and then moved our position about a 100 yards closer to the batteries still through a storm of shell and musketry which killed and wounded five or six men; and just as I had formed my company in line and was dressing and making them step up to the line and preventing them from lying down for the shell and minie balls were coming over our heads powerful, I saw a shell coming about three feet from the ground right towards us which was spent sufficiently to let me see it as it went. I only had time to say "You fellow" when it struck a man in the company on my left sending him to his final resting place. We were then ordered to lie down and while lying down two spent minie balls struck a color corporal lying on my right side and a spent shell about a foot long came tumbling over the ground right in front of me and if it had not struck an oak post that had been pulled up the night before for fire wood in all probability I would not now be here to write you.

PRIVATE PHINEAS P. WHITEHOUSE

6TH NEW HAMPSHIRE INFANTRY, NAGLE'S BRIGADE

After Ferrero's direct assault had stalled behind a slight rise in the ground, division commander Samuel Sturgis ordered his other brigade, under James Nagle, to swing farther to the left. Nagle's men braved the storm of lead, but they, too, were soon forced to take cover behind a shallow rise that offered as much cover as any Federal soldier would find that day on the battlefield.

Marching a short distance through two or three streets, we were soon in rear of the town, and within the sound of the flying bullets. Scenes pitiful and shocking met our gaze, as we neared the field of battle. The returning wounded, with powerless arms, shattered legs, or bloody and fearfully disfigured faces, were objects so dreadful to look upon, as to cause the bravest soldier to tremble, the stoutest heart to flutter, as, with floating banners, we hastened to the front. Halting a few moments behind a fence and high woodpile, to dress our files, we marched out into the open plain, in full view of the enemy's works. Here quickly facing to the front and moving in line of battle, we met with so terrible a fire, it seemed that our whole regiment must be cut down. A shell burst among our men on the right, doing much damage. The man next to me on my right, fell dead. These death-messengers often broke our ranks, but our brave Colonel, on foot and on the double-quick, was leading us, and we hastily closed up to fill the places made vacant by our fallen comrades, and made our way as rapidly as possible over that bloody plain where so many had fallen before us. Across the plain—some three hundred yards wide—was a little ridge occupied by our advance, who had been fighting bravely. These troops, whose ammunition was nearly exhausted, it was now our object to relieve. We gained the ridge at last, and commenced firing at the rebel infantry, who were seen swarming the heights beyond.

Our position now slightly favoring us, we were not subject to quite so galling a fire as when marching up over the plain. We were permitted to lie down in line of battle, and load and fire at will. We were thus protected, for two-thirds of the time or more, by the ridge before us. When standing or sitting up to fire, however, we found the zipping visitors more plentiful than was either safe or agreeable. Sometimes they would come so near that we could almost feel them graze the hair about our ears, and we would dodge back involuntarily, forgetting, for the instant, that that peculiar sound was ample proof that the ball could not harm us.

SERGEANT S. MILLETT THOMPSON

13TH NEW HAMPSHIRE INFANTRY, HAWKINS' BRIGADE

Close to sunset George Getty's division of the IX Corps entered the fray, with Colonel Rush C. Hawkins' brigade spearheading the division's only attack. The New York, New Hampshire, and New Jersey regiments in Hawkins' command raced into the withering gantlet of Confederate gunfire, accomplishing nothing beyond adding 255 more names to the Federal casualty rolls.

Advance now means advance to a grave, or upon scant and bad rations in a rebel prison. We can see the heads of the rebels now and then in the flashes of light, and distinctly hear their officers' words of command. We could easily throw a stone over among them. . . .

. . . We are so near to the muzzles of the enemy's cannon and muskets, that the wild scene is considerably lighted up by the incessant flashes of burning powder, and we can see our men lying about. . . . We are so near the enemy that his gun wads, or cartridge bags, fly over us, and some of them fall burning, smoking and stinking among us, and we feel upon our faces and hands the wind of the discharges of his cannon. Our men here pick up these burning wads or bags upon their bayonets and toss them away. We constantly hear the rebel commands. Their cannon are depressed, the muzzles well down, and we can see them jump back as they are fired. All that saves the portion of the Thirteenth now directly around the colors is their nearness to the rebel cannon and rifles, which cannot be depressed sufficiently to reach us with their fire, and a little dry hollow, dropping less than two feet, in the surface of the field just where the men are lying. The shelter is just enough to permit a man to rise a little from the ground, support himself upon his elbow, and look about him, as some of us do, and have quite a clear view, for a few seconds at a time, of the near surrounding scene. . . .

. . . We are in the midst of a magnificent exhibition of fireworks, their flashes of flame ranging from the bright spark of a rebel explosive bullet, to the instant glare of a locomotive headlight, as the cannon discharge and the shell burst, the blaze and roaring about the same on every hand and front and rear. The many crazy Union bullets are just skimming over our heads, from the rear, while the flashes of the Union guns only serve to provoke an increasing fire from the enemy on our front, their bullets also just skimming over our heads. The Union bullets are as dangerous for us to face in retreating, as the enemy's bullets are in following us. The situation is a trying one; but our interest in this scene, so new and strange to us raw troops, robs the dangers of half their terrors. And so we lie and wait. Think of spending half an hour in such a place! . . .

Andrew A. Werts (above) of the 3d South Carolina aided his commander, Colonel James Nance, by using the colonel's handkerchief to make a tourniquet for his wounded leg. Nance was hit as the regiment filed into position around the Marye house.

. . . While we are here one large Union shell, that comes rushing, screaming, the nearest of all to our heads, plunges into the ground about twenty-five or fifty feet to our front, bursts upon striking, jarring the ground and giving us a shower of gravel; as usual the most of the pieces take the direction of the shell, and we can hear the enemy scream, curse and swear. Since the first volleys, the enemy in dense ranks, in large numbers, and firing at will, have produced a perfect roar of musketry; but as they fire high and about all their shots go over, the result is more threatening than harmful. . . . We can occasionally, in the flashes of light, see the hands and arms of the rebels working, as they ram their cartridges home; and the multitude of their commands indicate many officers "present for duty." Our interest in the situation is greatly enhanced by knowing that they would instantly shoot us all at sight, if they could possibly do so!

PRIVATE DAVID E. HOLT

16TH MISSISSIPPI INFANTRY, FEATHERSTON'S BRIGADE

Featherston's men, entrenched along the ridgeline to the left of Marye's Heights, were well positioned both to enfilade the Federals advancing against the sunken road and to engage those Yankees who had worked their way over to the north side of the Plank road to find shelter, among other places, in the cemetery. Holt soldiered with the 16th until August 1864, when he was taken prisoner south of Petersburg.

We opened fire immediately, the enemy having the protection of the canal bank and cemetery. A large brick factory located in front of our right wing afforded them a vantage point which was quickly utilized by the enemy who fairly swarmed around it. They were as venomous as hornets, while the zipping bullets nipped the top of our breastworks, scattering dirt, and passing to the rear as though they had discovered something and were in a hurry to get to it.

Many Yanks crawled out of the canal up to the [Mary] Washington

As the 3d South Carolina lay in reserve in front of Brompton—the Marye home (right)—the regiment was exposed to heavy fire, mostly from Yankees overshooting the stone wall. This barrage scarred the home's bricks and columns and cost the 3d many dead and wounded. One of those struck was William G. Peterson (above) of Company B, hit in the leg by a bullet. Peterson limped behind the house and eventually ended up in a Richmond hospital. Wounded again at Gettysburg and the Wilderness, Peterson was discharged in April 1865.

This monument to Mary Washington, mother of the first president, was damaged during the battle, most likely by the Union bombardment of December 11 and later when Yankee troops used it for cover. George Washington, who spent much of his youth here, bought a home for Mary on Charles Street in 1772. She died in 1789 and was buried just outside the town. The monument, dedicated by President Andrew Jackson, was erected at her grave site in 1833. In the 1890s a new memorial that still stands was placed on the site and dedicated by Grover Cleveland.

tomb [which] afforded shelter for many. A message came to the Washington Artillery, asking them to direct fire on the tomb and the graveyard and flush the covey of blue bellies so we could take them on the wing. The request to shell the grave of the mother of the "Father of His Country" was refused, but they consented to fire a few shots into the cemetery. Soon a great noise of bursting marble was heard and double results obtained, as a fragment of marble was as good for killing purposes as a shell. Many a Yank doubtless had this inscription on his tomb, "Killed by a tombstone that broke loose at Fredericksburg." When the artillery flushed them we got in some deadly work with our rifles. But they stuck to the tomb as though it contained some sort of fascination. Soon the word was passed: "You fellows on the left get busy and concentrate your fire around that tomb."

I, being a little fellow, was on the left, [and I] took a lively hand in the fight. We aimed low, and a bullet on the ricochet was as good as a direct hit. In a short time the Yanks ceased fire and cleared the graveyard. But they still held out along the canal and improved their position at the mill, managing to get inside where they opened fire from every vantage point. We had to keep our heads down but lost quite heavily from their snipers. Our artillery opened up and gave us a chance to catch the enemy on the jump. As shells struck the wall and bricks began to fly, the Yanks decided to move out. Many were there, some in too big a hurry to go down the steps, [and they] fell out the windows. After having crawled in one by one, they attempted to go out altogether. The shooting at short range, afforded excellent hits, but it was sad. I never enjoyed the sport of shooting at men. There was no spirit of murder in my heart. But the heavy guns, on Stafford Heights kept up their steady fire and had our range down pat, while the invading Yankee infantry tried to drive us back. I pigeon-holed my sentiments and shot for keeps.

LIEUTENANT COLONEL WILLIAM W. TEALL

Staff, Major General Edwin V. Sumner

During the battle Teall remained on the east side of the Rappahannock along with General Sumner, who had set up his headquarters at Chatham, an impressive plantation house situated on the bluffs overlooking the river. Also on that side of the river were the balloons of Professor Thaddeus S. C. Lowe's Aeronautics Corps, which provided reconnaissance for the Army of the Potomac. Invited to go aloft, Teall gained perhaps the best view of the battlefield enjoyed by anyone that day.

At 8 minutes past 11 the balloon "Eagle" was brought in front of our HdQrs. It was a beautiful sight & at 11:12 it went up with 2 men in it. It was up but 3 minutes. At 1/2 past 11 it ascended again, carrying this time, Professor Low's assistant & yr *loving husband* who for the first time in his life, assumed a hazard yr father declared was greater than marching in front of the cannon's mouth. The atmosphere was somewhat smoky but the view was beautiful. . . .

At 1 P.M. I made a second reconnoisance in the balloon but it was too windy either to be entirely safe or to make good observations & I therefore soon descended. I then went to the signal station & through that powerful glass observed the Infantry fight for the crest of the hill directly in front of yr father's Right Grand Division. The wounded & killed were as plainly visible as if I stood on the field itself. I saw one poor fellow badly wounded limping from the field accompanied by some friend, towards the gorge on the left through which the Rail-Road passes & as they reached the brink how quickly they slid down the bank. I could not but rejoice to see them sink suddenly from the murderous fire of the rebel sharpshooters. . . .

At 4 P.M. Professor Low called on me & said it was so clear & still I had better make another reconnoisance with the balloon which I immediately did. I remained up this time for 20 or 25 minutes & at an altitude of from 800 to 900 feet. A view of the entire line of battle from the extreme right to the extreme left, say from 6 to 8 miles was spread out before me. The scene from this height & at this moment of the battle was magnificent beyond description. Language could not do it justice & any attempt to describe it would be useless & impotent in the extreme. It was a scene I never expect to live to see again. Surely no mortal ever witnessed one so fearfully sublime. Several shots were fired at the balloon & one from a battery undisclosed before. But on the instant several of our own poured into it & no further demonstration from that quarter was known.

Lieutenant Colonel Elbert Bland, the scion of a wealthy South Carolina planter family and a prominent physician, commanded the 7th South Carolina at Fredericksburg. Bland narrowly escaped suffering a serious wound while standing in front of the Marye house when his binoculars (far left), stuffed into his left breast pocket, stopped a bullet. Bland entered the war as a surgeon but after two months transferred to a field command. Pain from an arm wound received at Savage's Station plagued him until he was killed in action at Chickamauga.

Aeronautics pioneer Thaddeus S. C. Lowe inaugurated and headed the Union's "Balloon Corps." Although Lowe's organization showed great promise for detecting troop movements and directing artillery fire, administrative bickering over how best to use the service led to its demise just after the Battle of Chancellorsville.

SERGEANT EDWARD SIMONTON

20TH MAINE INFANTRY, STOCKTON'S BRIGADE

Although the better part of two corps had already been savaged in front of Marye's Heights, Burnside ordered an advance by the V Corps, leading off with the three brigades of Charles Griffin's division, as the sun was setting. Simonton was promoted to lieutenant in January 1863, but later that year he resigned to take command of a company of U.S. Colored Troops. Severely wounded at Petersburg, he later transferred to the Regular Army.

All at once our brigade bugler sounds the bugle-call, so familiar to the members of Butterfield's old brigade, and thus repeated by the boys: "Dan, Dan Butterfield, Butterfield, Dan, Dan Butterfield, Butterfield." This means that our time has come to cross the river and join in the battle. "Fall in!" shouts the colonel; "Fall in!" repeats the company commander. The men obey with alacrity, feeling that they have been inactive witnesses of the battle-scene quite long enough. At three o'clock in the afternoon of Saturday, the 13th, our brigade and division descend the river-bank, cross the pontoon-bridge, ascend the river-bank on the other side, and march through the suburbs of Fredericksburg in the direction of the advance lines of our troops. When within about half a mile of the enemy's position, our column of fours halts and hastily forms in line of battle. Then, after a brief rest, comes the command, scarcely heard above the roar of battle in our front, "Attention, battalion; fix bayonets; forward, guide centre, march!" and away we go, up the rising ground in our front, over fences, across ditches, gardens, and fields, but in the face of a storm, it seems to us, of crashing shot and shell and whistling bullets. We pass by and over several lines of battle of the Second and Ninth Corps, who had charged and fought manfully before us, and been repulsed with heavy loss in killed and wounded. Their thinned ranks now lie on the ground under the shelter of the slight elevation of ground in their front, and they willingly make way for the onward march of our fresh troops, and cheer us on. We hear them say, "Don't mind stepping on us, boys; march right on; the Johnnies are waiting for you right over there behind that stone wall. You'll find them there all right."

We see scattered all along the way our dead and wounded soldiers, lying where they had fallen. Still we keep our ranks unbroken, and march on in a well-preserved line of battle, under the leadership of our regimental and brigade commanders, our brigade having the lead of this advancing column. Finally, at about sunset on that short December day we reach the crest of a slope some distance in advance of those lines of our troops we have passed. At this point we are separated from the rebel intrenchments by a narrow vale, or field, only some one hundred yards across. Here our line is halted, and the soldiers are ordered to lie down and fire, which order we obey promptly, and commence firing; loading and firing, with all the energy we can command, at the rebel position across the way. We cannot now see distinctly any rebels to fire at, as they seem to seek the shelter of their works; but we can see puffs of smoke all along their line, and hear the storm of musketry and shot and shell over our heads, and we know the Johnnies are there, so we blaze away at the puffs of smoke and the earthworks on the hill-side opposite. This opportunity to fire at something in the enemy's direction has the effect to give the soldier confidence in himself, even if his own fire does no material execution.

SERGEANT WILLIAM H. PEACOCK

BATTERY E, MASSACHUSETTS LIGHT ARTILLERY, GRIFFIN'S DIVISION

To add some punch to the attacks of Griffin's division, several batteries were brought forward to pound the Rebel line from close range. But Peacock and the rest of the exposed Union artillerymen quickly felt the effects of Confederate counter-battery fire. Peacock served as a wagoner before being promoted to sergeant in March 1862, and shortly afterward he became chief of one of the battery's gun crews. He left the army when his term of service expired in October 1864.

The way Shell and balls flew around us was a caution. on my Gun two horses were Killed but none of my men hurt, the Shell that Killed the horses passed through one of them striking near me as I was getting the time on a patent shell. I had it between my Knees when something hit me knocking myself and shell over in the mud. picked myself up felt of my head found that all right, then my breast and legs and they were whole. but at the moment it seemed as if I could feel something go into me. it proved to be nothing more than stones and mud which the shell had kicked up when it struck the ground. one of our men was Killed, Eddie Platts of Boston. a pretty little boy only 16 years old. he was a great pet with the boys by his being so young and always having such a pleasant smile on his face even in death. he was under me over a year and a short time ago was promoted to Gunner in another Detachment. he had just given the order to fire when a Schrapnel ball passed through his body. we carried him to the rear and he died in about 12 hours. he was buried in a garden on one of the principal streets of the City amidst a terrible shelling of the place by the Rebels. I think the last gun he fired fully revenged his death as it was a splendid shot amidst the Rebel Infantry.

PRIVATE ALEXANDER HUNTER

17TH VIRGINIA INFANTRY, CORSE'S BRIGADE

As twilight neared, the two brigades of Humphrey's V Corps, composed primarily of green Pennsylvania regiments, mounted two rushes against the sunken road, by now almost overflowing with Rebels. The bravery of these troops impressed even the Confederates, many of whom, like Hunter, were never on the firing line.

In company with Bob Willis, we straggled to the front and lay in the rear of the Washington Artillery of New Orleans, which hurled grape and canister at the attacking force. All that day we watched the fruitless charges, with their fearful slaughter, until we were sick at heart.

As I witnessed one line swept away by one fearful blast from Kershaw's men behind the stone wall, I forgot they were enemies and only remembered that they were men, and it is hard to see in cold blood brave men die.

Just before sunset, everything being quiet along the line, many of the reserve, without orders, crowded to the front and were spectators of that last forlorn hope led by the gallant Humphries. . . .

. . . Every soldier knew the Rebel position was impregnable; they had seen charge after charge repulsed, they had seen brigade after brigade rush forward with deadly determination, only to recoil before the hailstorm of iron and of lead; their very route lay over a field where the dead lay thick "as the leaves in Vallombrosa." . . .

From the hill back of the heights the division of Pickett watched the advance, filled with wonder and a pitying admiration for men who could rush with such unflinching valor, such mad recklessness into the jaws of destruction. . . .

. . . Across the plain, with no martial music to thrill them, only a stillness that would strike terror into spirits less gallant—across the plain still onward sweeps the dauntless brigade with serried lines and gleaming steel.

"I forgot they were enemies and only remembered that they were men, and it is hard to see in cold blood brave men die."

During Humphrey's attack, depicted here by Alfred Waud, he ordered his officers to remain mounted in order to better direct their untried soldiers. Edward O'Brien, a one-armed Mexican War veteran and the colonel of the 134th Pennsylvania, had a narrow escape from harm when a bullet passed through his saddle from front to rear directly under him. The 134th, raised in the vicinity of New Castle, suffered 148 of the division's 1,019 casualties.

It was superb!

Still closer they advanced, while twice one thousand veterans lay beyond yon stone wall, with eyes ranged along the deadly barrel and fingers pressing the trigger.

Men held their breath.

There was no smoke or battle-fume to obstruct the view, nor wood to mask the movement; but as in a grand review, the whole advance could be seen in all its glory and in all its horror.

The brigade came on a run, and bent as it moved until it was the shape of a half moon with the concave toward the town. Batteries opened upon them; and then broke out the murderous musketry. Men staggered, reeled and fell but the others pushed on. From the wall and road came a living sheet of fire . . . at every foot they dropped by scores; some almost reached the wall and then fell dead with their feet to the foe; human nature could stand no more, for the number of killed was fast counting up by thousands, and half of them were down; the ranks broke and each man sought safety in flight.

LIEUTENANT CHARLES S. POWELL

24TH NORTH CAROLINA INFANTRY, RANSOM'S BRIGADE

Although in on the heaviest fighting, Powell's regiment, positioned in rifle pits to the left of the stone wall, lost only 28 men. Armed to the teeth in this 1861 photo, the youthful Powell had been released from Federal captivity just two weeks before the battle. He later transferred to a heavy-artillery battalion.

Brigadier General Robert Ransom Jr., a West Pointer and veteran of frontier army service, commanded one of Longstreet's divisions that helped repulse Federal attacks all afternoon. Ransom boasted that his troops had sent Humphrey's Pennsylvanians "actually howling, back to their beaten comrades in the town."

They were brave men. On their last charge some fell within a few feet of our line, and it looked like a pity to kill such brave men. Around that brick house and peach orchard the dead were thick enough to walk over the gound on. The cries of the wounded were heartrendering but unheaded. Our casualties were small. Lieutenant Brown killed and two wounded in my company. One of them Bill Worley is now living. Gen. Cobb on our right was killed. Each one of us fired over one hundred rounds that day. The muskets becoming so foul that they frequently had to be wiped out, using parts of our clothing. The boys were as black as burnt cork minstrels. This was from biting the end of the paper cartridges, and though cold under foot we were sweating through excitement and exertion. The planks around the peach orchard were shot so full of holes that you could stick every finger through at once. The peach twigs hung by little strips of bark. Blood and brains were scattered everywhere. It was gruesome and sickening. Our shoulders were kicked blue from the muskets and were sore for many days. When the battle first began a negro woman came running by our company going up Mayre's Heights in our rear and in full view and range of the Yankees and they were giving her "hot peas" too.

"They writhe a few hours or days, are rudely tumbled into a trench half filled with water their graves unknown."

PRIVATE ERSKINE M. CHURCH

27TH CONNECTICUT INFANTRY, ZOOK'S BRIGADE

Although nightfall halted the fighting, the suffering was far from over for Federal wounded on the bloody fields. The horrible scene Church describes affected many, including his commander, Colonel Zook, who wrote that while it was bad enough to see men "torn into shreds" during battle, it was even worse to "walk alone amongst the slaughtered brave in the 'still small hours of the night.'" Church deserted in 1863 while serving with the 12th Connecticut in Louisiana.

Those who say they would like to visit a battlefield seldom know what they are talking about. After darkness has put an end to the struggle a hush settles over the field. Such a contrast to the roar of the fight. Never is silence more oppressive, more eloquent. You hear the cries of the wounded which is never distinguished in the roar of battle. A stray shot hurles through the darkness overhead. You hear the ambulance wheels . . . grinding through the soil with a sullen muffled sound like some monster craunching the bones of his victims. You see the outlines of forms gliding through the gloom carrying on litters pale bloody men. Or perhaps your friend with his hair matted with blood over his white face and his dead eyes starring blindly up to the sky. You are startled by the yells of those lifted about after becoming cold and stiff in their blood. Follow to the hospital and see those dissected alive and buchered. They writhe a few hours or days, are rudely tumbled into a trench half filled with water their graves unknown. With the hoot Owl to sing their recquiem, with no kind friend to shed a parting tear . . . their funeral rites are attended by a few hard hearted Soldiers. A volly fired over their grave if grave it can be called, unknown forgoten, forgotten forever.

Among the casualties suffered during the late-afternoon pounding of the Rockbridge Artillery on the Rebel right was Private Randolph Fairfax, killed when struck in the head by a shell fragment. Around nightfall the battery moved to the rear carrying Fairfax's body on a caisson. Having found a bivouac for the night, the artillerymen buried their fallen comrades "with much difficulty," according to battery commander Poague, "in the tired broken down sleepy condition of the men."

CAPTAIN GEORGE HILLYER

9TH GEORGIA INFANTRY, G. T. ANDERSON'S BRIGADE

Positioned well forward in the mostly quiet center of the Rebel line, Anderson's brigade suffered only a handful of casualties and had a superb view of the fighting on both flanks. Hillyer, seen here in an unusual "wintertime" pose, commanded his regiment at both Fredericksburg and Gettysburg but resigned in October 1863 to take a position in his native state.

We lay all day and witnessed the fight; we were pretty severely cannonaded at times, and had to hug the ground with great firmness to let the minnie balls pass over us, and though our skirmishers were almost constantly engaged, yet the enemy did not attack us in force—well for him that he did not. We were advantageously posted behind a hedge and ditch. The men were in splendid condition and eager for the fight; (and it is not often that veterans are so.) But it was our lot to be inactive. It was a sight soul-stirring and exciting beyond conception. Those crowded hours in which years of life are compressed into a moment. I saw that day artillery duels in all their horrible perfection.

I saw exhibitions of individual valor and heroism, such as makes a nation famous. I saw a few, very few, dastards fly from the field, but I saw the enemy driven back and defeated, and heard the loud huzzars of our sons of the sunny South, as they drove him from the plain. I saw the columns of infantry charge, and this, when seen in the open field, is by all odds the most horrible and sublime exhibition of man's power and passion, the panorama of war can display.

SERGEANT WILLIAM A. MCCLENDON

15TH ALABAMA INFANTRY, HOKE'S BRIGADE

As a precaution against further Federal advances, the Confederates pushed forward vedettes, or pickets, into the gloomy darkness beyond their lines, where these troops often found themselves surrounded by dead and dying Union infantrymen. Although many Yankees had no reservations about searching their own dead for valuables, most of the stripping of bodies was done by Confederates eager to secure a better pair of shoes or a warm overcoat.

I was detailed to go on vidette. I was told to advance out in front about twenty-five yards, and there watch until I was relieved. I knew by going that far out I would be near the Yankees. It was dark, except the star-light. I did not know then that any one else from the regiment had been sent out, but I afterwards ascertained that similar details had been made from each company. I crawled as low as I could in the scattering broom sage as far as I thought I was ordered to go. I kept looking back to see if I could, how far I was out. I was in constant dread for fear I would crawl into the Yankee lines, for I knew they were nigh and I had to be cautious. When I decided that I was far enough out I halted and crouched down until I could just look above the top of the straw. I was not there long before I discovered something dark just ahead of me lying on the ground. I decided that it was a Yan-

"There I sat beside my dead enemy in the dark, one who had lost his life in trying to subdue a people who asked for nothing more than 'Equality in the Union, or Independence out of it.'"

kee lying there in silence to take me in. I cocked my gun, and took position to shoot at the first word or movement that might be done. I sat and watched for a minute or more without discovering any movement from whatever it was. I had a thousand thoughts in a minute. I would look back occasionally. I was not going to surrender without a difficulty. I eased up a little nearer, enough that I punched him gently with my bayonet, then it was that I ascertained that it was a dead Yankee that had been killed about four hours. I eased up to where I could lay my hands on him. The thought struck me to rifle his pockets and take off his shoes, but upon examination I found his pockets wrong side out, and his shoes gone. He had been robbed by his own people. There I sat beside my dead enemy in the dark, one who had lost his life in trying to subdue a people who asked for nothing more than "Equality in the Union, or Independence out of it." While there, meditating over our condition, the thought entered my mind that neither our parents, kindred or friends at home, could draw the picture in their imaginations of our condition and situation at that time. Nothing but the "All Seeing Eye" could do it. I was near enough to the Yankees to hear them cough and clear up their throats. We had no orders to shoot unless they advanced. There was wounded Yankees lying between our lines sending up the most pitiful cries for help I ever heard. Some were calling for water, some calling the names of his friends, but none answered or went to their relief. Neither side could help. The night was cold and there is no telling how some of them suffered. Some of them may have died during the night by freezing.

LIEUTENANT HENRY E. HANDERSON

9TH LOUISIANA INFANTRY, HAYS' BRIGADE

From his bivouac near Hamilton's Crossing, Handerson passed through what was for many men on both sides an unforgettable night filled with the cries of the wounded and the dying. Throughout the night, Federal soldiers worked to retrieve as many of their suffering comrades as they could, often using shutters torn from houses as improvised stretchers.

The night was again cold and clear, and as we huddled together in line of battle to make the most of our scanty blankets, even fatigue scarcely sufficed to bring any continuous sleep to my eyes. At last, chilled to the marrow, and weary of turning from side to side in the vain effort to extract a little warmth from my companions, I rose from the ground and paced up and down the line of battle in the hope of stimulating the sluggish blood-currents by a little exercise. It must have been one or two o'clock in the morning, and the bright moonlight varnished with a silvery sheen the bare twigs and withered leaves of the forest, defining them almost as distinctly as the day. Apparently I was the only soul awake, and as I looked down the long white line of battle, where the men lay wrapped in their blankets, it seemed more like a row of corpses wrapped in their winding-sheets than a line of living and breathing warriors. Scarcely a sound disturbed the intense silence. Even the owls and other birds of the night seemed to respect the slumbers of my exhausted comrades. Our bivouac was situated at the head of a broad and rather shallow ravine or valley, filled with undergrowth and small trees and debouching into the broad plain which bordered the Rappahannock. As I looked across the tops of the brush and trees a dense veil of misty clouds shut out the valley beyond, but occasionally the solemn stillness of the night was broken by a faint and ghostly wail, which located itself at no special point, but seemed to rise like a mist from the face of the whole field of battle and conveyed the impression of wide spread and terrible anguish.

The unutterable sadness of that midnight wail from the battlefield of Fredericksburg has never left, and will never leave, my mind and memory. After a time, wearied and somewhat warmed by my exercise, I again lay down and fell into a deep sleep, from which I was awakened by the stir of the opening day.

CAPTAIN HENRY L. ABBOTT

20th Massachusetts Infantry, Hall's Brigade

Abbott, who regarded Leander Alley "almost as a brother," wrote this letter to the young lieutenant's mother from the field only hours after her son's death. Abbott tried to tell his father about the death of his close friend, but stopped, stating that he couldn't "say anything more about [Alley], . . . for thinking on such a subject makes a man bluer than he ought to be in the presence of the enemy."

Lieutenant Leander Alley, a capable and well-liked officer in the 20th Massachusetts—pictured here before his promotion—was killed instantly by a bullet through his left eye during Howard's attack. Alley's regiment suffered 163 casualties, the largest loss of any in the division.

Dear Madam,

Private Josiah F. Murphey, who brings the dead body of your son, will tell you fully all the particulars. I know by judging of my own feelings, how bitterly you will feel his loss. I can say from an intimate acquaintance with him, that he was as brave, resolute, and energetic, and at the same time as tender-hearted a man as I ever knew. When I first heard of his death (I didn't see him fall), I felt the same kind of pang as when I first heard of my brother's death, who was killed at Cedar Mountain. It was only a few nights before his death, that he was telling me about his family, and speaking of you in terms of the strongest affection. Every man in the regiment, from the col. to the men of other companies, respected and admired him as much as any officer that has ever belonged to the regiment. He was a most invaluable officer. A great deal of the superiority of Co. I . . . is due to Lieut. Alley. I shall never cease to think of him with love, to my dying day. I hope after this bloody war is over, I shall live to express to you, personally, what I have been writing in this letter.

I remain, my dear madam,
Yours very respectfully, &c.,
H. L. Abbott
Capt. Co. I

LIEUTENANT JAMES P. SMITH

Staff, Lieutenant General Thomas J. Jackson

After spending a trying day crisscrossing the battlefield with orders and messages, the exhausted Smith hoped for a much needed rest. But while most of the army slept, the haggard officer was kept busy preparing for the morrow. For his final task of that long night he accompanied Jackson to the Yerby house, six miles southeast of Fredericksburg, so that Stonewall could pay a visit to the dying Maxcy Gregg, who wished to make amends for some past criticism of his commander.

General Jackson wished me to go to the front at once and find our four division commanders and communicate to them the wishes of General Lee as to supplying the troops with rations and ammunition before morning. He added his own message to General Early to move his division into the front line along the railroad before the moon rose, about 2 A.M. I had difficulty in finding the generals commanding divisions, A. P. Hill, Early, Taliaferro and D. H. Hill. The night was dark and the troops were sleeping on the ground. Two recollections I have distinctly: one is that of finding General Early by the striking of matches by several couriers, who were trying to make a fire for the general, and his own profane abuse of his staff, who were not with him. The other incident I recall is that, greatly wearied and almost asleep, I allowed my horse to turn not to the rear but to the front of our lines; and I thus rode out on the plain until a Confederate picket halted me and in a low tone told me that if I went two rods farther I should be in the enemy's hands. This woke me up thoroughly and I turned and came back, most thankful that I was not a prisoner, to be carried off to a hard prison life.

It was nearly daybreak when I returned to the headquarters camp, and wrapped myself again in my blankets. But I was not yet asleep, when again an orderly at my tent door said, "Captain, the general wants you." Struggling into my boots once more, I found the general making his toilet, with a tin basin of water and a rough towel.

He said, "I have just had a message from General Gregg, who is nearing his end at the Yerby house, asking that I call to see him as I go to the front this morning. I wish you to ride with me, captain!"

Dressing hurriedly, I got into the saddle and rode with General Jackson to the Yerby house.

There was an affecting interview between Jackson and Gregg, a large man, who was suffering greatly and failing rapidly. Gregg wished to explain and express regret for an endorsement he had written on some paper which he feared was offensive to General Jackson. Jackson did not know to what Gregg referred, and soon interrupted the sufferer to say that it had given him no offense whatever, and then, with Gregg's hand in his, he added, "The doctors tell me that you have not long to live. Let me ask you to dismiss this matter from your mind and turn your thoughts to God and to the world to which you go." Both were much moved. General Gregg with tears said: "I thank you; I thank you very much." Silently we rode away, and as the sun rose, General Jackson was again on the hill near Hamilton's Crossing.

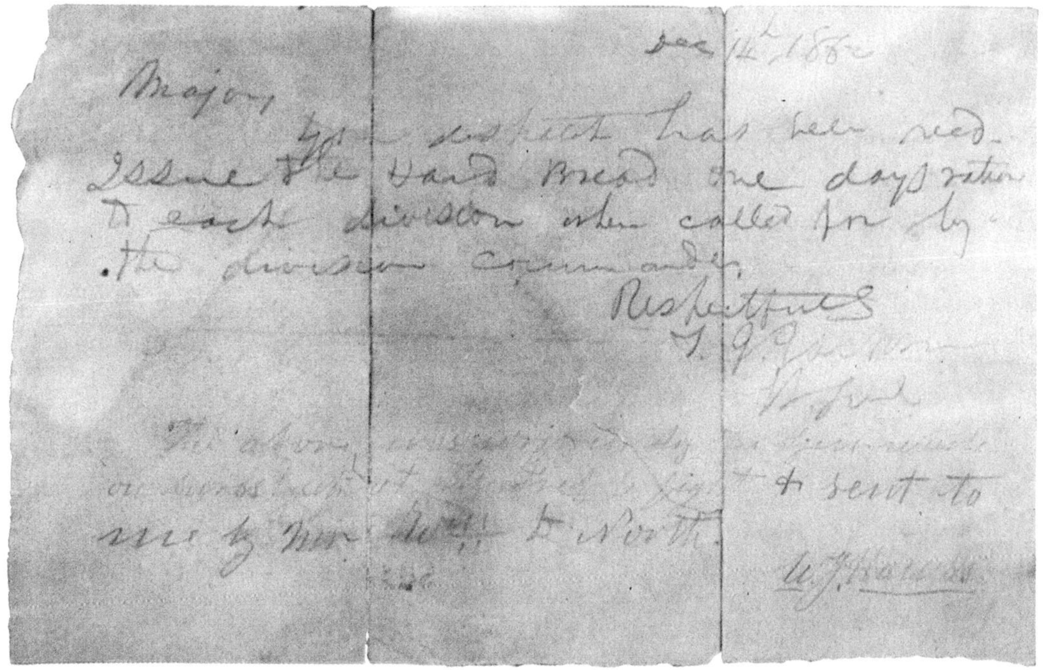

Dec 14th 1862

Major,
Your dispatch has been recd.
Issue the hard bread one days ration to each division when called for by the division commander.

Respectfully
T. J. Jackson

& sent to me by ... North

W. J. Hawks

Standing at arms for more than two days and drained by battle, the Rebel army was in need of replenishment by nightfall on December 13. Shown at left is an order from Jackson, written on horseback early the next morning, for his chief commissary officer, Major Wells J. Hawks, authorizing the distribution of "hard bread," or hardtack, to the four divisions of the Second Corps.

The Tragic Reckoning

On the bitter cold night of December 13, thousands of dead and dying Federal soldiers lay on the bloody slopes leading up to the heights. Beside them lay able-bodied comrades who had been ordered to hold their ground and others too frightened to move lest they draw deadly Rebel fire. As corpses froze, the living stacked them up like logs to form shields against the Rebel bullets and the biting wind.

That night and into the next day, the suffering wounded cried out for help, for water, even for death. Federal stretcher bearers roamed the field, carrying off as many wounded as they could. Scavengers from both sides skulked about, stripping the dead of their uniforms. Other soldiers braved the sporadic gunfire to move among the wounded offering water or whiskey.

A distraught General Burnside spent most of the night of December 13 conferring with his commanders and agonizing over his next move. "It was plain that he felt he had led us to a great disaster," said Darius N. Couch, II Corps commander, "and one knowing him so long and well as myself could see he wished his body was also lying in front of Marye's Heights."

For a time Burnside actually thought of resuming the attack at dawn, intending in his despair to lead the advance in person. But his top commanders rejected further bloodshed, and Burnside relented. There would be no more attacks. The campaign had failed, and the Army of the Potomac would withdraw.

By the night of December 15 the Federals had managed quietly to get their men off the battlefield. And under the cover of a driving rainstorm the forlorn troops evacuated Fredericksburg, crossing the Rappahannock on pontoon bridges that had been covered with dirt and straw to muffle the sound of their march.

The next morning Lee's Confederates awoke and prepared for battle, expecting the Federals to resume their attack. They were amazed to discover that the entire enemy army had melted away.

The news from Fredericksburg was greeted with great jubilation throughout the South. The Richmond *Examiner* proclaimed a "stunning defeat to the invader, a splendid victo-

Defeated at Fredericksburg, the demoralized Federals were forced to endure another winter in the field, a bitter sequel captured here by artist Edwin Forbes in a sketch entitled "Winter camp at Stoneman's Switch, Falmouth, Va.—Jan. 25, 1863."

ry to the defender of the sacred soil." The Charleston *Mercury* trumpeted that "General Lee knows his business and the army has yet known no such word as fail."

When the tidings reached the North, a pall of gloom descended. Burnside and his generals were denounced in the press for the bloody defeat, but President Lincoln bore the brunt of the criticism. The president, exclaimed a Republican senator from Michigan, "is a weak man, too weak for the occasion, and those fool or traitor generals are wasting time and yet more precious blood in indecisive battles and delays."

The president himself was reported to be despondent over the tragedy. After listening to an account of the carnage from an eyewitness, Lincoln said, "If there is a worse place than hell, I am in it."

On December 17 Burnside sent a report of the battle to General in Chief Halleck, blaming the failure of his plan on the tardy arrival of the pontoons. At the same time, he accepted full responsibility for the disaster because he alone, he wrote, had pressed for shifting the Federal offensive to Fredericksburg.

After reading the report, Lincoln framed a response that barely mentioned Burnside. His words were meant to console the soldiers of the Army of the Potomac: "Although you were not successful, the attempt was not an error, nor the failure other than accident," he wrote to the men. "The courage with which you, in an open field, maintained the contest against an entrenched foe, and the consummate skill and success with which you crossed and recrossed the river in the face of the enemy, show that you possess all the qualities of a great army."

Burnside was determined to compensate for the failure by renewing the offensive in the Fredericksburg area. He devised a plan to move his army upriver, then cross and circle southward behind Lee's army. He drew up the details and ordered supplies for the advance. The cavalry, in the lead, moved out as planned on December 30.

That same day, Burnside received a puzzling telegram from the president: "I have good reason for saying that you must not make a general movement of the army without letting me know." Burnside was astonished. He called a halt to the advance and headed to Washington for an explanation.

As it happened, the telegram from Lincoln was the result of scheming by two of Burnside's subordinates—officers in Franklin's grand division—who had taken it upon themselves to pay a visit to the president. The two told Lincoln of Burnside's new offensive, predicting failure and expressing their fears that another catastrophe might destroy the army. Although Lincoln had no taste for intrigue, he was persuaded to send the message restraining Burnside.

When Burnside heard the story, he demanded that the two officers be dismissed from the service—and then offered his own resignation to Lincoln, citing a loss of confidence in him on the part of his grand division commanders. The president asked for some time to ponder the matter, then turned to Halleck for advice about the army's next move.

The general in chief, as usual, declined to commit himself to a specific course of action. Halleck took no stand beyond agreeing with Burnside that the army should make some kind of move against the Rebels before going into winter quarters.

In the end, Lincoln refused to accept Burnside's resignation and halfheartedly endorsed his plan of action—but urged him to be cautious. This response could hardly have reassured Burnside, but he nevertheless resolved to implement his plan to move upriver, cross the Rappahannock, and outflank Lee.

On January 20 Burnside addressed his gathered troops: "The auspicious moment seems to have arrived to strike a great and mortal blow to the rebellion, and to gain that decisive victory which is due to the country." A band played "Yankee Doodle," and the columns marched off.

Burnside's plan might have succeeded had he launched it weeks before, as planned. But winter had set in, and the weather conspired to make a mockery of his venture. On the first night of the march, rain began to fall, and the wind rose. By morning the rain was falling in torrents, and it did not stop for four days.

The Army of the Potomac subsided into the resulting muck. Supply wagons sank to their wheel hubs, and artillery pieces became so mired that neither teams of draft animals nor gangs of men could pull them out. Dozens of horses and mules died of exhaustion.

By the time the storm abated, the army and its animals had no strength left, and there was nothing to do but call off the advance. This offensive—derisively dubbed the Mud March—had ended in yet another ignominious failure.

Burnside's officers, of course, blamed their superior for the debacle, and they became more and more scathing in their criticism. The most vocal of them, General Hooker, told a newspaper reporter that Burnside was incompetent and the administration weak. What the country needed, Hooker asserted, was a dictator.

All this was more than Burnside, finally, could stand, and on January 23 he lashed back, writing a general order for the dismissal of no fewer than eight senior officers—Hooker and Franklin chief among them. He bitterly painted Hooker as "a man unfit to hold an important commission during a crisis like the present, when so much patience, charity, confidence, consideration and patriotism are due from every soldier in the field."

The incensed Burnside hurried to Washington with his document and presented it—and his resignation—to the president, insisting that he accept one or the other. Lincoln concluded that the situation could not be salvaged, and he regretfully prepared the order relieving Burnside of his command.

His replacement would be none other than Joseph Hooker, chosen—despite his demonstrable flaws—for his reputation as a fighter. The disgraced Ambrose Burnside, meanwhile, went home to await reassignment, his unhappy place in history assured as the engineer of the tragedy at Fredericksburg.

FREDERICKSBURG CAMPAIGN CASUALTIES

FEDERAL

Killed	1,284
Wounded	9,600
Captured or Missing	1,769
Total	12,653

CONFEDERATE

Killed	608
Wounded	4,116
Captured or Missing	653
Total	5,377

BRIGADIER GENERAL JOSEPH B. KERSHAW

Brigade Commander, First Corps

As Kershaw's South Carolinians sat in their positions at the base of Marye's Heights, wounded Yankees lay on the ground between the lines unattended—until a lone Rebel Samaritan risked sniper fire to help them. Recalling the incident some 18 years later, Kershaw published the following account in the Charleston News and Courier.

All that day those wounded men rent the air with their groans and their agonizing cries of "Water! water!" In the afternoon the General sat in the north room, up stairs, of Mrs. Stevens' house, in front of the road, surveying the field, when Kirkland came up. With an expression of indignant remonstrance pervading his person, his manner and the tone of his voice, he said, "General! I can't stand this."

"What is the matter, Sergeant?" asked the General.

He replied, "All night and all day I have heard those poor people crying for water, and I can stand it no longer. I come to ask permission to go and give them water."

The General regarded him for a moment with feelings of profound admiration, and said: "Kirkland, don't you know that you would get a bullet through your head the moment you stepped over the wall?"

"Yes, sir," he said, "I know that; but if you will let me, I am willing to try it."

After a pause, the General said, "Kirkland, I ought not to allow you to run a risk, but the sentiment which actuates you is so noble that I will not refuse your request, trusting that God may protect you. You may go."

The Sergeant's eye lighted up with pleasure. He said, "Thank you, sir," and ran rapidly down stairs. The General heard him pause for a moment, and then return, bounding two steps at a time. He thought the Sergeant's heart had failed him. He was mistaken. The Sergeant stopped at the door and said: "General, can I show a white handkerchief?" The General slowly shook his head, saying emphatically, "No, Kirkland, you can't do that." "All right," he said, "I'll take the chances," and ran down with a bright smile on his handsome countenance.

With profound anxiety he was watched as he stepped over the wall on his errand of mercy—Christ-like mercy. Unharmed he reached the nearest sufferer. He knelt beside him, tenderly raised the drooping head, rested it gently upon his own noble breast, and poured the precious life-giving fluid down the fever-scorched throat. This done, he laid him tenderly down, placed his knapsack under his head, straightened out his broken limb, spread his overcoat over him, replaced his empty canteen with a full one, and turned to another sufferer. By this time his purpose was well understood on both sides, and all danger was over. From all parts of the field arose fresh cries of "Water, water; for God's sake, water!" More piteous still the mute appeal of some who could only feebly lift a hand to say, here, too, is life and suffering.

For an hour and a half did this ministering angel pursue his labor of mercy, nor ceased to go and return until he relieved all the wounded on that part of the field. He returned to his post wholly unhurt.

For his selfless efforts to aid the Federals who fell in the Confederate firestorm on December 13, Sergeant Richard Kirkland of the 2d South Carolina was hailed by both sides as the "angel of Marye's Heights." After Gettysburg Kirkland was promoted to lieutenant, but two months later he was mortally wounded in the Battle of Chickamauga. Of the young man formerly in his command, General Kershaw would later write: "He has bequeathed to the world an example which dignifies our common humanity."

PRIVATE BENJAMIN BORTON

24TH NEW JERSEY INFANTRY, KIMBALL'S BRIGADE

Ordered with the rest of the 24th to storm the Confederate position on Marye's Heights on December 13, Borton became separated from his company amid the hellish Rebel fire and twice tried unsuccessfully to rejoin the regiment at the firing line. He was reunited with it the next day and later wrote, "I have never forgiven myself for not proceeding out to the firing line; but had I gone on and faced those flying bullets, to-day I might have been lying at the foot of Willis Hill."

It was a common thing in the army for a soldier to cast aside his blanket, overcoat or knapsack before starting in a charge. Having flung my haversack away in the assault the day before, how was I to carry my rations if I did not procure another?

"Boys," I remarked to my companions, "I guess I will go out on the battlefield and get somebody's haversack; I cannot get along without one."

"Bring me a blanket, won't you, Ben?" called out Isaac Ridgway, who had lost his the same way.

"Yes, Ike, I will," I replied, as I started away.

The tumult of battle had ceased the evening before. Troops were now moving hurriedly about the city, led by excited officers; but the great death-roll was increasing all the time. The hospitals were giving up their dead—which laid in rows in front of those buildings, awaiting burial in the trenches which gangs of men were digging in gardens and vacant lots. As I approached the battlefield by way of Hanover street, which makes an abrupt descent at the edge of the town, I heard the Confederate sharpshooters all the way along the stone wall, up at the heights, firing at every Union soldier that appeared in sight. Not suspecting any immediate danger, I continued my course down the hill until I reached the open field, where I stopped at the ruins of a small brick house, destroyed by shells. Inside the walls a dead soldier laid on a heap of crumbled bricks. To find the coveted haversack, and a blanket for Comrade Ridgway, further search was unnecessary. They were lying all around. Upon the breast of the lifeless body lay a prettily-bound volume of "The Book of Common Prayer."

Covering the ghastly corpse with a cast-off garment, I turned away to gaze over the field where death had not yet ended its appalling feast, for the well-aimed bullets from the sharpshooters now and then whizzed across the plain. On a near-by hill-side, at the right of Hanover street, I counted fifteen Union dead, where a regiment had made a futile attempt to capture a battery. Away off at my left, near the railroad, in one place and another among the dead, a severely-wounded soldier could be seen creeping or limping, in a low, stooping posture, trying to get back into the town. Whether any succeeded in getting away alive, the writer does not know; their progress was so slow I did not watch them long. While surveying different parts of the field, and contemplating the awful realities of war, a ball from a sharpshooter's rifle crashed through a small frame shed which I had just entered, barely missing my limbs. My whereabouts had become known to the enemy, who were bent on driving me from cover, for a fair and open shot. Believing my situation very dangerous, I resolved upon flight back to the city. So catching up my trophies, I sprang out into the road and hurried back up Hanover street on double-quick. The fun was then on the sharpshooters, but they didn't succeed in bringing down their game. Bullet after bullet whizzed past my head and buried in the hill, but by the providence of God I escaped them all.

In 1861 the prestigious New York City jewelry firm Tiffany & Company began to produce war-related objects, including swords, medals, and flags, such as this embroidered green silk camp color, or guidon, of New York's 69th "Irish" Regiment. It was picked up in front of Marye's Heights by Kershaw's men.

In this sketch by Arthur Lumley, Burnside (seated, right) instructs Franklin to withdraw his grand division. Shown in the distance are Federal units and, on the ridge in the far background, the Confederate positions. By the evening of December 15, Burnside had accepted the need to pull his entire army back across the Rappahannock River.

"I could not minister to all who desired it, and often had to turn a deaf ear to the most earnest cries for help."

CHAPLAIN JOHN H. W. STUCKENBERG

145TH PENNSYLVANIA INFANTRY, CALDWELL'S BRIGADE

Although the roar of massed fire had ceased, sniping by both sides denied the soldiers complete peace and safety. Stuckenberg risked his life to try to identify the bodies of men from his regiment. He then plunged into the misery of the field hospitals and became a nurse as well as a minister.

The 14th of Dec was a beautiful day. It was Sunday too, But no day of rest to me. Immediately after breakfast I went on the battle field hoping to identify the bodies of some of our men. It was dangerous, as sharpshooters were picking off all within reach of their guns, so I did not venture very far, but saw enough to shock any feeling being. Bodies were lying about in all directions fearfully mutilated. The wounded were all or nearly all off the field. In a shed on the edge of the battle field I found several wounded whom I had conveyed to hospitals. One afterwards recognized me in a hospital in Washington and was very grateful.

From an elevated position I had a full view of the field. Dead bodies, blankets, overcoats, canteens, arms were scattered about every where. I spied many bodies lying flat on their faces and in rows, which I at first took for dead bodies, but they were our men lying down to avoid being shot. As soon as one arose the rebels fired. One man got up and came toward the city. Instantly a number of guns were fired at him by the rebels—and he fell flat on the ground wounded I supposed; but he jumped up again. As soon as a rebel appeared our men fired at him.

Leaving the field I again went from hospital to hospital, to hunt up our wounded and minister to their wants. In some large hospitals where there were but few nurses, I could not take a step without being called on from all sides to assist some wretched sufferer—some calling for water, for with the wound comes fever, with the fever thirst, some wanting their wounds dressed or moistened to relieve the pain; some desiring to change position, some wishing me to write or speak to their friends. It made my heart ache to see so much suffering, crowded in a small compass, and the means to relieve it so totally inadequate. I could not minister to all who desired it, and often had to turn a deaf ear to the most earnest cries for help. This was the most painful of all. I found many of the wounded of our regiment whom I had not before seen, and who were very glad to see me. I had never had any thing to do before this with the wounded; but I soon learned how to handle them, to move them from place to place, to cut off their shoes and socks, to bandage their wounds and make their position comfortable.

MATILDA HAMILTON

RESIDENT OF FREDERICKSBURG

Forced from their home by intermittent shelling, Hamilton and her family sought refuge on December 14 at Belle Voir, located six and a half miles southeast of Fredericksburg. There Hamilton and her fellow refugees offered comfort to the dying General Gregg. Later, the house was the setting for a reunion of Stonewall Jackson and his family, shortly before the Battle of Chancellorsville.

Sunday, 14th Dec. We never thought of its being Sunday. . . . We were all hurried off this morning to Belvoir, where we were out of range of shells. Forest Hill is almost immediately in their range. Indeed, the gentlemen of the family, the Maryes, say we ought not to come back to Forest Hill, even at night. Jane and myself rode out to Mr. Robt. Stevens about 11 o'clock and took breakfast. Most of

The Swiss-made, gold-cased pocket watch of General Gregg bears the posthumous engraving "The dying gift of Gen. Maxey Gregg to his faithful servent William Rose. Fredricksburg, Va. Decb' 13, 1862." Rose had served Gregg during the Mexican and Seminole Wars and was at his bedside when he died. Every Confederate Memorial Day thereafter, Rose laid a wreath at Gregg's grave in Columbia, South Carolina.

our things were deposited there for safety. I tried to compose my thoughts there and read out the 39th Psalm. The Bible opened at it. "Lord, make me to know my term of days. How frail I am," which is certainly very appropriate to these death-dealing days. We soon returned to Belvoir. The house and yard filled with the dying and wounded. Young Capt. Haskell of South Carolina, aide to General Gregg, fainted at Mr. Yerby's today. It produced great excitement. Mrs. Neale, who fed the wounded, got him a cup of tea. We proffered our refreshments. We had the carriage, which Jane sat in all the time, plentifully provided with provisions and Patsy to cook for us too. Sister Maria went into the parlor to see General Gregg. Mrs. Neale went in once with Ella and did something for him. She said he remarked, " 'Twas pleasant to feel the soft touch of woman." He is a single man who devoted his life to his widowed mother, who has lately died from distress at his exposed situation. . . . We all returned as usual to stay all night at Forest Hill, as we did not like to burden Mr. Yerby, whose house is as full as it can well be.

Monday, 15th Dec. Our friend Rev. Dr. Stuart stays at Forest Hill and helps to take care of the house which has been repeatedly struck by balls or shells. We have friends and foes (Yankee prisoners) to stay there at night. We were hurried off as usual after an uncomfortable breakfast to Belvoir. The first thing we heard when we got to Belvoir was that the gallant Maxey Gregg died this morning at 5 o'clock. At 11 his mortal remains, dressed in his regimentals, and in a coffin, were taken to Richmond on their way back to his home. His faithful servant, William, a free black, went with him and seemed much distressed. He looked very handsome as he lay in his last sleep, the battle of life fought and over.

LIEUTENANT WILLIAM H. MORGAN

11TH VIRGINIA INFANTRY, KEMPER'S BRIGADE

Morgan was a 24-year-old tobacconist from Campbell County, in central Virginia, when he enlisted. Standing six feet two inches tall, he ran more risk than his fellow Rebels of being picked off by a sniper as both sides exchanged potshots for two days after the battle on the 13th. In May 1864 Morgan was taken prisoner when Federal troops overwhelmed his unit at Milford Station, Virginia. Held in several prisons, he was released after taking the Oath of Allegiance in 1865.

At dark the brigade went around the hill to the left and relieved the troops who had been fighting all day. The Eleventh Regiment was placed in a cut in the road on the outskirts of the town, just to the left of the stone wall, remaining here that night, and the next day, sharp-shooting with the Yankees posted in the houses of the town. If a head was raised above the bank for half a minute, "sip" would come a minie ball, the Confederates returning the fire, giving the Yankees tit-for-tat—shot for shot.

It was fun for some of Company C to place a hat or cap on a ramrod, raise it slowly above the bank, and as soon as the Yankee ball whizzed by, rise up and fire at the door or window from whence the puff of smoke came. Some of them would raise a hand above the bank and say, "Look boys, I am going to get a furlough wound," but they would hold it there only a second, lest it be struck sure enough. I saw here one of the men fire upon two Yankees, one on the back of the other, who let his charge drop at the crack of the gun. I have often regretted not preventing this shot. It was a case of one comrade helping a sick or wound-

"Clothing in the Southern Confederacy was just about as scant as our rations; and fig leaves, even if available, did not suit a Virginia climate."

ed friend. Then we looked upon them as deadly enemies, and they were, too; revengeful, vindictive, and cruel.

All that day and the next, the 14th and 15th, the two armies lay still, only engaging in sharp-shooting and picket-firing along some parts of the line. On the night of the 15th, the Yankees, like the Arab, folded their tents and quietly stole away in the night, re-crossing the river on their pontoon bridges, which they drew ashore on the north bank, and again all was quiet along the banks of the Rappahannock; "no sound save the rush of the river." But many a soldier was "off duty forever."

SERGEANT CHARLES C. CUMMINGS

17TH MISSISSIPPI INFANTRY, BARKSDALE'S BRIGADE

Cummings survived Fredericksburg unharmed but lost his right arm on the second day of the fighting at Gettysburg and was left to be nursed by the enemy. Writing of his experiences a half-century later, Cummings, then a judge in Fort Worth, Texas, recalled the grisly aftermath of the Battle of Fredericksburg. Amid the black humor and macabre carryings-on of a burial party, Cummings witnessed an extraordinary expression of loyalty and grief.

The next morning, the 14th, the ground of this slaughter pen was covered in some places with as many as three deep, lying cross and pile, in cerulean hue.

On the morning of the 15th the blue had been transferred from the forms of the dead to those of living Confederates. They had just drawn their winter clothing, the blues, and we were just off our Maryland campaigns—Sharpsburg, South Mountain, and Harper's Ferry—and needed a new outfit of clothing; and if there is anybody at this late day to rise up and say we should not have gotten into the coverings of those who needed them not, all we have to say is that this was the second year of the war, and clothing in the Southern Confederacy was just about as scant as our rations; and fig leaves, even if available, did not suit a Virginia climate, especially at that season of the year, for it was in bleak December.

So what wonder, on the morning of the 15th, that this forty-acre plot which was blue the first morning after the battle should be white the second? They lay so thick on the ground that General Lee sent over a flag of truce to General Burnside, asking him to send over a detail to bury his dead there. A remnant of what was left of the Irish brigade came over with their native farming implement, the spade. They dug a long trench the length of a modern dreadnaught and the width of the height of a man and were as long a time in placing the bodies side by side as it took the gunners to lay them out there.

It was a cold, bleak, dreary winter day, with a fog over the plain from the Rappahannock so dense that we could discern an object only a few feet away from our place of concealment behind the sunken road. Our boys stood by, watching the biggest funeral it had ever been our lot to witness. There was much of the natural man in us, so much that it required restraint not to appear hilarious over our victory. In fact, our orderly sergeant, in whose veins ran a strain of Irish, got jubilant when they brought up a headless corpse to go in the trench, and exclaimed: "There's one with his head shot off." "Yes," replied Pat, one of the funeral cortege, "and he has his clothes shot off." We laughed at Pat's ready repartee and jeered our comrade's bad break. . . .

. . . The saddest mourner in all this long funeral train was a large New Foundland dog who had escaped the shot and shell of battle, and for those two days and nights he had kept faithful vigil by the side of his dead master, an officer. With mournful mien and downcast countenance he followed the corpse to the trench, and when he saw the hostile dirt cover his master's remains in a hostile land he exhibited a human sympathy in his mourning, more so than any there in human shape.

CAPTAIN WILLIAM J. NAGLE

88TH NEW YORK INFANTRY, MEAGHER'S BRIGADE

Nagle survived the brutal pounding suffered by his regiment during their advance on the stone wall in the second wave of the Federal attack. Taking advantage of the lull in the fighting on December 14, Nagle wrote the letter below to his father in Brooklyn. For more than a year afterward, Nagle was plagued by unexplained and persistent fevers and was granted several extended medical leaves to recuperate.

Dear Father—Thank God for his great mercy; I came out of the most terrible battle-day of the war without a scratch. My Brother Edmund is also unhurt. I can hardly realize the fact that I am so blessed. Oh! it was a terrible day. The destruction of life has been fearful, and nothing gained. The battle opened about ten o'clock yesterday morning with a terrific fire of artillery. As we were drawn up in line of battle on the front of the city, Gen. Meagher addressed us in words of inspiration and eloquence I never heard equalled, after which he ordered every one of the brigade to place a bunch of green boxwood at the side of his cap, showing the example himself. Every man appeared fired with determined zeal and a firm resolution, which the result proves to have been carried out in a manner scarcely paralleled in the annals of war. The 88th Regt. this morning numbers ten officers and forty-one men; the 69th, seven officers and fifty-nine men; the 63d, six officers and sixty-four men; the 116th, thirteen officers and fifty-seven men. The 28th Massachusetts also suffered heavily; but I have not the returns. Irish blood and Irish bones cover that terrible field today. . . . The whole-souled enthusiasm with which General McClellan inspired this army is wanting—his great scientific engineering skill is missing—his humane care for the lives of his men is disregarded. We are slaughtered like sheep, and no result but defeat. . . .

Lieutenant O'Brien, of my company, is, I believe, mortally wounded. All I can find of my once fine company of brave men is two Sergeants and three men. That noble, brave man, Major Horgan, was one

UNION FORCES BURYING THEIR DEAD ON THE BATTLEFIELD, IN FRONT OF STONEWALL JACKSON'S BATTERIES, AT FREDERICKSBURG, VA.

In the aftermath of the bloody contest, Federal burial parties under a white flag inter the dead. As troops dig trenches for mass graves beneath a hill held by Jackson's artillery, corpses awaiting their final rest lie in a row, many having been divested of their shoes and uniforms during the night by Confederate scavengers eager to replace their tattered garb with better material. A Virginia soldier writing in his diary recalled that "all the Yank dead had been stripped of every rag of their clothing and looked like hogs that had been cleaned. It was an awful sight."

of the first to fall, shot through the head. Every field officer of the brigade in action was killed or wounded, except Colonel Kelly, and he had a very narrow escape. Lieutenant Granger was struck by a piece of shell, tearing through all his clothes and the flesh over his bowels—one inch closer and he would have been killed. A piece of shell struck my haversack, tearing it off me, and throwing me over. To-day has been comparatively quiet, from a mutual desire on each side to attend to the wounded and bury the dead; but to-morrow morning it will, no doubt, be renewed with increased force and hotter fire on both sides.

I do not know what disposition will be made of us now in our shattered condition. Colonel Kelly is in command of the remnant of the brigade, which does not number half a regiment. We are under arms since six o'clock this morning. I have got cold in my limbs, and have felt very sick all morning; but it is nothing more than the results of exposure and want of regular food, which a couple of day's rest will remedy. . . . —Your affectionate son,

W. J. Nagle

This blanket belonging to the Union army's medical service was used at Mansfield, the Bernard family home situated near the west bank of the Rappahannock. The house, which served as Franklin's headquarters, was used briefly as a hospital.

SERGEANT OSCAR D. ROBINSON

9th New Hampshire Infantry, Nagle's Brigade

Robinson was a student when he joined the service in August 1862. Throughout the war he suffered from bouts of chronic diarrhea and was often away from his unit on medical leave. Here he vividly describes the gruesome procession of Federal wounded at Fredericksburg and recalls the remarkable stoicism of the sufferers.

Witnessed today some of the horrors of war in a new form, or rather in a new light. About sunrise commenced removing the wounded to the Falmouth side My God! Spare us the pain of another such a sight. For eight long hours the streets were crowded with the mutilated victims of Saturday's fighting. Those who have the use of their limbs are hobling along as best they can, many on crutches of their own manufacture (hastily improvised from fence boards or any thing that would serve their purpose) many are leaning for support on those but slightly wounded, and thousands are being borne along on stretchers and in ambulances. The heart sickens at such a sight of suffering. Some are pale and ghastly, and all more or less mangled. Some have lost their legs some their arms, hundreds with wounded heads, one poor fellow seemed to have lost both eyes. In one instance I saw a man but slightly wounded carrying another upon his back. And yet from all these bleeding suffering thousands I have not heard a groan or a complaint. Hundreds are left dead about the hospitals.

"Deliver me from ever being marched into such useless wholesale murder as that was."

MAJOR FRANCIS E. PIERCE

108TH NEW YORK INFANTRY, PALMER'S BRIGADE

Pierce did not mince words when he wrote home expressing disgust and frustration with the leadership of the Union army—sentiments undoubtedly shared in the ranks. In an afterthought, the officer voiced concern about airing his opinions when he added, "Don't have any of this published." Despite his disillusionment, Pierce fought through the war and remained in the Regular Army until his death in 1896.

Monday night Lt. Col. Powers and myself had just lain down together on some boards torn from a fence to keep up out of the mud when an order came to him "Have your men fall in as quickly and quietly as possible. We are going back to our old camp." Not a word was spoken above a whisper—not a single noise was made and in almost no time the men had their blankets on and all other traps and we were starting for this side of the river. . . . You can't tell the feeling of relief that I experienced when we were on this side of the river. For 5 long, long days we were in great danger every moment, had lost 15,000 killed and wounded, were awfully whipped and had not a moments quiet. Lame, sore, sick, tired, frightened and wounded after a horrible march of 4 miles in the dark, frequently sinking in mud over my boots, I reached our old camp, entered the tent, fell down and remained there until morning. I never want to go through another such 5 days. I am willing to go almost anywhere and endure anything but deliver me from ever being marched into such useless wholesale murder as that was. Crossing the river in face of an enemy in superior force, strongly fortified is an experiment that I don't think Burnside will attempt again very soon. I don't dare to express my opinions now—the whole army is disheartened and discouraged and it is certain that by arms the S.C. can *never* be subdued. Their troops are, of course, hopeful and jubilant. It is useless lieing to say that they have not supplies, ammunition and courage.

LIEUTENANT COLONEL E. PORTER ALEXANDER

ARTILLERY BATTALION COMMANDER, FIRST CORPS

Ordered to conserve ammunition lest the fighting resume on December 14, Alexander and his men itched to again pepper the battered Federal army from their line just outside Fredericksburg. When more ammunition arrived on Sunday evening, Alexander's gunners jumped at the chance to fire a few rounds the next day "to make the enemy unhappy." The zeal and anti-Yankee passion of the Rebel soldiers was seemingly shared by the few civilians who had remained in the town.

One amusing incident happened to me as we entered the town. Quite a few citizens of the place, from one cause or another, had remained in the city during the whole period of the battle, taking refuge in cellars when either we or the Federals shelled it. As I went in with the skirmish line, I saw a citizen coming with a musket & bayonet, marching in front of him a Federal soldier. The prisoner was a rather small Dutchman, in bran new uniform & with a most complete & extensive equipment of knapsack, haversack, canteen, overcoat, rubbercloth, tin cup, bags of ground coffee & sugar, & all sorts of little tricks I never saw before. And everything was that neat that it was plain the man was one of the old maid types, with a genius for making himself comfortable. And that was how he came to be a prisoner. His captor gave me the impression, but I don't know how, of being a clerk in a drug store. "Where did you get this man?" said I, as he came near. "He slipped into my cellar last night & went to sleep there. All the rest of the Yankees went across the river during the night & he never knew it. I found him still asleep there this morning & I just took him prisoner & marched him out to give him to you all." "Very good," I said, & turning to the prisoner I asked him, "To what regiment do you belong?" "One hundred forty fort Pensilvany," said he, with a very Dutch accent. Immediately his captor levelled the bayonet on him, & actually yelled, "God damn you! Did not I tell you, if you said that again I'd bayonet you! You damned lying ——" & he was apparently really about to give the fellow a taste of the steel when I stopped him. "Hold on! What's the matter? What are you threatening the man for?" "Why, didn't you hear what he said?" "He only answered my question. I asked his regiment & he was obliged to reply." "But didn't you hear what the son of a bitch said? That he said the *hundred & forty-fourth* Pa.? Don't you see that it's just a dam Yankee trick. That they've just left this fellow here on purpose to tell that lie, & try & demoralize our men by making them think there are 144 regiments in their army from Pa.?" "Pshaw," said I. "They've got over 200 from some states, but it isn't half enough yet to whip this army. So don't stick him but take him along to the line. Our boys would not care if he was in the 500th regiment." So I sent him on & I hope the prisoner made the trip safely, but I never heard more of either of them.

CAPTAIN CHARLES M. BLACKFORD

2D VIRGINIA CAVALRY, F. LEE'S BRIGADE

Blackford, a Lynchburg attorney, was one of four brothers present at Fredericksburg. Positioned on the Rebel extreme right, his unit was not engaged on December 13 but was under cannon fire all day. The next day Blackford, seeking word of his brothers, rode first to Marye's Heights and then to the ruined town, where he visited the house he had lived in as a child. Writing to his wife, Blackford described the battle damage and his efforts to aid the victims of the devastation.

I have been doing all I could for the sufferers in Fredericksburg. I gave one hundred and fifty dollars to relieve some suffering women and children. Besides my subscription the regiment has given about two thousand dollars, which is very liberal for one regiment of poor soldiers. On the 19th, I went into Fredericksburg, and the sight is woeful, but really the damage is not quite as bad as it appears—I mean not as permanent. Every fence is broken down, the doors and windows of the houses broken up and much of the furniture pulled out into the streets and badly used up and scattered. Some twenty-five houses have been burned and almost every house shows the mark of having been struck by some kind of missile, most of them shell or solid shot.

The part of the town known as Sandy Bottom was the scene of the most terrible fighting and every house facing Marye's Hill is covered with bullet marks. Mr. Marye's house, Brompton, which is of brick, is raked by musket balls until it looks as if a hail storm had scoured it. The heaviest carnage of the enemy was upon the street which passes by Rowe's house and in the field in front of the house. On one square the yankees left four hundred and eighty dead bodies, though they had been burying their dead during the two days they occupied the town

Head-Quarters Kemper's Brigade
Jany 31st 1863

Hon. M. Slaughter
Mayor of Fredericksburg
Sir,

Enclosed herewith I have the honor to send you two thousand two hundred and ninety one dollars and fifty cents ($2291.50/100), being a part of the Subscription of this Brigade to the Sufferers of your City.

The Brigade Subscribed as follows:

Head-Quarters	$170.00
1st Va. Regt.	421.00
7th " "	776.00
11th " "	401.50
24th " "	523.00
	$2291.50
3d	505.00
Total for the Brigade	$2796.50

The Subscription of the 3d Va. Regt. has already been handed to the Rev. Mr. August by the Col. of the Regiment.

I have the honor to be Sir
Very Respy
Yr. Obt. Servt
[illegible]

This letter, sent by Kemper's brigade to the mayor of Fredericksburg six weeks after the battle, itemizes charitable contributions made by its various regiments for the relief of the residents of the ravaged town. Combined with funds collected earlier from the 3d Virginia, the money put up by the men of the 1st, 7th, 11th, and 24th Virginia made for a total donation of $2,796.50 to the grateful citizens.

Residents of Fredericksburg return to their shell-shattered home in this painting by Jefferson County, Virginia, native David English Henderson. Some 6,000 residents fled the city for the safety of the countryside. Many, as one cavalry officer reported, preferred "the place to be burnt to the ground rather than it should be surrendered to the yankees." When the townspeople returned, they found that their homes had been devastated by artillery fire and their possessions ransacked and looted by the Federals.

"I do not wonder since seeing our position from the stand-point of Burnside, that his troops and Generals rebelled at having again to 'beard the lion in his den.' "

after the battle. The town was full of dead men when evacuated. It seems very strange to see a deserted town, with nothing but corpses of dead men and horses for inhabitants.

Our house was only struck by one cannon ball, and that was a solid shot fired by one of our batteries. It did not go through but buried itself in the brick, but fell out and was lying on the ground just below. A fragment of a shell broke a window blind. A shell struck a house in the yard known as "Uncle John's Study," went through the wall, knocking a number of books on the floor, then went through the front door, struck the pavement, ricochetted, tore down our front fence, and then exploded as it struck the top of Mr. Caldwell's on the other side of the street, tearing it to pieces very much.

Our house was used as an operating hospital and many yankees were buried in the back yard, one just at the foot of the back steps. In the dining room the large table was used as an operating table and a small table by its side had a pile of legs and arms upon it. I poured them out into the back yard and managed to get the table out to camp and will send it home in a few days. I also got a large Church of England prayer-book printed in 1745 which had belonged to my grandfather, General Minor. I further found an empty box and packed up a number of old law books which had belonged to my grandfather, and had them put aside to be sent home. The yankees had been up in the cuddy of the house and taken out barrels of old letters which were scattered all over the yard. Among them I found a letter from Light Horse Harry Lee to my grandfather. The whole house was covered with mud and blood and it was hard to realize it was the dear old house of my childhood.

LIEUTENANT R. CHANNING PRICE

STAFF, MAJOR GENERAL J. E. B. STUART

Price began his service with a brief stint in the 3d Company of the Richmond Howitzers. In August 1862 he joined the staff of his cousin, cavalry commander Stuart. On May 1, 1863, during an artillery duel at Chancellorsville, Price was mortally wounded by a shell fragment that struck him behind the knee, severing an artery.

I rode into Town . . . looking over our positions & other objects of interest to me, as it was the first time I had visited Fredericksburg, having neglected to do so before the fight. Quite a large working-party was over under Flag of Truce & had nearly completed the task of burying their dead. From Town Dr E. and I rode to the Crossing, thus passing over nearly our whole front, and I do not wonder since seeing our position from the stand-point of Burnside, that his troops and Generals rebelled at having again to "beard the lion in his den." The Town is a perfect wreck of what it was I suppose, houses burnt & battered fences & boarding of every description torn down and laid in the streets, and on this the wretches laid the bedding stolen out of the houses and slept during their occupancy of the place. Add to all these horrors that in numbers (a hundred I suppose) of the once tastily laid off gardens and yards of Fredericksburg, the bodies of these scoundrels have been laid for their last sleep. But it is worse than useless to talk of it and as an article I glanced at in one of the Richmond papers expressed it, if we desire a bloody revenge, we have gotten it, as I do not think we have yet begun to realize the amount of damage we have inflicted on Burnside's Army.

"Gastly were the numbers of amputated limbs found in great numbers in several places of the town."

In this Arthur Lumley sketch, Confederate and Union officers share a toast after signing the terms for parole and exchange of prisoners on December 19. The agreement provided for the return of bodies, thus enabling the widow of Rebel captain Edward P. Lawton to accompany his remains from an Alexandria, Virginia, hospital and cross over the Rappahannock at Fredericksburg, escorted by a Federal guard of honor. Lee wrote a letter of condolence to the Lawton family on January 8.

EDWARD I. HEINICHEN

Resident of Fredericksburg

Heinichen owned a mercantile business in Fredericksburg when war broke out. Awarded a commission by the governor, he raised a company of volunteers, only to lose all but one when an exemption for farmers was declared. In April 1862 the Heinichens moved to Columbia, South Carolina, but returned to Virginia after the Rebel victory at Second Manassas. Heinichen recorded what he saw after the Yankees recrossed the Rappahannock and Fredericksburg's residents returned.

We now had ample time, not only to view the battle-field, but also could enter our beloved F— with perfect safety. Here we found numbers of Union soldiers hidden away in cellars & other out of the way places with their arms & accoutrements, who requested us, to take them prisoners. Gastly were the numbers of amputated limbs found in great numbers in several places of the town. We now had leisure to examine the damage done by the shelling & during the presence of the Union army. A number of houses were burned down, many more made untenable by shot & shell, hardly one having escaped entirely. The few stores that did business were despoiled of their contents. . . . Private houses, pianos were smashed, pictures wantonly ruined, clocks broken, books torn. But for all this loss the losers considered themselves amply repaid, when they viewed the thousands of the enemy's corpses upon the battle field. It is generally concluded that the fiercest attacks were made upon Marye's Hill, & here some of the Federal dead did lie within a few yards of the famous Stonewall. The prisoners were at once set to work to bury the dead, which in many instances was done so superficially, that parts of them after a short time showed above ground, & dogs brought home many a limb. Some corpses were entirely overlooked, & I recollect, to have seen two of them untouched as late as the following April.

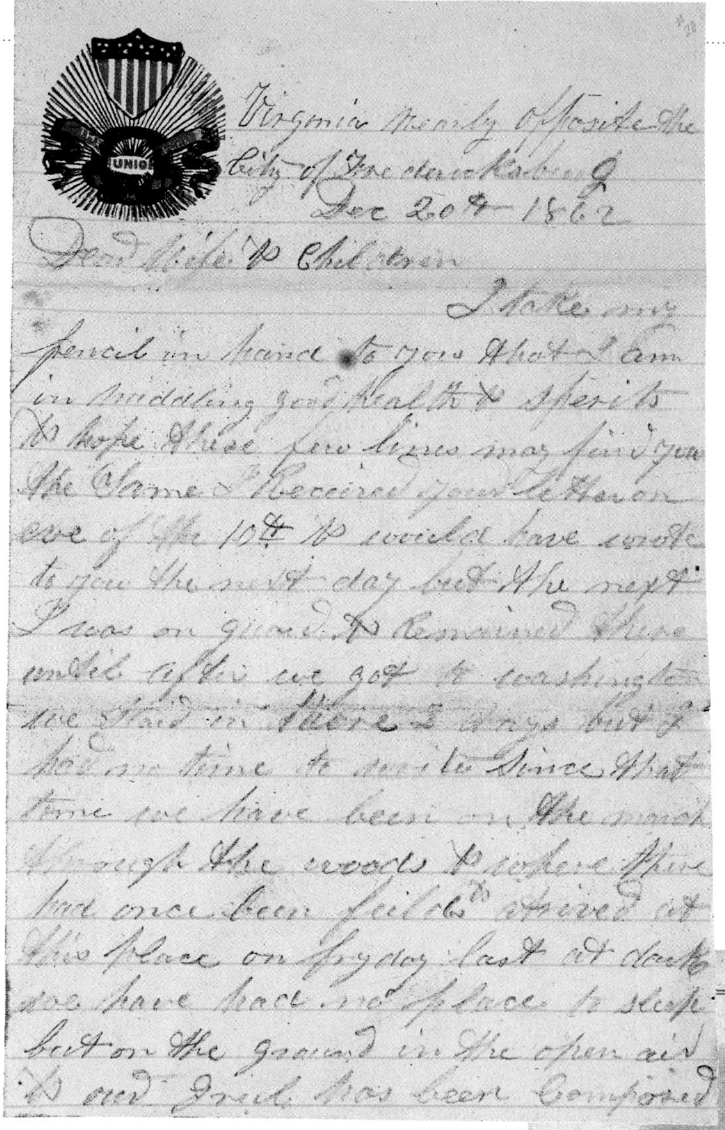

Virginia nearly Opposite the city of Fredericksburg
Dec 20th 1862

Dear Wife & Children

I take my pencil in hand to you that I am in middling good health & spirits & hope these few lines may find you the same I Received your letter on eve of the 10th & would have wrote to you the next day but the next I was on guard & Remained there until after we got to washington we staid in there 2 days but I had no time to write since that time we have been on the march through the woods & where there had once been fields arrived at this place on fryday last at dark we have had no place to sleep but on the ground in the open air & our grub has been Composed

PRIVATE COSTON ROHRER

62d Pennsylvania Infantry, Sweitzer's Brigade

Rohrer saw action late on December 13 in one of the last assaults on the stone wall. Four days after the battle, as the troops awaited orders and Rohrer contemplated the merits of the Federal army's leadership, Burnside filed a report to General in Chief Halleck, accepting blame for the fiasco at Fredericksburg. In this letter, dated December 17, Rohrer's musings may have had an element of prescience: Six weeks later Burnside relinquished command of the Army of the Potomac.

We are here once more in our old camp and probably will remain some time. What will the people say now about going ahead at full speed? McClellan would have dug before the fight, while Burny digs after a fight, but 't is graves for his men and then runs off before he can bury them. Our loss in this affair is not less than 1,500 killed and 5,500 wounded. The loss of our regiment is 96 in killed and wounded. In our company two were killed and five wounded. None of our officers got a scratch and out of 570 guns carried in the regiment I don't think over 420 went into the fight. We draw rations for 67 men

FRANK LESLIE'S ILLUSTRATED NEWSPAPER. [Jan. 10, 1862.

CONVEYING THE UNION SOLDIERS WOUNDED AT THE BATTLE OF FREDERICKSBURG ON BOARD THE GOVERNMENT STEAMER AT AQUIA CREEK, ON THEIR WAY TO THE HOSPITALS AT WASHINGTON. SKETCHED BY OUR SPECIAL ARTIST, HENRI LOVIE.

In the engraving at right, made from a sketch by artist Henri Lovie, Union troops help comrades wounded at Fredericksburg onto a government steamer bound for Washington, D.C. One soldier who helped transfer the wounded was Private David V. M. Smith of the 12th New Jersey Infantry. In a letter (above) to his wife, Elizabeth, Smith recalled the onerous duty: "We loaded 4 large steamers with wounded. They say there was 5000 of them. It took us nearly all night. It was the most heart sickening job I ever undertook so much so that I will not try to Discribe it at present."

"I have often read of sacked and pillaged towns in ancient history, but never, till I saw Fredericksburg, did I fully realize what one was."

PRIVATE TALIAFERRO N. SIMPSON

3D SOUTH CAROLINA INFANTRY, KERSHAW'S BRIGADE

In the letter below, Simpson longs for happier times and the war's end. The son of a South Carolina congressman, Simpson fought in all the major engagements in the eastern theater before being sent west. There he was killed at the foot of Snodgrass Hill during the Battle of Chickamauga.

and I have counted 27 men that were in the fight not counting the officers nor the men killed and wounded. That was the way with every regiment in the fight. The rebs probably lost 1,000 men in killed and wounded. I suppose the north will be satisfied now with the removal of McClellan, but I believe, and so do all the rest of the army, that had he had command of the army the thing would have ended far differently, but they will crowd ahead every man that takes command and will not give him time to work as the work ought to be done.

Give my respects to the folks and tell them that I am all right yet. I could write more but I have not time now. I suppose we will have a new commander now. I only wish McClellan was back. I hardly feel safe under Burny. He will have to cut off his Presbyterian whiskers and raise a moustache before he can take that hill with the Army of the Potomac. . . . Lee gave Burny three hours to withdraw his army from the town. Burny's answer was, "I am not going to leave this town, but I want five hours to get away my sick and wounded." This was at one o'clock on Monday. The next morning at the break of day the army was across this side of the river under the flag of truce like the rebs at Antietam. Has Burnside saved us?

Camp near Fred'burg
Dec 25th 1862
My dear Sister

This is Christmas Day. The sun shines feebly through a thin cloud, the air is mild and pleasant, a gentle breeze is making music through the leaves of the lofty pines that stand near our bivouac. All is quiet and still, and that very stillness recalls some sad and painful thoughts.

This day, one year ago, how many thousand families, gay and joyous, celebrating Merry Christmas, drinking health to the absent members of their family, and sending upon the wings of love and affection long, deep, and sincere wishes for their safe return to the loving ones at home, but today are clad in the deepest mourning in memory to some lost and loved member of their circle. If all the dead (those killed since the war began) could be heaped in one pile and all the wounded be gathered together in one group, the pale faces of the dead and the groans of the wounded would send such a thrill of horror through the hearts of the originators of this war that their very souls would rack with such pain that they would prefer being dead and in torment than to stand before God with such terrible crimes blackening their characters. Add to this the cries and wailings of the mourners—mothers and fathers weeping for their sons, sisters for their brothers, wives for their husbands, and daughters for their fathers—how deep would be the convictions of their consciences.

Yet they do not seem to think of the affliction and distress they are scattering broadcast over the land. When will this war end? Will another Christmas roll around and find us all wintering in camp? Oh! that peace may soon be restored to our young but dearly beloved country and that we may all meet again in happiness.

But enough of these sad thoughts. We went on picket in town a few days ago. The pickets of both armies occupy the same positions now as they did before the battle. Our regt was quartered in the market place while the others occupied stores and private houses. I have often read of sacked and pillaged towns in ancient history, but never, till I saw Fredericksburg, did I fully realize what one was. The houses, especially those on the river, are riddled with shell and ball. The stores have been broken open and deprived of every thing that was worth a shilling. Account books and notes and letters and papers both private and public were taken from their proper places and scattered over the streets and trampled under feet. Private property was ruined. Their soldiers would sleep in the mansions of the wealthy and use the articles and food in the house at their pleasure. Several houses were destroyed by fire. Such a wreck and ruin I never wish to see again.

JOSEPH HENRY LUMPKIN

Chief Justice, Georgia Supreme Court

When General Thomas R. R. Cobb was killed in action at Fredericksburg, it fell to Lumpkin, his father-in-law, to inform the family of the circumstances of the soldier's death and burial. Writing to his daughter, Callie, Lumpkin, a former law school professor, described Cobb's last hours and funeral. Cobb was survived by his wife, Marion (another Lumpkin daughter), and three children.

Athens Decr 30, 1862

Dearest I wrote you last night that my letter might go off by mail this morning—They are only a few hurried lines—I wish to give you the particulars of Mr. Cobb's death. After the repulse of the enemy the third time a random cannon shot was fired at the House behind which he was standing at the time. It was a conical ball fired by a fuse. It entered the House at the Fredericksburg side penetrated both rooms & exploded just as it came out of the building on the side where he was standing, killing Gen'l Cook of N.C. and wounding several others—It just grazed—that is a piece of the shell—the right thigh and struck the left where it lodged, breaking the bone & lacerating the femoral artery. This was about two o'clock. Mr. Cobb raised himself on his right elbow—asked tranquilly for a tourniquet—the instrument used for binding a limb to prevent the effusion of blood—none was at hand but a handkerchief was substituted. He was carried off on a litter . . . which crossed over the Hills just in the rear of the House, till they met an ambulance to which he was transferred & borne to the Hospital in the rear of the Hills. He expired a little after two—The Rev. Mr. Porter, his chaplain supported his head in his arms. He spoke not a word of his family nor did he seem conscious that death was so near—For about a quarter of an hour before he died he became speechless . . . but Eddy thinks he was conscious for he says he looked steadfastly at him and pressed his hand three times. Mr. Porter who accompanied his body home thinks he died from the summary effect of the blow upon his nervous system. But from all I can learn and the appearance of his corpse, I think he bled to death. He died on Saturday & arrived here Thursday afternoon & was buried Friday and his body exhibited no signs of mortification or decay. It seemed to be entirely exhausted of blood. It was brought in a box to Richmond & then put in a metallic case & had not bled a drop from the time it was washed at Fredericksburg. . . . When it reached the Depot and we were assured by Dr. White who had come across & met the party at the Point—that it could be taken to the house and remain one night with the family—you can't imagine what a relief it was to us all & to Marion—such a scene I never witnessed. Thursday afternoon and Friday every store was closed in Athens and every man, woman, and child met to witness the arrival and burial of the Town favorite. The body was exposed to view in the church which was hung in mourning—and everybody permitted to take a last look at his familiar and beloved face. There was not a tearless person present. Dr. Hoyt preached a capitol & most appropriate sermon Mr. Porter followed with a most feeling and appropriate address & the Methodist minister, Mr. Scott closed the meeting. Letters of condolence pour in from everybody. . . . Ladies wrote poetry and the press in Richmond & Georgia seemed to vie with each other in their eulogies. Still all this Callie does not & cannot reconcile poor Marion & her dear children to their irreperable loss. A kind of apathy seems to pervade Marion. She cares not for the world nor the things of the world. And God does not see fit to reveal to her now His mysterious Providence.

PRIVATE WILLIAM A. ALLISON

61st Pennsylvania Infantry, Cochrane's Brigade

Some weeks after the Federal debacle at Fredericksburg, Allison, a student before enlisting in May 1862, recorded this opinion of the decline in morale of the Union army. Just three days earlier, on January 1, 1863, the Emancipation Proclamation had gone into effect. As Allison saw it, the fighting man in the field viewed this act of moral rectitude with battle-weary cynicism. Taken prisoner at the Battle of the Wilderness in 1864, Allison was paroled in February 1865.

Friend Stock,

I will take advantage of a pleasant day and a little leisure time to answer your welcome letter. Since the battle of the Rappahannock we have remained in camp reconciling our exhausted energies after a wearisome and fruitless campaign. The campaign I said had been a fruitless one, but I will take that back. It has been productive of much evil to the Union Army. While in Maryland their ardor had been cooled and their confidence in their generals gradually diminished by mismanagement, but the Virginia campaign has rendered them indifferent and has caused them utterly to distrust any one with a star on his shoulder. This may be a dark picture but it is a true one. I have heard troops, from every loyal state in the Union (with one or two exceptions), give their opinion on this subject and it is the same old song "The war is played out." Desertions are frequent. In our Regiment alone 21 deserted in a

In this sketch by Alfred R. Waud, made on New Year's Day 1863, a Federal wagon train makes its way into camp near Falmouth. As supplies arrived from Washington, the battered Army of the Potomac, still numbering about 100,000, settled into winter camp north of the Rappahannock, spreading out to points north and northeast of Fredericksburg. Eager to erase the memory of the recent trouncing, Burnside had begun an advance on Lee's forces two days earlier, only to be halted in his tracks by word from the president. As Burnside hurried to Washington to sort out machinations of near-Machiavellian proportions, the army looked forward to a rest, ignorant of the additional indignities and suffering it would experience in the weeks to come.

single day. The men are heartsick and tired of a struggle that they deem worse than useless. I have heard around the campfire opinions that we have consigned a citizen to a dungeon within Fort LaFayette. Yet these very men will fight to the death if led on to battle. They fight because they are soldiers, not because they think they can gain anything by it. I tell you this that you may know the truth, because I see so many lies on this subject in the newspapers. We are waiting patiently for something to be determined upon and for the cabinet to settle its little troubles.

The President's proclamation is not very favorably received by the army, it is looked upon by the majority as a party scheme rather than a war measure. The weather has been changeable since we have stopped here, some very pleasant and some bitterly cold but, thank Heavens, we have had very little rain. If there is anything the soldier dreads, it is wet weather and it always helps to fill the Regimental hospitals. The boys did not have their ingenuity at home when they enlisted. In the camp one can see a thousand contrivances to increase comfort. Some build log houses with fireplaces, others log their tents up, etc. . . . The army is very healthy now, there are very few cases of sickness among the men. Several of my Philadelphia friends were wounded in the last blunder, among them Corporal Gordon of Gregory's regiment. How is fun this winter? I should like to have one good evening's sport at your house as of older time. Remember me to your sisters and tell them I will answer their letters as soon as I get any time. Remember me to your father's family—to all our acquaintances.

Please write soon and often.

I am

Your friend,

Wm. A. Allison

LIEUTENANT WILLIAM R. WILLIAMS

82D PENNSYLVANIA INFANTRY, COCHRANE'S BRIGADE

Williams took up arms in fall 1861, saw duty as a recruiter the following summer, and was promoted to lieutenant days before Fredericksburg. The Philadelphia native believed that notwithstanding poor leadership, the Union soldier had nothing to be ashamed of. The letter below underscores his refusal to accept defeat, as well as his unbridled optimism—an uncommon view in the Army of the Potomac, and among Northerners generally, during the winter of 1862–1863.

This talk about McClellan not losing the battle if he had been in command is all bosh. The men never have nor cannot fight better than they did under Burnside. If those men who think and talk so much of McClellan will only recruit an army for him, maybe we could get along better. They had better enlist under McClellan and fight for their country and their little god than stay in their comfortable homes and talk of army movements of which they know no more of than does a mule of astronimy.

Tell father that their is really no reason for being discouraged at our last repulse. We were not defeated but only repulsed. We crossed the river and gave the enemy battle and found their works too strong for us to take. We remained there two days waiting for the enemy to come out of their intrenchments and give us battle which they would not do. We recrossed the river in splendid order without the least panic or demoralization and did not lose a single peice of artillery and have been here in sight of the rebel camps ever since, and they dare not come out and fight us. We will soon be on the move again and test rebel courage at some other point. I am just as sure of success now as I was when I first enlisted.

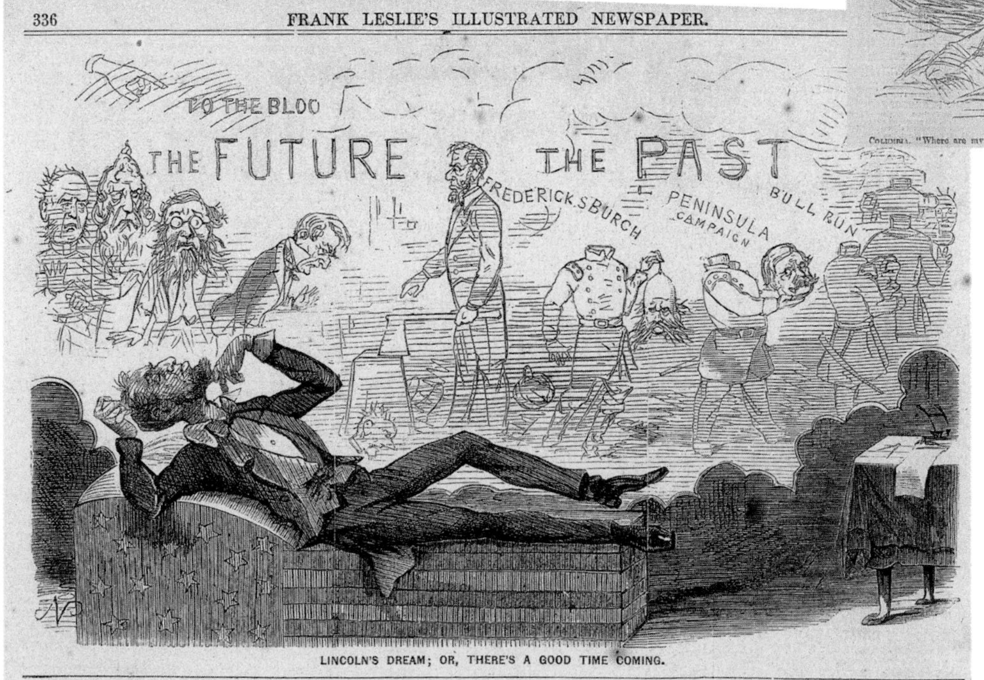

Cartoons published in early 1863 attest to Northern frustration following Burnside's defeat at Fredericksburg. Above, the national symbol, Columbia, denounces President Lincoln, General in Chief Henry Halleck, and Secretary of War Edwin Stanton. The caption alludes to Lincoln's bent for anecdotes, suggesting he return to Illinois to tell his jokes. The cartoon at left depicts a supposed fantasy of the president's in which he deals with his problem of finding effective leadership, both civilian and military, for the conduct of the war.

NEW YORK TABLET

On January 16, 1863, a high requiem mass was celebrated at St. Patrick's Cathedral in New York City to honor the men of the Irish Brigade who had died in the war. Following the mass an announcement was made in the name of the 69th New York's chaplain about the creation of a relief fund to benefit the families of the fallen. A week later, in its January 24 issue, the New York Tablet published an account of the moving tribute, noting, "The last solemn rites were performed and the vast multitude seemed deeply impressed with the solemnity of the celebration."

During the service, the scene in the Cathedral was most imposing; the solemn grandeur of the venerable edifice—a perfect gem of the florid Gothic style so consonant to the majesty of the Catholic worship, the mournful catafalque before the altar, representing the dead soldiers of the Irish Brigade; the rich uniforms of the officers present; and the motionless forms of the Marines who lined the aisle on either side of the catafalque; these, with the crowd of sorrowing relatives and sympathizing friends, who filled all the available space in the nave and in the aisles, formed altogether a solemn and impressive sight. Here and there might be seen living members of the Brigade, still suffering from the effects of their wounds, and distinguished from the other soldiers present by a sprig of evergreen in their hats. These formed not the least affecting feature in the scene.

As the long swell of the organ filled the Church, and the voice of prayer and praise resounded through the sacred edifice, and the funeral tapers floated torch-like over the catafalque, then memory was busy, and hearts were full, and eyes were dimmed with tears.

"And is this," we asked ourselves, "all that remains of the thousands of brave men who fell under the banners of the Irish Brigade on the bloody plains of Maryland and Virginia?—who marched so gaily through our city a few months ago? Is yonder mournful memento all that we shall ever see of them who so well sustained Ireland's honor—America's right on so many a battlefield?" As the sad response rose up from the hearts' depths we thought of the high hopes and the brave light hearts that buoyed the soldiers of the Brigade all through their perilous career—ending all in death and that mournful show. It was sad to think that of the thousands there commemorated, not even one was present in their mortal remains—all, all mouldering in Southern clay far from home and kindred. A few—a very few of the officers have been recovered from the battlefields of the South and laid in consecrated earth, but all the rank and file of the Brigade sleep where they fell, their graves scarcely distinguishable from the desert waste around.

And yet there was something grand, as well as affecting in the thought "we mourn them to-day who fell at Fair Oaks, at Gaines' Mill, at White Oak Swamp, Turkey Bend and Malvern Hill—we mourn the heroes of Antietam, the slaughtered dead of Fredericksburg, no less brave and heroic than those who fell in the arms of victory—on these bloody fields they lie, far apart, though in death united, but here their memory is cherished—here we honor them all." . . . And have we not reason to be proud of these dead Irish soldiers who fell fighting for two glorious principles—the eternal principle of union and the no less exalted principle of gratitude? Have they not paid with their lives the debt of gratitude the Irish people owe to this great Republic? Have they not vindicated the undying fidelity of the Irish race—the gratitude that warms, or ought to warm, Irish hearts? . . . They loved their adopted country even unto death—they fought, and bled, and died to save her from disruption. . . . "Our noble little Brigade" has almost disappeared.

On the morning of December 13 Colonel Robert Nugent of the 69th New York had little suspected the slaughter in store for the Irish Brigade. As the men awaited orders, Nugent had joked with Colonel Edward Cross of the 5th New Hampshire that the first of them to get to Richmond would order dinner for two. Nugent fell severely wounded on Marye's Heights, which he recalled as a "living hell from which escape seemed scarcely possible." He was later brevetted for his performance at both Gaines' Mill and Petersburg.

308 FRANK LESLIE'S ILLUSTRATED NEWSPAPER. [FEB. 7, 1863.

GRAND REQUIEM MASS IN ST. PATRICK'S CATHEDRAL, NEW YORK, FRIDAY, JANUARY 16, FOR THE REPOSE OF THE SOULS OF THE OFFICERS AND MEN OF THE IRISH BRIGADE KILLED IN THE WAR.—SEE PAGE 305.

This engraving depicts New York City's St. Patrick's Cathedral during the high requiem mass held for the dead of the Irish Brigade. Symbolizing the remains of the Irishmen who had given their lives at Gaines' Mill, Malvern Hill, Antietam, and Fredericksburg, a catafalque adorned by a cross-emblazoned velvet cloth stands in the middle aisle, flanked by funeral tapers and an honor guard drawn from the marines serving aboard the USS North Carolina. Musicians from the ship accompanied the organ, filling the church with the strains of a dirge, and the choir sang the Dies Irae from Mozart's Requiem. The mass, celebrated jointly by the brigade's chaplain and the clergymen of the cathedral, was attended by brigade commander Meagher and the surviving members of the brigade, among whom were Colonel Robert Nugent and Captain John Donovan of the 69th New York.

SERGEANT J. FRANKLIN MANCHA

122D PENNSYLVANIA INFANTRY, PRATT'S BRIGADE

Enlisting in August 1862, Mancha kept an almost daily chronicle of his activities througout his nine-month term of service, written down in several small, leather-bound volumes. Below is Mancha's almost comical account of the notorious "Mud March," which was initiated by Burnside but endured by the Army of the Potomac.

"I have walked through mud before but never such as this."

Wednesday, Jan. 21st.

We were aroused long before day & instructed to be ready to move in one hour. In less than half an hour we had orders to strike tents & very soon the long roll summoned the men to *fall* in. It was still raining as it had been during all the night. We started on the march but the officers soon found it next to impossible to keep the Reg. in good order, they were soon all mixed up so that we could not distinguish one Co. from the other. In the start each one tried to keep the mud & water out of his shoes & sometimes it got too deep so those who had shoes on, in trying to cross the place, (generally low places) without filling his shoes, detained others, and thus threw all into confusion. This lasted only a short distance, however. After we got on the way traveled by other troops ahead of us, we found we were only getting into mud, so those who had no boots nor leggins found their efforts nothing more than wasting strength so they grew perfectly reckless and waded on with a hundred weight of mud to their pant legs, both in & outside mud to the knees & shoes *full.* Now came the tug of war with those who were favored with boots & leggins, particularly with those whose bootlegs were lower than the knees, for the struggle to keep mud & water out of them was not a very insignificant one. I have walked through mud before but never such as this. It was worse than the march from Harpers Ferry. At some places the mud was so thin that one was uncertain was it mud or water. Some places it reminded one of shoemaker's wax, all but the color. It was so tough that it was a matter of considerable difficulty to draw out the foot without leaving the boot stick. This was a work, or rather, a getting along under difficulties with two woolen blankets, one gum blanket & two shelter tents with a gallon of water in from the rain & besides all this load, 60 rounds of cartridges, musket, sword, accoutrements & a store of other trash, such as wearing apparel, "stationary" (Book & paper depot) & hard tack. It rained all day.

Refrain of Burnside's
Mud March Jan. 1863

Now. I Lay me down to Sleep
In Mud & water Six feet deep
If Im not here when you awake
Look for me with an Oyster Rake
John. O'Connell Co I 2 Me Vols
1st Brigade 1st Division
5. A. C.

Another soldier who suffered through Burnside's "Mud March" was Private John O'Connell of the 2d Maine, a veteran who claimed to have fought from First Bull Run until Lee's surrender at Appomattox. After mustering out of the 2d Maine in 1863, O'Connell served in two other Maine regiments—the 20th and the 11th—the latter until February 1866. In this parody of the well-known child's bedtime prayer, O'Connell asks to be rescued with the use of a tool familiar to shellfish harvesters.

In this Alfred Waud sketch, troops of the Army of the Potomac struggle through rain and mud in a vain attempt to reach a crossing on the Rappahannock. Giving in to pressure from the Northern press and to his own desire for redemption following Fredericksburg, Burnside launched a poorly conceived drive on January 20 that he hoped would trump the Rebels. But the Union effort was a short-lived farce, foiled by an unrelenting winter storm that left roads impassable. "I don't know how the world's surface looked after the flood in Noah's time," wrote an officer, "but I am certain it could not have appeared more saturated than does the present surface of the Old Dominion." Burnside's Mud March—as the event would thereafter be called—sealed his fate: Days later, he was relieved of command.

CORPORAL DAYTON E. FLINT

15TH NEW JERSEY INFANTRY, TORBERT'S BRIGADE

Born in New Hampshire and plying the tinsmith's trade in Michigan, Flint chose a New Jersey regiment when he enlisted in August 1862. He found the hellish march through mud too much to endure, and in this January 27 letter to his father, Flint bitterly described the ordeal. Later cited for bravery at Petersburg, Flint ended the war as a captain.

You have probably heard by this time of this last strategic movement. We returned yesterday to our encampment where we have been laying ever since the brush at Fredericksburg. Such roads and marching no one has ever seen who has not followed an army in Virginia. The day we started the weather was cold, the ground frozen hard, and the roads smooth. We moved at noon and marched near to the intended crossing place, about seven miles, and encamped, waiting for the pontoon and supply train to come up, which were behind. About dark it commenced raining, and rained steady all night. As if by magic there was a sudden transformation in the surface of Virginia. The mud was knee deep, the wagons were up to their bodies in it, and were as immoveable as if they were frozen fast. Then came a destruction of horse flesh. Thousands of horses and mules dropped down dead in their harness. To give you an idea of it, within a distance of one mile from the river on one road alone there were 52 dead horses and mules. Our way back to camp was plainly marked by their bodies. In one place I counted ten horses but twenty yards apart. I think it was the hardest march we have had. We started about half past one and got in camp before dark. I believe that on that day two-thirds of the prominent officers were drunk. The day before they kept us on the move all day, within a circle of a mile, mud over our boot tops, for the purpose of helping the trains out. Horses were of no use. Seventy-five or one hundred men had hold of each pontoon wagon to get them out of the worst places.

I have said that I would not write home of the true state of affairs in the army should they prove to be different from what I imagined them

Union soldiers mill around the smoldering ruins of the Phillips house after hauling out what contents they could save. Used by Burnside as his headquarters during and after the Battle of Fredericksburg, the house was accidentally set ablaze by troops cooking a meal in the attic in February 1863. The soldiers were unable to save the building. "Not a bucket of water could be had to quench the fire," mourned Burnside's provost marshal, General Marsena R. Patrick. "Wells all dry."

before coming, but this last hair has broken the camel's back, and I must give vent to my thoughts, or rather, those of a majority of the army, officers included. . . .

The Army of the Potomac is no more an army. Its patriotism has oozed out through the pores opened by the imbecility of its leaders, and the fatigues and disappointments of a fruitless winter campaign. Its faith in the ability of the command is gone and the confidence in the government is even being weakened. They believe that this question will never be settled by fighting, that every life lost either in battle or by disease is only an additional and useless sacrifice to the shrine of the disappointed ambition and avarice of a few politicians. In a word, the Army of the Potomac is demoralized. They will never do the fighting they have done. It is only a sense of honor and self-respect and an adherence to their oath to support and obey those over them that keep them from deserting enmasse. If our other armies are in the same condition as this, there is no hope of a successful prosecution of the war.

After the battle, Private Marquis L. Beam of the 38th North Carolina faced a more terrible duty than that of enduring the harsh conditions in camp. On February 23, 1863, Beam and some mates were formed into a firing squad to execute deserters from their home state who, as another North Carolinian put it, "got satisfied that fighting was not a very pleasant thing & . . . thought they would not stay."

COLONEL ZENAS R. BLISS

7th Rhode Island Infantry, Nagle's Brigade

On December 31, 1862, Bliss assumed temporary command of his brigade, relinquishing it three weeks later to Simon G. Griffin. Reassigned to an administrative post at army headquarters, Bliss encountered Burnside and later recalled the bitterness with which the discredited commander took the news of his replacement by Hooker, and the unusual way in which he marked the event.

One day while in camp, I received an order detailing me as President of a Court Martial to meet at Army Headquarters, and I went up there. It was early in the morning, perhaps nine o'clock when I approached General Burnside's tent, which stood at the head of a little street, formed of the tents of his staff officers. As I went towards his tent, I saw the General in his shirt sleeves standing in the door of his tent, with a tumbler and a bottle of champagne in his hands. He called me to him and said in a very familiar and jolly sort of a way, "Come in, Bliss, and take some wine." I went in. The floor of the tent was covered with bottles, and straw from the champagne bottles. He filled a glass for me and one for himself, and I said, "Is this the usual morning custom at Army Headquarters, or what is the meaning of all this celebration?" He seemed surprised and asked if I did not know what it meant, and I told him I had not the slightest idea, unless there was some great victory that I had not heard of. He said, "Why, I am relieved of the Army of the Potomac, and the orders are being circulated now, that Hooker is to be my successor." I was very much surprised and sorry, and told him so. He thanked me, and said, "Well, Bliss, they will find out before many days, that it is not every man who can command an Army of one hundred and fifty thousand men." He filled the glasses, and I again expressed my regret at his being relieved, and bade him good morning and went to my court.

"They will find out before many days, that it is not every man who can command an Army of one hundred and fifty thousand men."

Fort Delaware
Del. Apr. 3. 1865

Mrs. H. Baldwin,

My Dear Friend;

I send you a poor sketch—for my hand is out of practice—of a scene I witnessed in a part of the Patent Office U.S.A. Hospital under my charge soon after the first battle of Fredericksburg. One of the soldiers, wounded through the lungs, at that battle, was dying. Two friends of his, fellow-soldiers of a cavalry regiment, were sent for to see him and arrived in time to speak with him a few minutes and to witness his death. I was attending another wounded man near him when they arrived. The eloquent expression of sympathy and sorrow in the action and faces of the visitors, and of mingled pain and heroic resignation in the countenance of the wounded man, induced me to make a hasty sketch of the group, which I thought to commemorate in a marble relief, should I live to see the end of the war. That sketch was lost. But while at the inauguration ball, which was held in the same hall where the scene occurred, in the midst of the throng of dancers, I could not but see it again as a reality, and have reproduced it as well as I could from memory.

Truly Your friend
Horatio Stone M.D.
U.S.A.

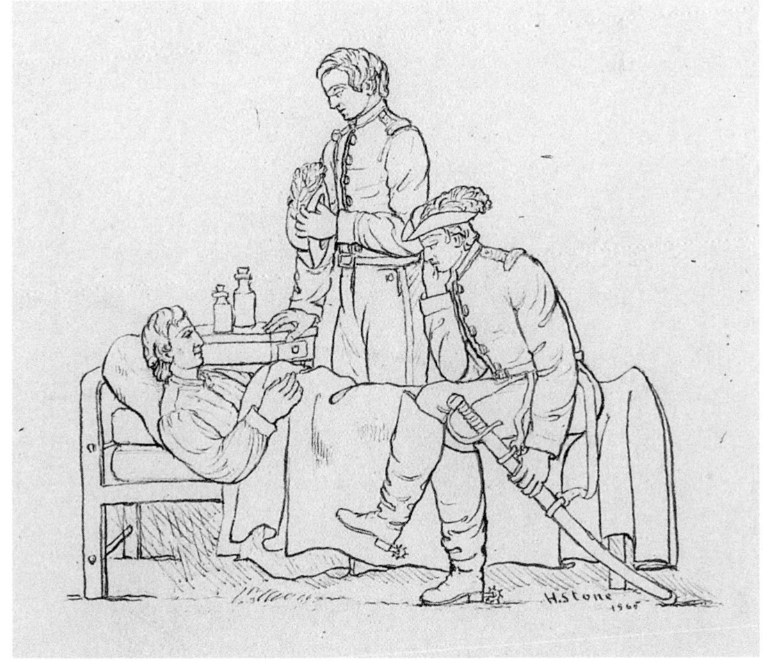

This letter and sketch were produced by Dr. Horatio Stone, a physician and sculptor whose statues of John Hancock and Alexander Hamilton stand in the U.S. Capitol. In 1862 Stone signed on for three years as a surgeon in the Union army. While serving at the Patent Office Hospital in Washington, he was moved by the sight of two soldiers attending a dying comrade wounded at Fredericksburg. Stone sketched the scene, hoping to sculpt a relief of it. In the letter he explains that the sketch was lost, but two years later, while attending a ball in the Patent Office Building to celebrate Lincoln's second inauguration, he recalled the moment and redrew the scene. The sculpture, however, was never done.

GLOSSARY

adjutant—A staff officer assisting the commanding officer, usually with correspondence.
battery—The basic unit of artillery, consisting of four to six guns.
bivouac—A temporary encampment, or to camp out for the night.
breastwork—A temporary fortification, usually of earth and about chest high, over which a soldier could fire.
brevet—An honorary rank given for exceptional bravery or merit in time of war. It granted none of the authority or pay of the official rank.
buck and ball—A round of ammunition consisting of a bullet and three buckshot.
caisson—A cart with large chests for carrying artillery ammunition; connected to a horse-drawn limber when moved.
canister—A tin can containing lead or iron balls that scattered when fired from a cannon.
color guard—a detachment of men chosen to carry and guard the regimental flags or colors.
corduroy road—A road with a surface of logs laid together transversely.
cuddy—A small room, cupboard, or closet.
double-quick—A trotting pace.
Dutchmen—A term, often pejorative, for Union soldiers of German descent.
enfilade—Gunfire that rakes an enemy line lengthwise, or the position allowing such firing.
flank—The right or left end of a military formation. Therefore, to flank is to attack or go around the enemy's position on one end or the other.
forlorn hope—A last-ditch, desperately difficult or dangerous assignment, or the body of soldiers given such a task.
furlough—A leave of absence granted to a soldier.
grapeshot—Iron balls (usually nine) bound together and fired from large-caliber coastal or siege cannon. Resembling a cluster of grapes, the balls broke apart and scattered on impact. The terms "grape" and "grapeshot" are commonly misapplied to the much smaller canister and case shot used in field artillery.
gum blanket—A waterproof blanket, treated with rubber and often in poncho form.
hardtack—A durable cracker, or biscuit, made of plain flour and water and normally about three inches square and a half-inch thick.
haversack—A shoulder bag, usually strapped over the right shoulder to rest on the left hip, for carrying personal items and rations.
howitzer—A short-barreled artillery piece that fired its projectile in a relatively high trajectory.
limber—A two-wheeled, horse-drawn vehicle to which a gun carriage or a caisson was attached.
Minié ball—The standard bullet-shaped projectile fired from the rifled muskets of the time. Designed by French army officers Henri-Gustave Delvigne and Claude-Étienne Minié, the bullet's hollow base expanded, forcing its sides into the grooves, or rifling, of the barrel. This caused the bullet to spiral in flight, giving it greater range and accuracy. Appears as minie, minnie, and minni.
musket—A smoothbore, muzzleloading shoulder arm.
muster—To assemble. To be mustered in is to be enlisted or enrolled in service. To be mustered out is to be discharged from service, usually on expiration of a set time.
oblique—At an angle. Units would be ordered to fire or move in a direction other than straight ahead.
orderly—A soldier assigned to a superior officer for various duties, such as carrying messages.
parole—The pledge of a soldier released after being captured by the enemy that he would not take up arms again until properly exchanged.
Parrott guns—Muzzleloading, rifled artillery pieces of various calibers made of cast iron, with a unique wrought-iron reinforcing band around the breech. Patented in 1861 by Union officer Robert Parker Parrott, these guns were more accurate at longer range than their smoothbore predecessors.
picket—One or more soldiers on guard to protect the larger unit from surprise attack.
provost guard—A detail of soldiers acting as police under the supervision of an officer called a provost marshal.
redoubt—An enclosed, defensive stronghold.
rifle—Any weapon with spiral grooves cut into the bore, which give spin to the projectile, adding range and accuracy. Usually applied to cannon or shoulder-fired weapons.
rifle pits—Holes or shallow trenches dug in the ground from which soldiers could fire weapons and avoid enemy fire. Foxholes.
right shoulder shift—A position for holding a musket in which the butt of the gun was held in the right hand at just below chest height, the breech area rested on the right shoulder, and the muzzle pointed skyward. The rough equivalent of the modern *shoulder arms.*
round shot—A solid, spherical artillery projectile.
salient—That part of a fortress, line of defense, or trench system that juts out toward the enemy position.
section of artillery—Part of an artillery battery consisting of two guns, the soldiers who manned them, and their supporting horses and equipment.
see the elephant—To participate in combat.
shelter tent—Also called a tente d'abri, pup tent, or dog tent, it consisted of two shelter halves (each carried by a single soldier)

buttoned together and hung over a ridgepole.
shrapnel—An artillery projectile in the form of a hollow sphere filled with metal balls packed around an explosive charge. Developed by British general Henry Shrapnel during the Napoleonic Wars, it was used as an antipersonnel weapon. Also called spherical case.
skirmisher—A soldier sent in advance of the main body of troops to scout out and probe the enemy's position. Also, one who participated in a skirmish, a small fight usually incidental to the main action.
small arms—Any hand-held weapon, usually a firearm.
solid shot—A solid artillery projectile, oblong for rifled pieces and spherical for smoothbores.
sponge—An artillerist's tool used to clear a cannon barrel of grime, smoldering cloth, and other detritus between rounds.
stack arms—To set aside weapons, usually three or more in a pyramid, interlocking at the end of the barrel with the butts on the ground.
worm fence—Also known as a snake fence, in which split rails were stacked alternately and at an angle producing a zigzagging line.
Zouaves—Regiments, both Union and Confederate, that modeled themselves after the original Zouaves of French Colonial Algeria. Known for spectacular uniforms featuring bright colors—usually reds and blues—baggy trousers, gaiters, short and open jackets, and a turban or fez, they specialized in precision drill and loading and firing muskets from the prone position.

ACKNOWLEDGMENTS

The editors wish to thank the following for their valuable assistance in the preparation of this volume:
Eva-Maria Ahladas, Museum of the Confederacy, Richmond; John Mills Bigham, Confederate Relic Room, Columbia, S.C.; Keith Bohannon, East Ridge, Tenn.; Harva Bryson, Pennsylvania Capitol Preservation Committee, Harrisburg, Pa.; G. Barry Davis, Erie, Pa.; Mary Wallace Day, Gritter's Library, Marietta, Ga.; Gail DeLoach, Georgia Department of Archives and History, Atlanta; Thomas Desjardin, Thomas Publications, Gettysburg, Pa.; Amy Fleming, Historical Society of Pennsylvania, Philadelphia; Janice Frye, National Park Service, Fredericksburg, Va.; Randy W. Hackenburg, U.S. Army Military History Institute, Carlisle Barracks, Pa.; Peter Harrington, Brown University Library, Providence; David T. Hedrick, Gettysburg College, Gettysburg, Pa.; Mary Ison and Staff, Library of Congress, Washington, D.C.; Joseph Loehle, Fredericksburg, Va.; Elsa Lohman, National Park Service, Fredericksburg, Va.; Michael Lynn, Stonewall Jackson Foundation, Lexington, Va.; Peter MacGlashan, Nantucket Historical Society, Nantucket, Mass.; Bonnie Moffat, Confederate Relic Room, Columbia, S.C.; Dorothy Olsen, Georgia State Capitol Collection, Atlanta; Don Pfanz, National Park Service, Fredericksburg, Va.; Patrick Reed, State House Flag Collection, Boston; Teresa Roane, Valentine Museum, Richmond; Paul Romaine, Gilder Lehrman Collection, New York; Kathy Schumacher, Emory University Library, Atlanta; Willie Sherrod, Confederate Relic Room, Columbia, S.C.; Leslie Sickels, Luther Memorial Church, Erie, Pa.; Dr. Richard Sommers, U.S. Army Military History Institute, Carlisle Barracks, Pa.; William Styple, Kearny, N.J.; Glen Swain, Sperryville, Va.; Sandra Trenholm, Gilder Lehrman Collection, New York; Emily Walhout, Harvard University, Cambridge, Mass.; George Whitely, Atlanta; Michael J. Winey, U.S. Army Military History Institute, Carlisle Barracks, Pa.; Mac Wyckoff, National Park Service, Fredericksburg, Va.; Jane Yates, The Citadel Museum and Archives, Charleston, S.C.

PICTURE CREDITS

The sources for the illustrations are listed below. Credits from left to right are separated by semicolons, from top to bottom by dashes.

Dust jacket: front, David D. Finney Collection at the U.S. Army Military History Institute (USAMHI), copied by A. Pierce Bounds; rear, Georgia Department of Archives and History, Atlanta, copied by George S. Whiteley IV.
All calligraphy by Mary Lou O'Brian/Inkwell, Inc.
6, 7: Art by Paul Salmon. 8: From *The Photographic History of the Civil War*, Vol. 1, Francis Trevelyan Miller, editor in chief, Review of Reviews, New York, 1911. 13: Map by Walter W. Roberts. 16: Massachusetts Commandery of the Military Order of the Loyal Legion and the U.S. Army Military History Institute (MASS-MOLLUS/USAMHI), copied by A. Pierce Bounds. 17: Meserve Collection of Mathew Brady negatives, National Portrait Gallery, Smithsonian Institution, Washington, D.C./Art Resource. 18: MASS-MOLLUS/USAMHI, copied by A. Pierce Bounds—courtesy Barry Jett, photographed by Andy Franck and Karen Jones of High Impact Photography. 19: Courtesy Doug Bast/Boonsboro Museum of History, photographed by Larry Sherer; courtesy Stonewall Jackson Foundation, Lexington, Va. 20: Frank and Marie-Thérèse Wood Print Collections, Alexandria, Va. 21: From *Four Years on the Firing Line,* by James Cooper Nisbet, McCowat-Mercer Press, Jackson, Tenn., 1963, copied by Philip Brandt George. 23: Library of Congress; Division of Military and Naval Affairs, New York State Adjutant General Office, Albany, N.Y., copied by A. Pierce Bounds. 24: Frank and Marie-Thérèse Wood Print Collections, Alexandria, Va. 25: National Archives—Library of Congress, Neg. No. LC-B8184-4167. 26: Courtesy collection of William A. Turner; The Citadel Archives

and Museum, Charleston, S.C. 27: Gettysburg National Military Park Museum, photographed by Larry Sherer at Fredericksburg and Spotsylvania National Military Park (FSNMP). 28, 29: Library of Congress, Waud #486. 30: Library of Congress, Waud #185; Historical Society of Pennsylvania, Philadelphia. 31: MASS-MOLLUS/USAMHI, copied by A. Pierce Bounds. 32: National Archives. 35: Map by Walter W. Roberts. 36: Library of Congress, Manuscript Division. 37: Library of Congress, Waud #326. 38, 39: From *Battles and Leaders of the Civil War*, Vol. 3, Century, New York, 1887—MASS-MOLLUS/USAMHI, copied by A. Pierce Bounds (2). 40, 41: Sketch by Frank Vizetelly, by permission of the Houghton Library, Harvard University, Cambridge, Mass. 42: FSNMP, photographed by Andy Franck and Karen Jones of High Impact Photography—MASS-MOLLUS/USAMHI, copied by A. Pierce Bounds. 43: Collection of Old Capitol Museum of Mississippi History, Jackson; from *Battles and Leaders of the Civil War*, Vol. 3, Century, New York, 1887. 44: From *The Civil War: The Nantucket Experience*, Richard F. Miller and Robert F. Mooney, Wesco, Nantucket, Mass., 1994. 45: Frank and Marie-Thérèse Wood Print Collections, Alexandria, Va. 46, 47: Courtesy David K. Hann, photographed by Marty Lerario; MASS-MOLLUS/USAMHI, copied by A. Pierce Bounds—Library of Congress, Waud #406. 49: Library of Congress, Lumley #12. 50: FSNMP, photographed by Andy Franck and Karen Jones of High Impact Photography. 51: From *Confederate Veteran*, January 1912. 52: Cook Collection, Valentine Museum, Richmond; MASS-MOLLUS/USAMHI, copied by A. Pierce Bounds. 53: Library of Congress, Waud #261. 55: Map by Walter W. Roberts. 56: From *The Long Arm of Lee: The History of the Artillery of the Army of Northern Virginia*, Vol. 2, by Jennings Cropper Wise, J. P. Bell, Lynchburg, Va., 1915, courtesy Kirk Denkler. 57: Library of Congress, Manuscript Division, Edwin V. Sumner Papers; National Archives, Neg. No. 111-B-4510. 58, 59: Gilder Lehrman Collection, on deposit at the Pierpont Morgan Library, GLC 3607, photographed by Robert D. Rubic; courtesy Barry Jett, photographed by Andy Franck and Karen Jones of High Impact Photography. 60: Library of Congress, Manuscript Division, Edwin V. Sumner Papers. 61: From *The Long Arm of Lee: The History of the Artillery of the Army of Northern Virginia*, Vol. 2, by Jennings Cropper Wise, J. P. Bell, Lynchburg, Va., 1915, courtesy Kirk Denkler—from *Battles and Leaders of the Civil War*, Vol. 3, Century, New York, 1887. 62: Courtesy Mark Katz, Americana Image Gallery. 63: Georgia State Capitol Museum, Office of the Secretary of State Lewis A. Massey. 65: Courtesy Dr. Charles V. Peery, copied by Henry Mintz. 66: Courtesy Scott Hann, photographed by Marty Lerario—from *Battles and Leaders of the Civil War*, Vol. 3, Century, New York, 1887. 67: Pennsylvania Capitol Preservation Committee, Harrisburg—courtesy Robert Schell Ulrich. 68: Alan R. Duke Collection at the USAMHI, copied by A. Pierce Bounds; courtesy James E. Martin, copied by Henry Mintz. 69: Courtesy Les Jensen Collection, photographed by Larry Sherer. 70: Courtesy Roger B. Hansen; Confederate Museum, Charleston, S.C., photographed by Michael Latil. 72, 73: Painting by C. Rochling, courtesy John Henry Kurtz; courtesy private collection. 74: Courtesy Frances Honeycutt, copied by Henry Mintz. 75: Courtesy James Alfred Locke Miller Jr., copied by Henry Mintz; collection of C. Paul Loane, photographed by Larry Sherer—courtesy William B. Styple. 76: From *The Story of a Cannoneer under Stonewall Jackson*, by Edward A. Moore, Neale, New York, 1907, courtesy Kirk Denkler, copied by Philip Brandt George. 77: B. N. Miller Collection at the USAMHI, copied by A. Pierce Bounds; courtesy Brian Pohanka. 79: Map by Walter W. Roberts. 80, 81: Special Collections, Musselman Library, Gettysburg College, Gettysburg, Pa.—MASS-MOLLUS/USAMHI, copied by A. Pierce Bounds. 82: Roger D. Hunt Collection at the USAMHI, copied by A. Pierce Bounds; MASS-MOLLUS/USAMHI, copied by A. Pierce Bounds. 85: Courtesy collection of William A. Turner, copied by Philip Brandt George. 86: From *Battles and Leaders of the Civil War*, Vol. 3, Century, New York, 1887. 87: Gil Barrett Collection at the USAMHI, copied by A. Pierce Bounds. 88: Anne S. K. Brown Military Collection, Brown University Library, Providence. 91: Courtesy Scott Hann, photographed by Marty Lerario; courtesy John D. Hemminger, photographed by Mike Brouse. 92, 93: MASS-MOLLUS/USAMHI, copied by A. Pierce Bounds; Museum of the Confederacy, Richmond. 94, 95: National Archives, Neg. No. 111-B-5252; Rance Hulshart Collection at the USAMHI, copied by A. Pierce Bounds—courtesy Michael G. Kraus (2). 96: USAMHI, copied by A. Pierce Bounds, MASS-MOLLUS/USAMHI, copied by A. Pierce Bounds. 97: Library of Congress, Lumley #10. 98: Cook Collection, Valentine Museum, Richmond. 99: Division of Military and Naval Affairs, New York State Adjutant General Office, Albany, N.Y., copied by A. Pierce Bounds; Stephen D. Rockstroh Collection at the USAMHI, copied by A. Pierce Bounds. 101: Courtesy Bureau of State Office Buildings, Commonwealth of Massachusetts, photographed by Douglas Christian—FSNMP, photographed by Andy Franck and Karen Jones of High Impact Photography. 102, 103: Courtesy Scott Hann, photographed by Marty Lerario. 105: Map by Walter W. Roberts. 107: Library of Congress, Lumley #14. 108, 109: Bob Bentley Sr. Collection at the USAMHI, copied by A. Pierce Bounds—sketch by Frank Vizetelly, by permission of the Houghton Library, Harvard University, Cambridge, Mass. 110: USAMHI, copied by A. Pierce Bounds—courtesy Bureau of State Office Buildings, Commonwealth of Massachusetts, photographed by Douglas Christian; courtesy William Gladstone Collection. 111: From *From Manassas to Appomattox*, by James Longstreet, Dallas Publishing, 1896. 112: USAMHI, copied by A. Pierce Bounds. 114, 115: Library of Congress, Waud #189. 116: Museum of the Confederacy, Richmond. 117: A. E. M. Adams via South Carolina Confederate Relic Room and Museum, Columbia. 118, 119: Barbara H. Smith, courtesy Sergeant Kirkland's Museum and Historical Society; MASS-MOLLUS/USAMHI, copied by A. Pierce Bounds (2). 120: South Carolina Confederate Relic Room and Museum, Columbia, photographed by Henry Mintz; courtesy Mary Wallace Day. 121: From *Above the Civil War: The Story of Thaddeus Lowe, Balloonist, Inventor, Railway Builder*, by Eugene B. Block, Howell-North Books, Berkeley, Calif., 1966. 122: Courtesy Kirk Denkler, copied by Evan H. Sheppard. 123: Library of Congress, Waud #751. 124: Courtesy William S. Powell, copied by Henry Mintz—MASS-MOLLUS/USAMHI, copied by A. Pierce Bounds. 125: From *The Story of a Cannoneer under Stonewall Jackson*, by Edward A. Moore, Neale, New York, 1907, courtesy Kirk Denkler. 126: Courtesy Georgia Department of Archives and History, Atlanta, photographed by George S. Whiteley IV. 127: From *Yankee in Gray: The Civil War Memoirs of Henry E. Handerson*, biographical introduction by Clyde Lottridge Cummer, Press of Western Reserve University, Cleveland, 1962, courtesy Cleveland Health Sciences Library, copied by Philip Brandt George. 128: Courtesy Nantucket Historical Association, Nantucket, Mass.; MASS-MOLLUS/USAMHI, copied by A. Pierce Bounds. 129: Old Courthouse Museum, Vicksburg, Miss., photographed by Henry Mintz. 130: Library of Congress, Forbes #050. 134: MASS-MOLLUS/USAMHI—South Caroliniana Library, University of South Carolina, Columbia. 135: New York State Division of Military and Naval Affairs, Military History Collection, photographed by Larry Sherer. 136: Library of Congress, Lumley #3. 137: Special Collections, Musselman Library, Gettysburg College, Gettysburg, Pa. 138: Courtesy McKissick Museum, University of South Carolina, Columbia. 140: Frank and Marie-Thérèse Wood Print Collections, Alexandria, Va. 141: William Howard Collection at the USAMHI, copied by A. Pierce Bounds—FSNMP, photographed by Andy Franck and Karen Jones of High Impact Photography. 143: FSNMP, photographed by Andy Franck and Karen Jones of High Impact Photography. 144: Gettysburg National Military Park Museum, photographed by Larry Sherer at

FSNMP. 145: Valentine Museum, Richmond. 146: Library of Congress, Lumley #8. 147: Gilder Lehrman Collection, on deposit at the Pierpont Morgan Library, GLC 4189 #20, copied by Robert D. Rubic—Frank and Marie-Thérèse Wood Print Collections, Alexandria, Va. 148 : Courtesy Ed and Maureen Simpson. 150, 151: Library of Congress, Waud #209. 152: Frank and Marie-Thérèse Wood Print Collections, Alexandria, Va. 153: David D. Finney Collection at the USAMHI, copied by A. Pierce Bounds. 154: Frank and Marie-Thérèse Wood Print Collections, Alexandria, Va. 155: USAMHI, photographed by A. Pierce Bounds. 156: Library of Congress, Waud #718. 157: Library of Congress, Neg. No. LC-B8171-677. 158: Courtesy Mary Gordon Elliot and Alison Elliot Mintz, copied by Henry Mintz. 159: Anne S. K. Brown Military Collection, Brown University Library, Providence.

BIBLIOGRAPHY

BOOKS

Abbott, Henry Livermore. *Fallen Leaves: The Civil War Letters of Major Henry Livermore Abbott.* Ed. by Robert Garth Scott. Kent, Ohio: Kent State University Press, 1991.

Alexander, Edward Porter. *Fighting for the Confederacy: The Personal Recollections of General Edward Porter Alexander.* Ed. by Gary W. Gallagher. Chapel Hill: University of North Carolina Press, 1989.

Allan, William. "Jackson's Valley Campaign." In *Southern Historical Society Papers.* Wilmington, N.C.: Broadfoot, 1991.

Battles and Leaders of the Civil War: Retreat from Gettysburg. Ed. by Robert Underwood Johnson and Clarence Clough Buel. New York: Castle Books, 1956.

Benson, Berry. *Berry Benson's Civil War Book: Memoirs of a Confederate Scout and Sharpshooter.* Ed. by Susan Williams Benson. Athens: University of Georgia Press, 1991.

Bilby, Joseph G. *Remember Fontenoy! The 69th New York and the Irish Brigade in the Civil War.* Hightstown, N.J.: Longstreet House, 1995.

Blackford, Susan Leigh, comp. *Letters from Lee's Army: Or Memoirs of Life in and out of the Army in Virginia during the War between the States.* Ed. by Charles Minor Blackford III. New York: Charles Scribner's Sons, 1947.

Borton, Benjamin. *On the Parallels: Or Chapters of Inner History, a Story of the Rappahannock.* Woodstown, N.J.: Monitor-Register Print, 1903.

Buck, Samuel D. *With the Old Confeds: Actual Experiences of a Captain in the Line.* Baltimore: H. E. Houck, 1925.

Burgwyn, William H. S. *A Captain's War: The Letters and Diaries of William H. S. Burgwyn, 1861–1865.* Ed. by Herbert M. Schiller. Shippensburg, Pa.: White Mane, 1994.

Caldwell, J. F. J. *The History of a Brigade of South Carolinians: Known First as "Gregg's," and Subsequently as "McGowan's Brigade."* Philadelphia: King and Baird, 1866.

Child, William. *A History of the Fifth Regiment New Hampshire Volunteers in the American Civil War: 1861–1865.* Bristol, N.H.: R. W. Musgrove, 1893.

Clark, Walter, ed. *Histories of the Several Regiments and Battalions from North Carolina in the Great War, 1861–'65,* Vol. 3. Wendell, N.C.: Broadfoot's Bookmark, 1982 (reprint of 1901 edition).

Cockrell, Thomas D., and Michael B. Ballard, eds. *A Mississippi Rebel in the Army of Northern Virginia: The Civil War Memoirs of Private David Holt.* Baton Rouge: Louisiana State University Press, 1995.

Cory, Eugene A. "A Private's Recollections of Fredericksburg." In *Personal Narratives of Events in the War of the Rebellion: Being Papers Read before the Rhode Island Soldiers and Sailors Historical Society,* Vol. 4. Wilmington, N.C.: Broadfoot, 1993 (reprint of 1883-1885 editions).

Currier, John Charles. *From Concord to Fredericksburg: A Paper Prepared and Read before California Commandery of the Military Order of the Loyal Legion of the United States, February 12, 1896.* San Francisco: N.p., 1896.

Davis, William C., ed. *The Confederate General,* Vol. 4. Harrisburg, Pa.: National Historical Society, 1991.

Dictionary of American Biography, Vol. 2. Ed. by Allen Johnson and Dumas Malone. New York: Charles Scribner's Sons, 1958.

Dictionary of American Biography, Vol. 6. Ed. by Dumas Malone. New York: Charles Scribner's Sons, 1961.

Dinkins, James:

"Barksdale's Mississippi Brigade at Fredericksburg." In *Southern Historical Society Papers,* Vol. 36. Ed. by R. A. Brock. Wilmington, N.C.: Broadfoot, 1991 (reprint of 1908 edition).

1861 to 1865: Personal Recollections and Experiences in the Confederate Army. Wilmington, N.C.: Morningside Bookshop, 1975 (reprint of 1897 edition).

"Griffith-Barksdale-Humphrey Mississippi Brigade and Its Campaigns." In *Southern Historical Society Papers,* Vol. 32. Ed. by R. A. Brock. Wilmington, N.C.: Broadfoot, 1991 (reprint of 1904 edition).

Favill, Josiah Marshall. *The Diary of a Young Officer Serving with the Armies of the United States during the War of the Rebellion.* Chicago: R. R. Donnelley & Sons, 1909.

Fletcher, William A. *Rebel Private: Front and Rear.* New York: Dutton, 1995.

Frassanito, William A. *Grant and Lee: The Virginia Campaigns, 1864–1865.* New York: Charles Scribner's Sons, 1983.

Goolrick, Frances Bernard. "Suffering in Fredericksburg." In *Southern Historical Society Papers,* Vol. 37. Ed. by R. A. Brock. Wilmington, N.C.: Broadfoot, 1991 (reprint of 1909 edition).

Handerson, Henry E. *Yankee in Gray: The Civil War Memoirs of Henry E. Handerson.* Cleveland: Press of Western Reserve University, 1962.

Harrison, Noel G. *Fredericksburg Civil War Sites: December 1862–April 1865,* Vol. 2 (Virginia Civil War Battles and Leaders series). Lynchburg, Va.: H. E. Howard, 1995.

Haynes, Martin A. *History of the Second Regiment, New Hampshire Volunteers: Its Camps, Marches and Battles.* Manchester, N.H.: Charles F. Livingston, 1865.

Hood, J. B. *Advance and Retreat: Personal Experiences in the United States & Confederate States Armies.* Ed. by Richard N. Current. Millwood, N.Y.: Kraus Reprint, 1981 (reprint of 1959 edition).

Hunter, Alexander. *Johnny Reb and Billy Yank.* New York: Neale, 1905.

Kepler, William. *History of the Three Months' and Three Years' Service from April 16th, 1861, to June 22d, 1864, of the Fourth Regiment Ohio Volunteer Infantry in the War for the Union.* Cleveland: Leader Printing, 1886.

Kershaw, J. B. "Richard Kirkland, the Humane Hero of Fredericksburg." In *Southern Historical Society Papers,* Vol. 8. Wilmington, N.C.: Broadfoot, 1990.

Krick, Robert K. *Lee's Colonels: A Biographical Register of the Field Officers of the Army of Northern Virginia.* Dayton: Morningside, 1992.

McClendon, William A. *Recollections of War Times.* San Bernardino, Calif.: California Church Press, 1973 (reprint of 1909 edition).

Marvel, William. *The Battle of Fredericksburg* (Civil War series). Conshohocken, Pa.: Eastern National Park and Monument Association, 1993.

Miller, Richard F., and Robert F. Mooney. *The Nantucket Experience: Including the Memoirs of Josiah Fitch Murphey.* Nantucket, Mass.: Wesco, 1994.

Moore, John H. "Fredericksburg." In *The Southern Bivouac,* Vol. 2. Louisville, Ky.: B. F. Avery & Sons, 1887.

Morgan, William H. *Personal Reminiscences of the War of 1861–5.* Freeport, N. Y.: Books for Libraries Press, 1977.

The New-York Historical Society's Dictionary of Artists in America: 1564–1860. Ed. by George C. Groce and David H. Wallace. New Haven, Conn.: Yale University Press, 1957.

Nisbet, James Cooper. *Four Years on the Firing Line.* Ed. by Bell Irvin Wiley. Jackson, Tenn.: McCowat-Mercer Press, 1963.

O'Reilly, Frank A. *"Stonewall" Jackson at Fredericksburg: The Battle of Prospect Hill, December 13, 1862* (Virginia Civil War Battles and Leaders series). Lynchburg, Va.: H. E. Howard, 1993.

Owen, William Miller. *In Camp and Battle with the Washington Artillery of New Orleans.* Boston: Ticknor, 1885.

Poague, William Thomas. *Gunner with Stonewall: Reminiscences of William Thomas Poague.* Ed. by Monroe F. Cockrell. Jackson, Tenn.: McCowat-Mercer Press, 1957.

Sauers, Richard A. *Advance the Colors! Pennsylvania Civil War Battle Flags,* Vol. 1. Harrisburg, Pa.: Capitol Preservation Committee, 1987.

Sawyer, Franklin. *Military History of the 8th Regiment Ohio Vol. Inf'y: Its Battles, Marches and Army Movements.* Cleveland, Ohio: Fairbanks, 1881.

Scharf, Jonathan Thomas. *The Personal Memoirs of Jonathan Thomas Scharf of the First Maryland Artillery.* Ed. by Tom Kelley. Baltimore: Butternut and Blue, 1992.

Simonton, Edward. "Recollections of the Battle of Fredericksburg." In *Glimpses of the Nation's Struggle.* Wilmington, N.C.: Broadfoot, 1992 (reprint of 1890 edition).

Simpson, Richard Wright, and Taliaferro Simpson. *"Far, Far from Home": The Wartime Letters of Dick and Tally Simpson, Third South Carolina Volunteers.* Ed. by Guy R. Everson and Edward W. Simpson Jr. New York: Oxford University Press, 1994.

Smith, James Power. "With Stonewall Jackson." In *Southern Historical Society Papers.* Wilmington, N.C.: Broadfoot, 1991.

Stuckenberg, John H. W. *I'm Surrounded by Methodists: Diary of John H. W. Stuckenberg, Chaplain of the 145th Pennsylvania Volunteer Infantry.* Ed. and comp. by David T. Hedrick and Gordon Barry Davis Jr. Gettysburg, Pa.: Thomas, 1995.

Thompson, S. Millett. *Thirteenth Regiment of New Hampshire Volunteer Infantry in the War of the Rebellion, 1861–1865: A Diary.* Boston: Houghton, Mifflin, 1888.

Wise, Jennings Cropper. *The Long Arm of Lee: The History of the Artillery of the Army of Northern Virginia.* New York: Oxford University Press, 1959.

Woodward, E. M. *History of the Third Pennsylvania Reserve: Being a Complete Record of the Regiment.* Trenton: MacCrellish & Quigley, 1883.

Wyckoff, Mac. *A History of the Third South Carolina Infantry, 1861–1865.* Fredericksburg, Va.: Sergeant Kirkland's Museum, 1995.

PERIODICALS

Alexander, Bates. "Seventh Regiment." *The Sun* (Hummelstown, Pa.), October 25, 1895.

Charles, R. K. "'Events in Battle of Fredericksburg." *Confederate Veteran,* February 1906.

Corbin, Roberta Cary. "Stonewall Jackson in Winter Quarters." *Confederate Veteran,* January 1912.

Cummings, C. C. "Battle of Fredericksburg, December 13, 1862." *Confederate Veteran,* August 1915.

Flint, Dayton E. Letter. *Washington Star,* January 26, 1911.

Guilford, S. H. "The 127th Penna. Infantry at the Capture of Fredericksburg." *Philadelphia Weekly Press,* June 16, 1886.

Hatton, Clarence R. "Gen. Archibald Campbell Godwin." *Confederate Veteran,* April 1920.

Hillyer, George. Letter. *Southern Banner* (Athens, Ga.), January 7, 1863.

Hull, A. L. "Gen. Thomas R. R. Cobb." *Confederate Veteran,* July 1899.

Jones, A. C. "Arkansas Soldiers in Virginia." *Confederate Veteran,* October 1912.

McCleland, William H. Letter. *New York Irish-American,* January 10, 1863.

Nagel, William J. Letter. *New York Irish-American,* December 27, 1862.

New York Irish-American, January 3, 1863.

New York *Tablet,* January 24, 1863.

Savas, Theodore P., and David A. Woodbury, eds. *Civil War Regiments: A Journal of the American Civil War,* Vol. 4, No. 4, 1995.

OTHER SOURCES

Allison, William A. Letter, January 4, 1863. Carlisle Barracks, Pa.: U.S. Army Military History Institute.

Anderson, James Monroe. Letter, January 9, 1863, Maxcy Gregg Papers. Columbia: University of South Carolina, South Caroliniana Library.

Beem, David. Letter, November 27, 1862. Fredericksburg, Va.: Fredericksburg and Spotsylvania National Military Park.

Bliss, Zenas R. Unpublished memoir, papers. Carlisle Barracks, Pa.: U.S. Army Military History Institute.

Campbell, William Oliver. Unpublished manuscript. Fredericksburg, Va.: Fredericksburg and Spotsylvania National Military Park.

Church, Erskine M. Letter, March 15, 1863. Fredericksburg, Va.: Fredericksburg and Spotsylvania National Military Park.

Crumley, William M. "Battle of Fredericksburg." Unpublished manuscript. Fredericksburg, Va.: Fredericksburg and Spotsylvania National Military Park.

Eames, Walter A. Letter, December 5, 1862, Murray Smith Collection. Carlisle Barracks, Pa.: U.S. Army Military History Institute.

Haas, Jacob W. Letter, December 18, 1862. Carlisle Barracks, Pa.: U.S. Army Military History Institute.

Hamilton, Matilda. "An Eyewitness Account of the Battle of Fredericksburg." Unpublished manuscript. Fredericksburg, Va.: Fredericksburg and Spotsylvania National Military Park.

Hatton, John W. F. Memoirs, n.d. Washington, D.C.: Library of Congress, Manuscript Division.

Heffelfinger, Jacob. Diary. Carlisle Barracks, Pa.: U.S. Army Military History Institute.

Heinichen, Edward L. Memoirs, n.d. Fredericksburg, Va.: Fredericksburg and Spotsylvania National Military Park.

Hill, Ambrose P. Letter to Jeb Stuart, November 14, 1862. Richmond: Virginia Historical Society.

Josiah, Tom. Letter, December 12, 1862. Fredericksburg, Va.: Fredericksburg and Spotsylvania National Military Park.

Kimble, June. Letter, n.d. Richmond: Museum of the Confederacy.

Lumpkin, J. H. Papers, Ms #192. Athens: University of Georgia, Special Collections.

McCarter, William. " 'My Life in the Army' 1862." Unpublished manuscript. Fredericksburg, Va.: Fredericksburg and Spotsylvania National Military Park.

McIntosh, David Gregg. "The Battle of Fredericksburg." Unpublished manuscript. Carlisle Barracks, Pa.: U.S. Army Military History Institute.

Mancha, J. Franklin. Diary. Carlisle Barracks, Pa.: U.S. Army Military History Institute.

Montgomery, William R. Letter, December 17, 1862. Columbia: University of South Carolina, South Caroliniana Library.
Nance, James D. Letter, November 30, 1862. Charleston, S.C.: The Citadel.
Owen, Thomas J. Letters, March 1897. Fredericksburg, Va.: Fredericksburg and Spotsylvania National Military Park.
Paige, Charles C. Diary, Wendell W. Long Collection. Carlisle Barracks, Pa.: U.S. Army Military History Institute.
Peacock, William H. Letters, December 1862. Carlisle Barracks, Pa.: U.S. Army Military History Institute.
Pierce, Francis. Letter, December 17, 1862. Washington, D.C.: Library of Congress, Manuscript Division.
Pollack, Curtis C. Letters, December 1862. Carlisle Barracks, Pa.: U.S. Army Military History Institute.
Powell, Charles S. Memoirs, Charles Steven Powell Papers. Durham, N.C.: Duke University, William Perkins Library, Special Collections.
Price, R. Channing. Letters, December 1862-January 1863, Douglas Southall Freeman Papers. Washington, D.C.: Library of Congress, Manuscript Division.
Robinson, Oscar D. Diary. Hanover, N.H.: Dartmouth College.
Rohrer, Coston. Letter, December 17, 1862. Atlanta: Emory University.
Shreve, George W. "Reminiscences of the Stuart Horse Artillery." Unpublished manuscript, R. Preston Chew Papers. Charlestown: Jefferson County, West Virginia, Museum.
Teall, William W. Letters, November-December 1862. Nashville: Tennessee State Library and Archives.
Whitehouse, Phineas P. "My First Battle." Unpublished manuscript, William O. Bourne Papers. Washington, D.C.: Library of Congress, Manuscript Division.
Williams, E. E. Letters, December 1862. Carlisle Barracks, Pa.: U.S. Army Military History Institute.
Williams, William R. Letter, December 26, 1862. Carlisle Barracks, Pa.: U.S. Army Military History Institute.
Zook, Samuel. Letters, December 1862. Carlisle Barracks, Pa.: U.S. Army Military History Institute.

INDEX

Numerals in italics indicate an illustration of the subject mentioned.

A

Abbott, Henry L.: 45, *128;* letter from, 128
Alexander, Bates: account by, 60, 65-68
Alexander, E. Porter: *26;* account by, 26, 37-38, 142-143
Alley, Leander: *128*
Allison, William A.: letter from, 150-151
Anderson, G. T.: 126
Andrews, John W.: 90
Antietam, Battle of: 9, 10
Aquia Creek: 24
Archer, James J.: 54, 63, 71
Army of Northern Virginia: discipline in, 158; fraternization in, 22, *23,* 26, *30;* marksmanship medal (Fredericksburg Greys), *18;* order of battle, 15; supply shortages in, 18-19
Army of the Potomac: fraternization in, 22, *23,* 26, *30;* Medal of Honor winners, 52; medical service blanket, *141;* morale in, 142, 147-148, 150-151, 152, 156-158; observation balloons, 120, 121; order of battle, 15; pontoon equipment, 11, 13, 14, 24, *25,* 33, 36, 132; regimental drum, *101;* supply lines for, 13; supply trains, *24, 150-151;* winter camp, *130*
Atkinson, Edmund N.: 54, 70, 71, 73

B

Babbit, Jacob: *52*
Barksdale, William: 33, 37, 38, 42, 43, 45, 90
Barr, George W.: china looted by, *50*
Bayard, George D.: *77*
Beam, Marquis L.: *158*
Beckwith, Robert S.: *46*
Belle Plain, Virginia: 11
Belle Voir. *See* Yerby house
Benson, Berry: account by, 64
Bernard, Francis: account by, 39-42
Bernard house: 59, 77; hospital blanket used at, *141*
Birney, David B.: 54
Blackford, Charles M.: account by, 143-145
Bland, Elbert: *120;* binoculars of, *120*
Bliss, Zenas R.: *52, 112;* account by, 52-53, 112-113, 158
Borton, Benjamin: account by, 87-88, 135
Bowling Green, Virginia: 12
Brady, Mathew: photographers working for, 16, 39, 81, 94
Brigham, George: map sketched by, *58-59*
Brockenbrough, John M.: 61
Brompton. *See* Marye house
Brown, Hiram L.: *82*
Burgwyn, William H. S.: *116;* account by, 116
Burnside, Ambrose E.: 9, 11, 12, 13, 14, *17,* 24, 28, 33, 34, 35, 37, 38, 60, 104, 105, 106, 121, 131, 132, 139, 147, 151, 152, 155, 156, 157; appointed Army of the Potomac commander, 10, 17; and Federal retreat, *136;* order by, *57;* replaced by Hooker, 133, 158
Butterfield, Daniel: 104

C

Caldwell, John C.: 78-79, 102, 103
Carpenter, Porter: 78
Cavanaugh, James: *99*
Charleston *Mercury:* 132
Charleston *News and Courier:* 134
Chatham: 120
Church, Erskine M.: account by, 125
Cobb, Howell: 93
Cobb, Thomas R. R.: 34, 78, 79, 85, 90, 92, *93,* 98, 104, 105, 149
Collis, Charles H. T.: *72-73*
Cooke, John R.: *98*
Cooke, Philip: 98
Corbin, Richard: 51
Corbin, Roberta Cary: account by, 51
Cory, Eugene A.: 78; account by, 22-23
Couch, Darius N.: 78, 79, 104, 131
Crombargar, Thomas S.: Bible looted by, *50*
Cross, Daniel K.: *103*
Cross, Edward E.: *102,* 103, 153; account by, 102
Crumley, William M.: account by, 108-109
Culpeper Court House, Virginia: 9
Cummings, Charles C.: account by, 139
Currier, John C.: *110;* account by, 110-111
Curtis, John B.: identification badge of, *59*
Cushing, Alonzo H.: *16*

D

Dana, Charles A.: 10
Davis, Jefferson: 12
Decker, Charles: *66*
Dinkins, James M.: account by, 42-43

Donovan, John H.: 154; account by, 98-100
Doubleday, Abner: 54
Duke, Charles W.: *68*
Durr, William W.: *42*
Dwyer, John: *99*

E

Early, Jubal A.: 21, 54
Elder, John: 42
Emancipation Proclamation: 150, 151

F

Fairfax, Randolph: *125*
Falmouth, Virginia: 11, 24, 29; Federal winter camp at, *130, 150-151*
Favill, Josiah M.: account by, 24-25, 50
Featherston, Winfield Scott: 118
Ferrero, Edward: 110, 112, 116
Flags: 19th Georgia Infantry, *63;* 21st Massachusetts Infantry, *110;* 28th Massachusetts Infantry, *101;* 17th Mississippi Infantry, *43;* 69th New York Infantry guidon, *135;* 7th Pennsylvania Infantry, *67*
Flint, Dayton E.: account by, 156-158
Flynn, John: sword and scabbard of, *94-95*
Forbes, Edwin: 131
Frank Leslie's Illustrated Newspaper. See Leslie's Illustrated Newspaper
Franklin, William B.: 10, 11, 33-34, 35, 53, 54, *57,* 60, 61, 77, 132, 133, *136,* 141
Fredericksburg, Battle of: *map* 6-7; "angel of Marye's Heights," 134; artillery fire at, 37-*38,* 61-62, 76, 78, *111,* 119, 122; burial details, 125, 139, *140,* 145, 146; campaign chronology, 14; campaign theater, *map* 13; casualties, 133; initial troop dispositions, *map* 35; Marye's Heights, final assaults on, 104-105, *map* 105-107, *108-109,* 110-113, *114-115,* 116-119, 121-122, *123,* 124; Marye's Heights, I Corps assaults on, 34, 78-79, *map* 79, 80-85, *86,* 87, *88-89,* 90-102; I Corps attack, 34, 54, *map* 55, 56-57, *map* 58-59, 60, *61,* 62-65, *66,* 67-69, 71, *72-73,* 74-77; parole and exchange agreement following, *146;* prisoners, 142-143, 146; sniping in aftermath of, 135, 137, 138-139; stone wall, *92-93;* wounded, *97,* 141, *147;* wounded and dead left between lines, 125, 126-128, 131, 134, 135, 137
Fredericksburg, Virginia: *32;* bombardment of, *40-41,* 42-43; civilian evacuation of, 13, 39-42; civilian life in, 12, 26, *144;* civilian refugees from, *27,* 42, 137, 144; Confederate defensive position at, 12, 26, *map* 35; Confederate troops in, *20;* damage to, *39,* 143, *144,* 145, 146, 149; efforts for civilian relief, 143; Federal advance on, 11, 12; Federal retreat from, 131, 136, 142; Federal troops in, 34, 48, *49, 107;* fighting in, *43,* 44, *45;* looting in, 34, 48-*49,* 50, 107; outskirts of, *80-81;* riverfront, *8, 20, 28-29;* shell fragment found at, *42*
French, William H.: 34, 78, 79, 82, 90, 97, 104
Fry, W. T.: letter from, *143*

G

Getty, George W.: 105, 117
Gibbon, John: 34, 54, 68, 74
Gibbons, Elijah: *91*
Gordonsville, Virginia: 11
Gregg, Maxcy: 54, 64, *65,* 69, 129, 137-138; pocket watch of, *138*
Griffin, Charles: 104, 121, 122
Griffin, Simon G.: *96,* 158
Guilford, Simeon H.: account by, 46-47

H

Hall, Edward D.: 79
Hall, Norman J.: 44, 45, 46
Halleck, Henry W.: 10, 11, 13, 17, 132, 147, 152
Hamilton, Matilda: account by, 137-138
Hamilton's Crossing: 61, 69, 127
Hancock, Winfield S.: 34, 78, 79, 95, 102, 104
Handerson, Henry E.: *127;* account by, 127-128
Hardie, James A.: message from, *60*
Harper's Weekly: 29, 46; page from, *45;* political cartoon from, *152*
Hatch, William: *75;* hat of, *75*
Haupt, Herman: 10
Hawkins, Rush C.: 14, 46, 105, 117
Hawks, Wells J.: 129
Heffelfinger, Jacob: *77;* account by, 77
Heinichen, Edward I.: account by, 146
Henderson, David English: 144
Hill, Ambrose P.: *18,* 54, 61; letter from, 18
Hillyer, George: *126;* account by, 126
Hoke, Robert F.: 69, 71
Holder, William D.: 43
Holt, David E.: account by, 118-119
Hood, John B.: *52;* account by, 52
Hooker, Joseph: 10, 11, 12, 17, 33, 34, 104, 105, 133; replaces Burnside as Army of the Potomac commander, 133, 158
Howard, Oliver O.: 34, 46, 47, 79, 104, 105, 128
Humphreys, Andrew A.: 104-105, 122, 123, 124
Hunt, Henry J.: 38
Hunter, Alexander: *122;* account by, 122-124

I

Illustrated London News: pages from, *20*
Innis house: *92-93*
Irish Brigade: green sprigs worn by, 78, 95; memorial mass held for, 153, *154*

J

Jackson, Thomas J.: 9, 12, 13, 18, *19,* 21, 22, 34, 35, 51, 52, 54, 61, 62, 65, 74, 76, 129; order from, *129*
Jones, Alexander C.: account by, 18-19
Jones, Hamilton C.: account by, 74-75
Jones, William G.: *16*

K

Kepler, William: account by, 83-84
Kershaw, Joseph B.: 78, 104, 105, 108, *134,* 135
Kimball, Nathan: 34, 78, 82, 83, *87,* 88, 90
Kirkland, Richard: *134*

L

Lane, James H.: 54, 63, 69
Law, Evander M.: 74, 75
Lawton, Alexander R.: 70
Lawton, Edward P.: 146; coat and ring of, *70*
Lee, Robert E.: 9, 11, 12, 13, 14, 19, 27, 33, 34, 35, 56, 79, 104, 111, 131, 133, 139, 146, 151
Lee Hill: Confederate artillery at, *111*
Leslie's Illustrated Newspaper: 49; page from, *147, 152, 154*
Lincoln, Abraham: 9, 10, 11, 13, 132, 133, 151, 159; political cartoons of, *152*
Longstreet, James: 9, 12, 13, 26, 33, 34, 35, 37, 78, 79, 104, 105, 124
Lovie, Henri: 147
Lowe, Thaddeus S. C.: 120, *121*
Lumley, Arthur: 22, 49, 97, 107, 136, 146
Lumpkin, Joseph Henry: letter from, 149

M

McCarter, William: *30:* account by, 30-31, 97, 100
McCleland, William H.: *95;* account by, 95
McClellan, George B.: 9, 10, 140, 147, 148, 152
McClendon, William A.: account by, 69, 126-127
McIntosh, David G.: *61;* account by, 61-62
McLaws, Lafayette: 90, 109
Mancha, J. Franklin: account by, 155
Mansfield. *See* Bernard house
Martin, William A.: *68*
Marye house: 115, 117, *118,* 120, 143
Marye's Heights: *28-29,* 30, *40-41, 80-81,* 135; Federal assaults on, 34, 78-79, *map* 79, 80-85, *86,* 87, *88-89,* 90-102, 104-105, *map* 105-107, *108-109,* 110-113, *114-115,* 116-119, 121-122, *123,* 124; view of battleground from, *32*
Mason, John S.: 83

Meade, George G.: 34, 54, 61, *62*, 63, 69
Meagher, Thomas F.: 78, *94*, 95, 97, 100, 101, 140, 154
Miles, Nelson A.: 79
Miller, Alfred A.: *75*
Montgomery, William R.: account by, 90-92
Moore, John H.: account by, 63
Morgan, William H.: account by, 138-139
Moss Neck: *51*
"Mud March": 133, 155, *156*
Murphey, Josiah F.: *44*, 128; account by, 44-45

N

Nagle, James: 96, 112, 116
Nagle, William J.: account by, 140-141
Nance, James D.: *26*, 117
New York Illustrated News: 22
New York *Tablet:* article from, 153
New York *Tribune:* 11
Nisbet, James C.: *21;* account by, 21-22, 71
North Anna River: 12
North Carolina, USS: marines from, *154*
Nugent, Robert: *153*, 154

O

O'Brien, Edward: 123
Occoquan Creek: 11
O'Connell, John: note by, *155*
Orange & Alexandria Railroad: *map* 13
Owen, Joshua T.: 46
Owen, Thomas J.: account by, 36
Owen, William M.: *85;* account by, 85

P

Paige, Charles C.: account by, 106
Palfrey, Francis W.: 10
Palmer, Oliver: 90
Parke, John G.: 57
Patrick, Marsena R.: 157
Peacock, William H.: account by, 122
Pelham, John: 54, *56*, 60
Pendley, Jesse M.: *109*
Perkins, Augustus S.: 36
Peterson, William G.: *118*
Phillips, William: 90, 109
Phillips house: *157*
Pierce, Francis E.: account by, 48-49, 90, 142
Plunkett, Thomas: *110*
Poague, William T.: *76*, 125; account by, 76
Pollack, Curtis C.: account by, 28
Port Royal, Virginia: 13
Potomac River: *map* 13
Powell, Charles S.: *124;* account by, 124
Price, R. Channing: *145;* account by, 145

R

Ransom, Robert: 78, 104, 105, 109, *124*
Rappahannock River: 11, 12, *map* 13, 14, 19, *20*, 24, 59, 133, 156; Confederate casualties at, *53;* Federal crossing of, 33-34, *map* 35, 36, *37*, 38, 43-44, *45*, *46-47;* Federal retirement across, 131, 136; fraternization along, 22, *23*, 26, *30*
Redwood, Allen C.: 43, 86
Richmond, Fredericksburg & Potomac Railroad: 30, 66
Richmond, Virginia: 9, 10, 11, 12
Richmond *Examiner:* 131
Robinson, John C.: 71, *72-73*
Robinson, Oscar D.: *141;* account by, 141
Rohrer, Coston: account by, 147-148
Rose, William: 138

S

St. Patrick's Cathedral: memorial mass for Irish Brigade held in, 153, *154*
Salem Church: 42
Sawyer, Franklin: *82;* account by, 82-83
Schell, Reuben: *67*
Shenandoah Valley: 9
Shreve, George W.: account by, 56
Simonton, Edward: account by, 121
Simpson, Taliaferro: *148;* letter from, 148-149
Skinker's Neck: 13
Smith, David V. M.: letter from, *147*
Smith, James P.: *19;* account by, 19-21, 129
Spaulding, Ira: 37
Stafford Heights: 41; Federal artillery on, 12, *38*, *53*, 62, 119
Stanton, Edwin M.: 12, 152
Stevens house: 92, 134
Stone, Horatio: letter and sketch by, *159*
Stratton house: *88-89*, 100
Stuart, Jeb: 19, 98, 145
Stuckenberg, John H. W.: *80*, *137;* account by, 80, 137
Sturgis, Samuel D.: 34, *47*, 104, 105, 116
Sturtevant, Edward E.: *103*
Sully, Alfred: 46
Sumner, Edwin V.: 10, 11, 12, 17, 33, 34, 35, 120; with staff, *16*
Sumner, Sam: *16*, 17
Sykes, George: 105

T

Taliaferro, William B.: 54
Taylor, Joseph H.: 14
Teall, William W.: *16;* account by, 17, 120
Tepe, "French Mary": *73*
Thompson, Gilbert W.: journal of, *36*
Thompson, S. Millett: account by, 48, 117
Throop, N. Garron: 22, *23*
Tiffany & Company: guidons made by, *135*
Torbert, Alfred T. A.: 74
Trask, Daniel W.: *103*
Tyler, Erastus B.: 104, 105

U

United States Ford: 12

V

Vizetelly, Frank: 20, 40, 41, 109

W

Walton, J. B.: 86
Warrenton, Virginia: 9, 11, 12
Washington, D.C.: 11, 147; Patent Office Hospital, 159
Washington, Mary: memorial monument for, *119*
Waud, Alfred R.: 29, 37, 46, 53, 115, 123, 151, 156
Wells, William: overcoat of, *69*
Werts, Andrew A.: *117*
Whitaker, William B.: *74*
Whitehouse, Phineas P.: *96;* account by, 96, 116
Willcox, Orlando B.: 104, 106, 107
Williams, Edward E.: account by, 71
Williams, William R.: account by, 152
Woodbury, Daniel P.: *38*
Woodward, Evan M.: 63
Wright, Hillery T.: *70*

Y

Yerby house: 129, 137, 138

Z

Zinn, Henry I.: *91*
Zook, Samuel: *31*, 78, 125; letter from, 31
Zouaves: 53, *72-73*, 85

Time-Life Books is a division of Time Life Inc.

TIME LIFE INC.
PRESIDENT and CEO: George Artandi

TIME-LIFE BOOKS
PRESIDENT: Stephen R. Frary
PUBLISHER/MANAGING EDITOR: Neil Kagan

VOICES OF THE CIVIL WAR

MARKETING DIRECTOR: Pamela R. Farrell

FREDERICKSBURG

EDITOR: Paul Mathless
Deputy Editors: Kirk Denkler (principal), Harris J. Andrews, Philip Brandt George
Design Director: Barbara M. Sheppard
Art Director: Ellen L. Pattisall
Associate Editor/Research and Writing: Gemma Slack
Senior Copyeditor: Judith Klein
Picture Coordinator: Lisa Groseclose
Editorial Assistant: Christine Higgins

Initial Series Design: Studio A

Special Contributors: Gary L. Ecelbarger, Brian C. Pohanka, Dana B. Shoaf, Henry Woodhead (text); Paul Birkhead, Charles F. Cooney, Robert Lee Hodge, Susan V. Kelly, Beth Levin, Henry Mintz, Dana B. Shoaf (research); Roy Nanovic (index).

Correspondent: Christina Lieberman (New York).

Director of Finance: Christopher Hearing
Director of Book Production: Marjann Caldwell
Director of Publishing Technology: Betsi McGrath
Director of Photography and Research: John Conrad Weiser
Director of Editorial Administration: Barbara Levitt
Production Manager: Marlene Zack
Quality Assurance Manager: James King
Chief Librarian: Louise D. Forstall

Consultants

Robert K. Krick is the author of more than 100 published articles and nine books, among them *Fredericksburg Artillery* and *Lee's Colonels.* His book *Stonewall Jackson at Cedar Mountain* won three national awards, including the Douglas Southall Freeman Prize. His most recent work is *Conquering the Valley: Stonewall Jackson at Port Republic.*

Frank A. O'Reilly is the historian at the Stonewall Jackson Shrine. In addition to numerous articles on the Civil War, O'Reilly is the author of *Stonewall Jackson at Fredericksburg,* and the coauthor of *The Atlas of the Civil War,* edited by James M. McPherson. He is currently working on an in-depth history of the entire Fredericksburg campaign.

First printing. Printed in U.S.A.
School and library distribution by Time-Life Education, P.O. Box 85026, Richmond, Virginia 23285-5026.

Library of Congress Cataloging-in-Publication Data
Fredericksburg / by the editors of Time-Life Books.
p. cm.—(Voices of the Civil War)
Includes bibliographical references and index.
ISBN 0-7835-4714-5
1. Fredericksburg (Va.), Battle of, 1862.
I. Time-Life Books. II. Series.
E474.85.F845 1997
973.7'33—dc21 97-30386
CIP

OTHER PUBLICATIONS

HISTORY
The Civil War
The American Indians
Lost Civilizations
The American Story
Mysteries of the Unknown
Time Frame
Cultural Atlas

SCIENCE/NATURE
Voyage Through the Universe

DO IT YOURSELF
The Time-Life Complete Gardener
Home Repair and Improvement
The Art of Woodworking
Fix It Yourself

TIME-LIFE KIDS
Library of First Questions and Answers
A Child's First Library of Learning
I Love Math
Nature Company Discoveries
Understanding Science & Nature

COOKING
Weight Watchers® Smart Choice Recipe Collection
Great Taste~Low Fat
Williams-Sonoma Kitchen Library

For information on and a full description of any of the Time-Life Books series listed above, please call 1-800-621-7026 or write:

Reader Information
Time-Life Customer Service
P.O. Box C-32068
Richmond, Virginia 23261-2068